CONFIGURING ACCOUNTS RECEIVABLE WITHIN DYNAMICS 365 FOR OPERATIONS

MODULE 1: CONFIGURING THE ACCOUNTS RECEIVABLE CONTROLS

Murray Fife

ISBN-13: 978-1973883937

ISBN-10: 1973883937ISBN-13: 978-1973883937

ISBN-10: 1973883937

DYNAMICS COMPANIONS
BARE BONES CONFIGURATION GUIDE

CONFIGURING ACCOUNTS RECEIVABLE WITHIN DYNAMICS 365 FOR OPERATIONS
MODULE 1: CONFIGURING THE ACCOUNTS RECEIVABLE CONTROLS

Preface

What You Need for this Guide

All the examples shown in this blueprint were done with the Microsoft Dynamics 365 for Operations hosted image that was provisioned through Lifecycle Services.

The following list of software from the virtual image was leveraged within this guide:

Microsoft Dynamics 365 for Operations

Even though all the preceding software was used during the development and testing of the recipes in this book, they should also work on later versions without any changes.

Errata

Although we have taken every care to ensure the accuracy of our content, mistakes do happen. If you find a mistake in one of our books—maybe a mistake in the text or the code—we would be grateful if you would report this to us. By doing so, you can save other readers from frustration and help us improve subsequent versions of this book. If you find any errata, please report them by emailing editor@dynamicscompanions.com.

Piracy

Piracy of copyright material on the Internet is an ongoing problem across all media. If you come across any illegal copies of our works, in any form, on the Internet, please provide us with the location address or website name immediately so that we can pursue a remedy.

Please contact us at legal@dynamicscompanions.com with a link to the suspected pirated material.

We appreciate your help in protecting our authors, and our ability to bring you valuable content.

Questions

You can contact us at help@dynamicscompanions.com if you are having a problem with any aspect of the book, and we will do our best to address it.

DYNAMICS COMPANIONS
BARE BONES CONFIGURATION GUIDE

CONFIGURING ACCOUNTS RECEIVABLE WITHIN DYNAMICS 365 FOR OPERATIONS
MODULE 1: CONFIGURING THE ACCOUNTS RECEIVABLE CONTROLS

www.dynamicscompanions.com
Dynamics Companions

- 4 -

www.blindsquirrelpublishing.com
© 2017 Blind Squirrel Publishing, LLC, All Rights Reserved

BLIND SQUIRREL
PUBLISHING

DYNAMICS COMPANIONS
BARE BONES CONFIGURATION GUIDE

CONFIGURING ACCOUNTS RECEIVABLE WITHIN DYNAMICS 365 FOR OPERATIONS
MODULE 1: CONFIGURING THE ACCOUNTS RECEIVABLE CONTROLS

Table of Contents

dyn

www.dynamicscompanions.com
Dynamics Companions

- 5 -

www.blindsquirrelpublishing.com
© 2017 Blind Squirrel Publishing, LLC, All Rights Reserved

BLIND SQUIRREL
PUBLISHING

DYNAMICS COMPANIONS
BARE BONES CONFIGURATION GUIDE

CONFIGURING ACCOUNTS RECEIVABLE WITHIN DYNAMICS 365 FOR OPERATIONS
MODULE 1: CONFIGURING THE ACCOUNTS RECEIVABLE CONTROLS

www.dynamicscompanions.com
Dynamics Companions

- 7 -

www.blindsquirrelpublishing.com
© 2017 Blind Squirrel Publishing, LLC , All Rights Reserved

BLIND SQUIRREL
PUBLISHING

DYNAMICS COMPANIONS
BARE BONES CONFIGURATION GUIDES

CONFIGURING ACCOUNTS RECEIVABLE WITHIN DYNAMICS 365 FOR OPERATIONS
MODULE 1: CONFIGURING THE ACCOUNTS RECEIVABLE CONTROLS

Introduction

Before we start adding customers and creating invoices within the Accounts Receivable module of Dynamics 365, there are a couple of codes and controls that need to be configured so that everything else later in the book will run smoothly. In this section, we will walk through everything that you need to set up to get the basic Accounts Receivable features working.

Topics Covered

- Configuring a Customer Payment Journal Name
- Configuring a Customer Write-Off Journal Name
- Configuring a General Customer Posting Profile
- Configuring a Prepayment Customer Posting Profile
- Configuring a Cash Terms of Payment
- Configuring a Cash on Delivery Terms of Payment
- Configuring Net Day Payment Terms
- Configuring Net Day of Month Term of Payment
- Configuring Equal Monthly Scheduled Payment Terms
- Configuring Proportional Monthly Scheduled Payment Terms
- Configuring Cash Discount Codes
- Configuring Cash Payment Methods
- Configuring Check Payment Methods
- Configuring Electronic Payment Methods
- Configuring Postdated Check Payment Methods
- Configuring Refund Payment Methods
- Configuring the Accounts Receivable Parameters

www.dynamicscompanions.com
Dynamics Companions

- 8 -

www.blindsquirrelpublishing.com
© 2017 Blind Squirrel Publishing, LLC , All Rights Reserved

BLIND SQUIRREL
PUBLISHING

DYNAMICS COMPANIONS
BARE BONES CONFIGURATION GUIDES

CONFIGURING ACCOUNTS RECEIVABLE WITHIN DYNAMICS 365 FOR OPERATIONS
MODULE 1: CONFIGURING THE ACCOUNTS RECEIVABLE CONTROLS

Configuring a Customer Payment Journal Name

Everything you do within the Receivables area of Dynamics 365 is controlled through Journals. So, it makes sense that the very first thing that we need to do is to configure some default Journal Names that we can then start using for our journal postings. If we want to receive customer payments, then we will want to create a **Journal Name** that we can use within the journals for this.

How to do it...

To do this, open up the navigation panel, expand out the **Modules** group, and click on **General Ledger** module to see all of the menu items that are available. Then click on the **Journal Names** menu item within the **Journal Setup** menu group.

Alternatively, you can search for the **Journal names** form by clicking on the search icon in the header of the form (or press **ALT+G**) and then type in **journal name** into the search box. Then you will be able to select the **Journal names** maintenance form from the dropdown list.

This will open up the **Journal names** maintenance form and we will see all of the other Journal names that we have already configured.

All we need to do to create a new Journal name record is click on the **New** button in the menu bar.

This will create a new Journal name record for us to start configuring.

Now we will want to start configuring our **Customer Payment** Journal name.

Start off by setting the **Name** for the Journal name to **CUSTPAY**.

Then set the Description to Customer Payment.

Next we will want to specify the **Journal type** that will be associated with the Journal name.

To do this, click on the **Journal Type** dropdown list box and select the **Customer Payment** value.

Now we will want to associate the Customer Payment Journal with a Bank.

So, within the **Offset Account Proposal** field group, click on the **Account Type** dropdown box and select the **Bank** option to identify that the journal will be posting to the bank accounts by default.

Now we will want to select the default bank account that we will want to associate the Customer Payment with.

To do this, click on the **Offset Account** dropdown, select the **Bank Account** that you want the customer payment to post to.

In this example, we set the **Bank Account** to be *OPER USD* since that is our operating bank account.

Now we need to give out Journal a number sequence. We don't have one right now, so we will create one by right-mouse-clicking on the **Voucher Series** field and selecting the **View details** option.

When the **Number Sequence** maintenance form is displayed, click on the **Number Sequence** button within the **New** group of the **Number Sequence** ribbon bar.

DYNAMICS COMPANIONS
BARE BONES CONFIGURATION GUIDES

CONFIGURING ACCOUNTS RECEIVABLE WITHIN DYNAMICS 365 FOR OPERATIONS
MODULE 1: CONFIGURING THE ACCOUNTS RECEIVABLE CONTROLS

This will open up the **Number sequence** maintenance form with a new **Number sequence** record that we can configure.

First we will want to assign our number sequence a reference code by setting the **Number sequence code** field.

For this number sequence we will set the **Number sequence code** to *CustPay_01*.

And then we can set the **Name** of the new Number sequence.

For this example, we will set the **Name** to *Customer Payment Journal*.

Now we will want to specify the Scope that the number sequence is tracked at.

We will want this number sequence to be unique by company, so click on the **Scope** dropdown list and select the **Company** option.

Since this is associated to the Company scope now, a new **Company** field will show up and we will be able to click on it to select the Company that this number sequence applies to.

Here we set the **Company** to our primary company of **AOT**.

Now we will tweak the **Segment** structure a little. The **Company** constant has already been added for us, but to make the Customer Payment Journals a little easier to see we can add a unique **Constant** value that we will use just for this journal.

In this example we will set the **Constant** field to *– CPJL-* which will allow us to recognize that these postings are customer payments.

Finally, we will want to make a slight tweak to the general number sequence settings. Then set the **Continuous** flag within the **General** tab group.

When you have done that, click on the **Close** button to exit from the form.

When you return to the Journal Names form you will be able to select your new **CustPay_01** Number Sequence from the **Voucher Series** dropdown list.

After we have done that we have set up

dyn
www.dynamicscompanions.com
Dynamics Companions

- 10 -

www.blindsquirrelpublishing.com
© 2017 Blind Squirrel Publishing, LLC, All Rights Reserved

BLIND SQUIRREL
PUBLISHING

DYNAMICS COMPANIONS
BARE BONES CONFIGURATION GUIDES

CONFIGURING ACCOUNTS RECEIVABLE WITHIN DYNAMICS 365 FOR OPERATIONS
MODULE 1: CONFIGURING THE ACCOUNTS RECEIVABLE CONTROLS

Configuring a Customer Payment Journal Name

How to do it...

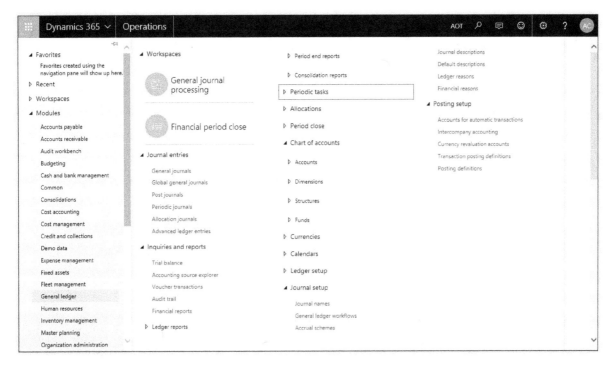

To do this, open up the navigation panel, expand out the **Modules** group, and click on **General Ledger** module to see all of the menu items that are available. Then click on the **Journal Names** menu item within the **Journal Setup** menu group.

www.dynamicscompanions.com
Dynamics Companions

- 11 -

www.blindsquirrelpublishing.com
© 2017 Blind Squirrel Publishing, LLC, All Rights Reserved

BLIND SQUIRREL
PUBLISHING

DYNAMICS COMPANIONS
BARE BONES CONFIGURATION GUIDES

CONFIGURING ACCOUNTS RECEIVABLE WITHIN DYNAMICS 365 FOR OPERATIONS
MODULE 1: CONFIGURING THE ACCOUNTS RECEIVABLE CONTROLS

Configuring a Customer Payment Journal Name

How to do it...

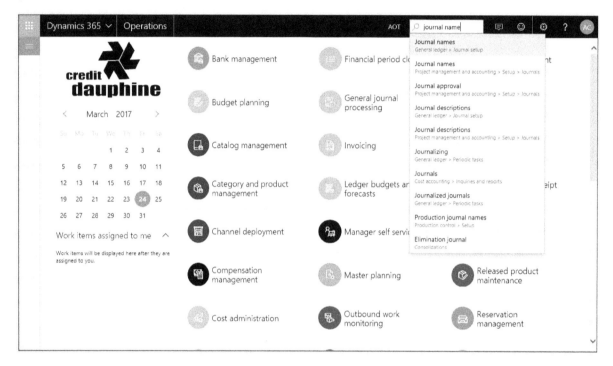

Alternatively, you can search for the **Journal names** form by clicking on the search icon in the header of the form (or press **ALT+G**) and then type in **journal name** into the search box. Then you will be able to select the **Journal names** maintenance form from the dropdown list.

dyn
www.dynamicscompanions.com
Dynamics Companions

- 12 -

www.blindsquirrelpublishing.com
© 2017 Blind Squirrel Publishing, LLC , All Rights Reserved

BLIND SQUIRREL
PUBLISHING

DYNAMICS COMPANIONS
BARE BONES CONFIGURATION GUIDES

CONFIGURING ACCOUNTS RECEIVABLE WITHIN DYNAMICS 365 FOR OPERATIONS
MODULE 1: CONFIGURING THE ACCOUNTS RECEIVABLE CONTROLS

Configuring a Customer Payment Journal Name

How to do it...

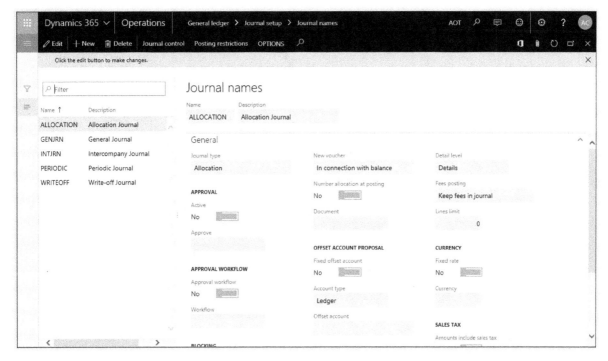

This will open up the **Journal names** maintenance form and we will see all of the other Journal names that we have already configured.

All we need to do to create a new Journal name record is click on the **New** button in the menu bar.

dync
www.dynamicscompanions.com
Dynamics Companions

- 13 -

www.blindsquirrelpublishing.com
© 2017 Blind Squirrel Publishing, LLC , All Rights Reserved

BLIND SQUIRREL
PUBLISHING

DYNAMICS COMPANIONS
BARE BONES CONFIGURATION GUIDES

CONFIGURING ACCOUNTS RECEIVABLE WITHIN DYNAMICS 365 FOR OPERATIONS
MODULE 1: CONFIGURING THE ACCOUNTS RECEIVABLE CONTROLS

Configuring a Customer Payment Journal Name

How to do it...

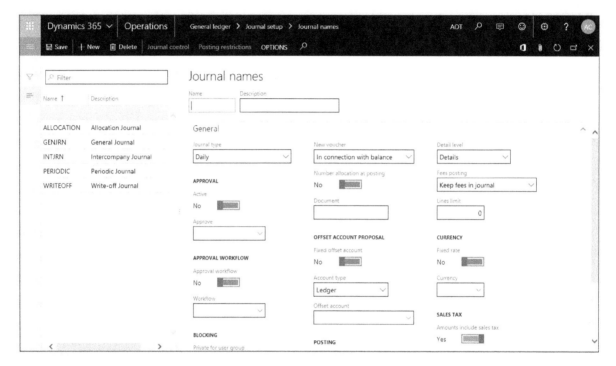

This will create a new Journal name record for us to start configuring.

dyn

www.dynamicscompanions.com
Dynamics Companions

- 14 -

www.blindsquirrelpublishing.com
© 2017 Blind Squirrel Publishing, LLC, All Rights Reserved

BLIND SQUIRREL
PUBLISHING

DYNAMICS COMPANIONS
BARE BONES CONFIGURATION GUIDES

CONFIGURING ACCOUNTS RECEIVABLE WITHIN DYNAMICS 365 FOR OPERATIONS
MODULE 1: CONFIGURING THE ACCOUNTS RECEIVABLE CONTROLS

Configuring a Customer Payment Journal Name

How to do it...

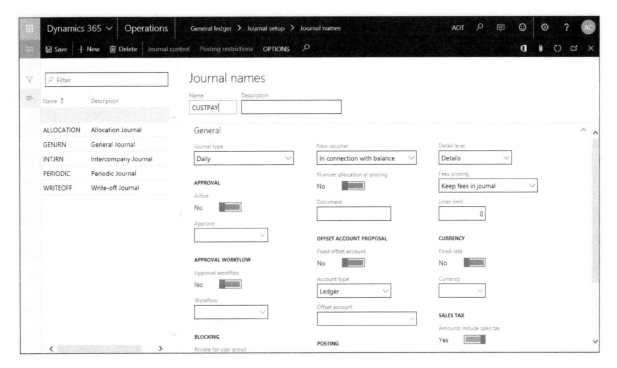

Now we will want to start configuring our **Customer Payment** Journal name.

Start off by setting the **Name** for the Journal name to **CUSTPAY.**

dyn c
www.dynamicscompanions.com
Dynamics Companions

- 15 -

www.blindsquirrelpublishing.com
© 2017 Blind Squirrel Publishing, LLC , All Rights Reserved

BLIND SQUIRREL
PUBLISHING

DYNAMICS COMPANIONS
BARE BONES CONFIGURATION GUIDES

CONFIGURING ACCOUNTS RECEIVABLE WITHIN DYNAMICS 365 FOR OPERATIONS
MODULE 1: CONFIGURING THE ACCOUNTS RECEIVABLE CONTROLS

Configuring a Customer Payment Journal Name

How to do it...

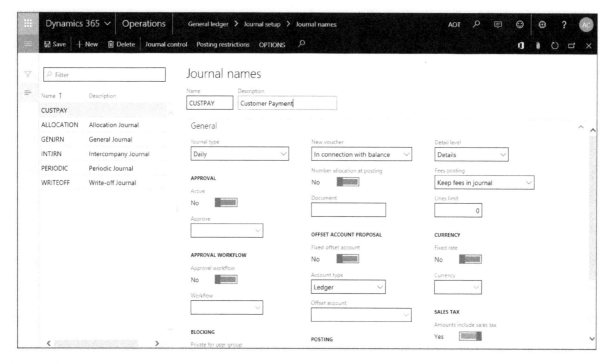

Then set the Description to Customer Payment.

DYNAMICS COMPANIONS
BARE BONES CONFIGURATION GUIDES

CONFIGURING ACCOUNTS RECEIVABLE WITHIN DYNAMICS 365 FOR OPERATIONS
MODULE 1: CONFIGURING THE ACCOUNTS RECEIVABLE CONTROLS

Configuring a Customer Payment Journal Name

How to do it...

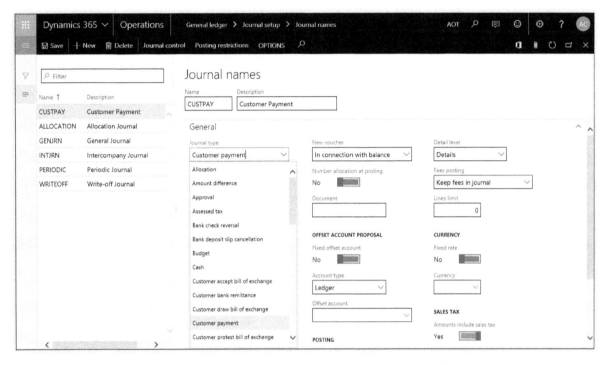

Next we will want to specify the **Journal type** that will be associated with the Journal name.

To do this, click on the **Journal Type** dropdown list box and select the **Customer Payment** value.

dyn c
www.dynamicscompanions.com
Dynamics Companions

- 17 -

www.blindsquirrelpublishing.com
© 2017 Blind Squirrel Publishing, LLC, All Rights Reserved

BLIND SQUIRREL
PUBLISHING

DYNAMICS COMPANIONS
BARE BONES CONFIGURATION GUIDES

CONFIGURING ACCOUNTS RECEIVABLE WITHIN DYNAMICS 365 FOR OPERATIONS
MODULE 1: CONFIGURING THE ACCOUNTS RECEIVABLE CONTROLS

Configuring a Customer Payment Journal Name

How to do it...

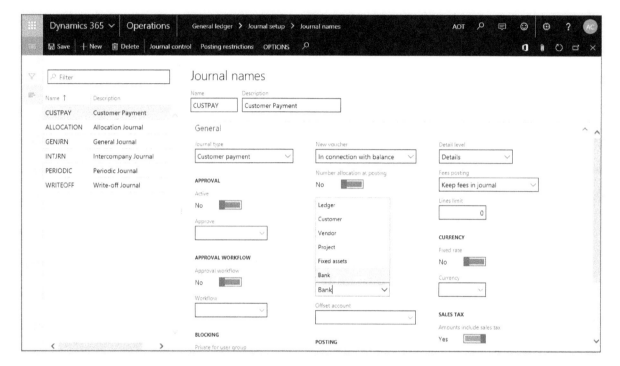

Now we will want to associate the Customer Payment Journal with a Bank.

So, within the **Offset Account Proposal** field group, click on the **Account Type** dropdown box and select the **Bank** option to identify that the journal will be posting to the bank accounts by default.

dyn c

www.dynamicscompanions.com
Dynamics Companions

- 18 -

www.blindsquirrelpublishing.com
© 2017 Blind Squirrel Publishing, LLC , All Rights Reserved

BLIND SQUIRREL
PUBLISHING

DYNAMICS COMPANIONS
BARE BONES CONFIGURATION GUIDES

CONFIGURING ACCOUNTS RECEIVABLE WITHIN DYNAMICS 365 FOR OPERATIONS
MODULE 1: CONFIGURING THE ACCOUNTS RECEIVABLE CONTROLS

Configuring a Customer Payment Journal Name

How to do it...

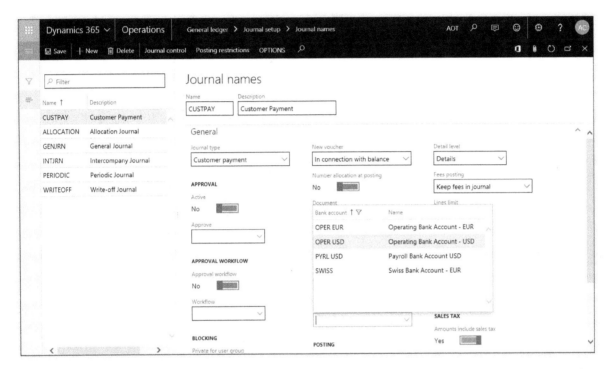

Now we will want to select the default bank account that we will want to associate the Customer Payment with.

To do this, click on the **Offset Account** dropdown, select the **Bank Account** that you want the customer payment to post to.

In this example, we set the **Bank Account** to be *OPER USD* since that is our operating bank account.

www.dynamicscompanions.com
Dynamics Companions

- 19 -

www.blindsquirrelpublishing.com
© 2017 Blind Squirrel Publishing, LLC , All Rights Reserved

BLIND SQUIRREL
PUBLISHING

DYNAMICS COMPANIONS
BARE BONES CONFIGURATION GUIDES

CONFIGURING ACCOUNTS RECEIVABLE WITHIN DYNAMICS 365 FOR OPERATIONS
MODULE 1: CONFIGURING THE ACCOUNTS RECEIVABLE CONTROLS

Configuring a Customer Payment Journal Name

How to do it...

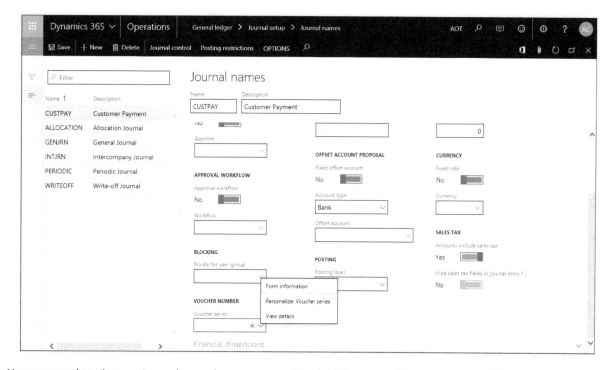

Now we need to give out Journal a number sequence. We don't have one right now, so we will create one by right-mouse-clicking on the **Voucher Series** field and selecting the **View details** option.

dyn

www.dynamicscompanions.com
Dynamics Companions

- 20 -

www.blindsquirrelpublishing.com
© 2017 Blind Squirrel Publishing, LLC, All Rights Reserved

BLIND SQUIRREL
PUBLISHING

DYNAMICS COMPANIONS
BARE BONES CONFIGURATION GUIDES

CONFIGURING ACCOUNTS RECEIVABLE WITHIN DYNAMICS 365 FOR OPERATIONS
MODULE 1: CONFIGURING THE ACCOUNTS RECEIVABLE CONTROLS

Configuring a Customer Payment Journal Name

How to do it...

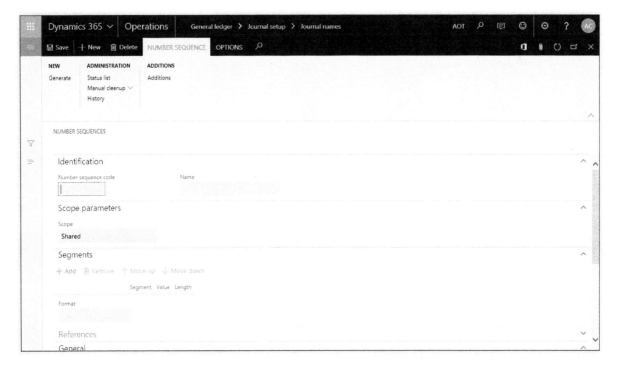

When the **Number Sequence** maintenance form is displayed, click on the **Number Sequence** button within the **New** group of the **Number Sequence** ribbon bar.

www.dynamicscompanions.com
Dynamics Companions

- 21 -

www.blindsquirrelpublishing.com
© 2017 Blind Squirrel Publishing, LLC , All Rights Reserved

BLIND SQUIRREL
PUBLISHING

DYNAMICS COMPANIONS
BARE BONES CONFIGURATION GUIDES

CONFIGURING ACCOUNTS RECEIVABLE WITHIN DYNAMICS 365 FOR OPERATIONS
MODULE 1: CONFIGURING THE ACCOUNTS RECEIVABLE CONTROLS

Configuring a Customer Payment Journal Name

How to do it...

This will open up the **Number sequence** maintenance form with a new **Number sequence** record that we can configure.

dyn

www.dynamicscompanions.com
Dynamics Companions

- 22 -

www.blindsquirrelpublishing.com
© 2017 Blind Squirrel Publishing, LLC , All Rights Reserved

BLIND SQUIRREL
PUBLISHING

DYNAMICS COMPANIONS
BARE BONES CONFIGURATION GUIDES

CONFIGURING ACCOUNTS RECEIVABLE WITHIN DYNAMICS 365 FOR OPERATIONS
MODULE 1: CONFIGURING THE ACCOUNTS RECEIVABLE CONTROLS

Configuring a Customer Payment Journal Name

How to do it...

First we will want to assign our number sequence a reference code by setting the **Number sequence code** field.

For this number sequence we will set the **Number sequence code** to *CustPay_01*.

DYNAMICS COMPANIONS
BARE BONES CONFIGURATION GUIDES

CONFIGURING ACCOUNTS RECEIVABLE WITHIN DYNAMICS 365 FOR OPERATIONS
MODULE 1: CONFIGURING THE ACCOUNTS RECEIVABLE CONTROLS

Configuring a Customer Payment Journal Name

How to do it...

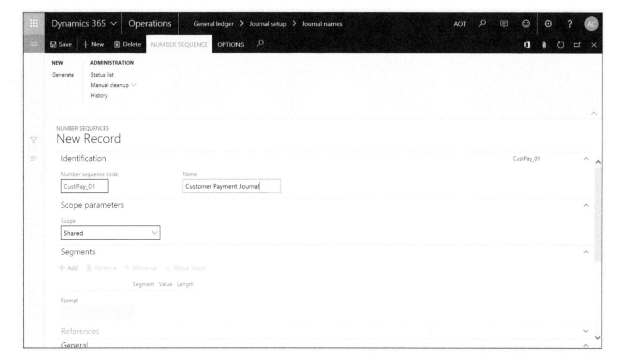

And then we can set the **Name** of the new Number sequence.

For this example, we will set the **Name** to *Customer Payment Journal*.

dyn☐
www.dynamicscompanions.com
Dynamics Companions

- 24 -

www.blindsquirrelpublishing.com
© 2017 Blind Squirrel Publishing, LLC , All Rights Reserved

BLIND SQUIRREL
PUBLISHING

DYNAMICS COMPANIONS
BARE BONES CONFIGURATION GUIDES

CONFIGURING ACCOUNTS RECEIVABLE WITHIN DYNAMICS 365 FOR OPERATIONS
MODULE 1: CONFIGURING THE ACCOUNTS RECEIVABLE CONTROLS

Configuring a Customer Payment Journal Name

How to do it...

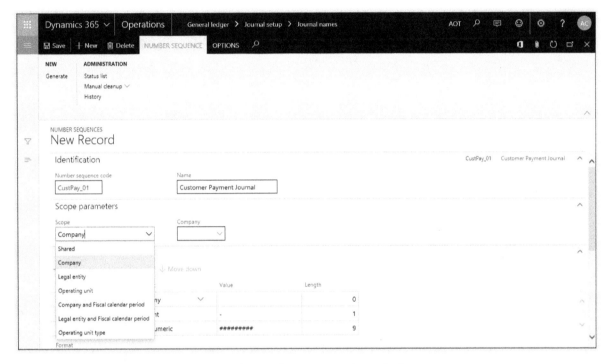

Now we will want to specify the Scope that the number sequence is tracked at.

We will want this number sequence to be unique by company, so click on the **Scope** dropdown list and select the **Company** option.

dynco
www.dynamicscompanions.com
Dynamics Companions

- 25 -

www.blindsquirrelpublishing.com
© 2017 Blind Squirrel Publishing, LLC, All Rights Reserved

BLIND SQUIRREL
PUBLISHING

DYNAMICS COMPANIONS
BARE BONES CONFIGURATION GUIDES

CONFIGURING ACCOUNTS RECEIVABLE WITHIN DYNAMICS 365 FOR OPERATIONS
MODULE 1: CONFIGURING THE ACCOUNTS RECEIVABLE CONTROLS

Configuring a Customer Payment Journal Name

How to do it...

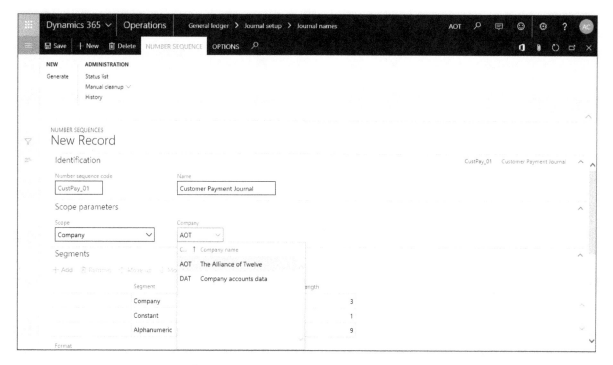

Since this is associated to the Company scope now, a new **Company** field will show up and we will be able to click on it to select the Company that this number sequence applies to.

Here we set the **Company** to our primary company of **AOT**.

www.dynamicscompanions.com
Dynamics Companions

- 26 -

www.blindsquirrelpublishing.com
© 2017 Blind Squirrel Publishing, LLC , All Rights Reserved

BLIND SQUIRREL
PUBLISHING

DYNAMICS COMPANIONS
BARE BONES CONFIGURATION GUIDES

CONFIGURING ACCOUNTS RECEIVABLE WITHIN DYNAMICS 365 FOR OPERATIONS
MODULE 1: CONFIGURING THE ACCOUNTS RECEIVABLE CONTROLS

Configuring a Customer Payment Journal Name

How to do it...

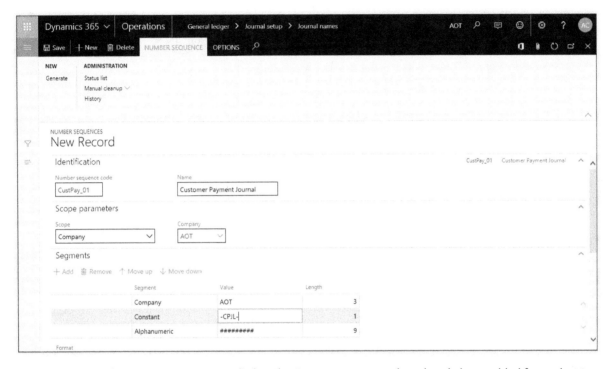

Now we will tweak the **Segment** structure a little. The **Company** constant has already been added for us, but to make the Customer Payment Journals a little easier to see we can add a unique **Constant** value that we will use just for this journal.

In this example we will set the **Constant** field to *–CPJL-* which will allow us to recognize that these postings are customer payments.

dync
www.dynamicscompanions.com
Dynamics Companions

- 27 -

www.blindsquirrelpublishing.com
© 2017 Blind Squirrel Publishing, LLC, All Rights Reserved

BLIND SQUIRREL
PUBLISHING

DYNAMICS COMPANIONS
BARE BONES CONFIGURATION GUIDES

CONFIGURING ACCOUNTS RECEIVABLE WITHIN DYNAMICS 365 FOR OPERATIONS
MODULE 1: CONFIGURING THE ACCOUNTS RECEIVABLE CONTROLS

Configuring a Customer Payment Journal Name

How to do it...

Finally, we will want to make a slight tweak to the general number sequence settings. Then set the **Continuous** flag within the **General** tab group.

When you have done that, click on the **Close** button to exit from the form.

dync
www.dynamicscompanions.com
Dynamics Companions

- 28 -

www.blindsquirrelpublishing.com
© 2017 Blind Squirrel Publishing, LLC, All Rights Reserved

BLIND SQUIRREL
PUBLISHING

DYNAMICS COMPANIONS
BARE BONES CONFIGURATION GUIDES

CONFIGURING ACCOUNTS RECEIVABLE WITHIN DYNAMICS 365 FOR OPERATIONS
MODULE 1: CONFIGURING THE ACCOUNTS RECEIVABLE CONTROLS

Configuring a Customer Payment Journal Name

How to do it...

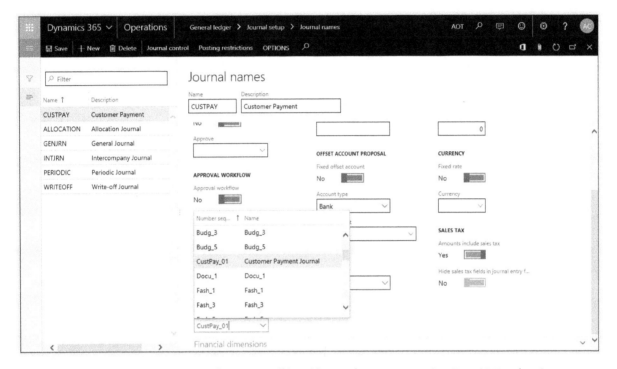

When you return to the Journal Names form you will be able to select your new **CustPay_01** Number Sequence from the **Voucher Series** dropdown list.

www.dynamicscompanions.com
Dynamics Companions

- 29 -

www.blindsquirrelpublishing.com
© 2017 Blind Squirrel Publishing, LLC, All Rights Reserved

BLIND SQUIRREL
PUBLISHING

DYNAMICS COMPANIONS
BARE BONES CONFIGURATION GUIDES

CONFIGURING ACCOUNTS RECEIVABLE WITHIN DYNAMICS 365 FOR OPERATIONS
MODULE 1: CONFIGURING THE ACCOUNTS RECEIVABLE CONTROLS

Configuring a Customer Payment Journal Name

How to do it...

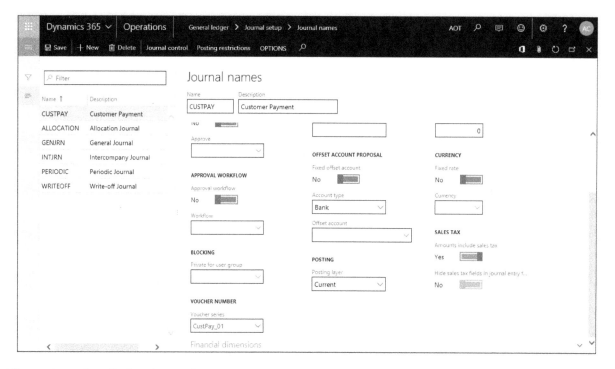

After we have done that we have set up

www.dynamicscompanions.com
Dynamics Companions

- 30 -

www.blindsquirrelpublishing.com
© 2017 Blind Squirrel Publishing, LLC , All Rights Reserved

BLIND SQUIRREL
PUBLISHING

DYNAMICS COMPANIONS
BARE BONES CONFIGURATION GUIDES

CONFIGURING ACCOUNTS RECEIVABLE WITHIN DYNAMICS 365 FOR OPERATIONS
MODULE 1: CONFIGURING THE ACCOUNTS RECEIVABLE CONTROLS

Configuring a Customer Payment Journal Name

Example Data

Field Name	Value
Name	CUSTPAY
Description	Customer Payment
Journal Type	Customer Payment
Account Type	Bank
Offset Account	OPER
Voucher Series	CustPay_01

Journal Name: CUSTPAY – Customer Payment

Field Name	Value
Number Sequence Code	CustPay_01
Name	Customer Payment Journal
Scope	Company
Company	AOT
Segment.Company	AOT
Segment.Constant	-CPJL-
Segment.Alphanumeric	########
Continuous	True

Number Sequence: CustPay_01 – Customer Payment Journal

dync
www.dynamicscompanions.com
Dynamics Companions

- 31 -

www.blindsquirrelpublishing.com
© 2017 Blind Squirrel Publishing, LLC, All Rights Reserved

BLIND SQUIRREL
PUBLISHING

DYNAMICS COMPANIONS
BARE BONES CONFIGURATION GUIDES

CONFIGURING ACCOUNTS RECEIVABLE WITHIN DYNAMICS 365 FOR OPERATIONS
MODULE 1: CONFIGURING THE ACCOUNTS RECEIVABLE CONTROLS

Configuring a Customer Payment Journal Name

Review

Now we have set up a Journal name that we can use to process all of our customer payments.

If you want to be really clever, you can create more journal names just like this to segregate out the different types of customer payments. This will allow you to see all of the different types simply by filtering out the view by journal name.

But for now we will stick with just one.

www.dynamicscompanions.com
Dynamics Companions

- 32 -

www.blindsquirrelpublishing.com
© 2017 Blind Squirrel Publishing, LLC , All Rights Reserved

BLIND SQUIRREL
PUBLISHING

DYNAMICS COMPANIONS
BARE BONES CONFIGURATION GUIDES

CONFIGURING ACCOUNTS RECEIVABLE WITHIN DYNAMICS 365 FOR OPERATIONS
MODULE 1: CONFIGURING THE ACCOUNTS RECEIVABLE CONTROLS

Configuring a Customer Write-Off Journal Name

Another **Journal name** that we will want to configure is a **Write-Off** journal name. We will use this to write off any customer payments that we cannot collect on, or amounts that are not worth collecting on.

How to do it...

To do this, return back to the **Journal names** maintenance form and click on the **New** button in the menu bar to create a new record.

This will create a new **Journal name** record for us to start configuring.

Now we will want to start configuring our **Write-Off** Journal name.

Start off by setting the **Name** for the Journal name to **WRITEOFF.**

Then set the Description to Write-Off Journal.

Next we will want to create a new **Number sequence** for the Write-Off Journal.

To do this, right-mouse-click on the **Voucher Series** field and select the **View details** menu item.

This will open up the **Number sequence** maintenance form for us.

All we need to do here is click on the **Generate** menu item within the **New** group to the **Number sequence** action panel.

This will create a new **Number sequence** record for us.

Now set the Number sequence code to *WriteOff01*.

Then set the **Name** of the number sequence to *Write-Off Journal*.

We will want this Number sequence to be associated with a particular Company, so we will want to click on the **Scope** dropdown list and select the *Company* option from the list.

Now that we have set the Scope to Company, we can now click on the **Company** dropdown list and select the company that we want to associate the number sequence to.

In this example we will select the **AOT** Company.

Now we will tweak the **Segment** structure a little just like we did with the other Journal Name.

The **Company** constant has already been added for us, but to make the Write-Off Journals a little easier to see we can add a unique **Constant** value that we will use just for this journal.

In this example we will set the **Constant** field to – *WOJL-* which will allow us to recognize that these postings are customer payments.

Finally, we will want to make a slight tweak to the general number sequence settings. Then set the **Continuous** flag within the **General** tab group.

When you have done that, click on the **Close** button to exit from the form.

When you return to the Journal Names form you will be able to select your new **WriteOff01** Number Sequence from the **Voucher Series** dropdown list.

DYNAMICS COMPANIONS
BARE BONES CONFIGURATION GUIDES

CONFIGURING ACCOUNTS RECEIVABLE WITHIN DYNAMICS 365 FOR OPERATIONS
MODULE 1: CONFIGURING THE ACCOUNTS RECEIVABLE CONTROLS

After we have done that we have set up of our new
Write-Off Journal name.

www.dynamicscompanions.com
Dynamics Companions

- 34 -

www.blindsquirrelpublishing.com
© 2017 Blind Squirrel Publishing, LLC , All Rights Reserved

BLIND SQUIRREL
PUBLISHING

DYNAMICS COMPANIONS
BARE BONES CONFIGURATION GUIDES

CONFIGURING ACCOUNTS RECEIVABLE WITHIN DYNAMICS 365 FOR OPERATIONS
MODULE 1: CONFIGURING THE ACCOUNTS RECEIVABLE CONTROLS

Configuring a Customer Write-Off Journal Name

How to do it...

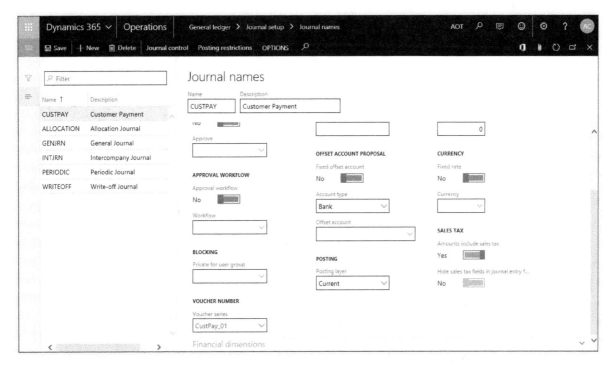

To do this, return back to the **Journal names** maintenance form and click on the **New** button in the menu bar to create a new record.

www.dynamicscompanions.com
Dynamics Companions

- 35 -

www.blindsquirrelpublishing.com
© 2017 Blind Squirrel Publishing, LLC , All Rights Reserved

BLIND SQUIRREL
PUBLISHING

DYNAMICS COMPANIONS
BARE BONES CONFIGURATION GUIDES

CONFIGURING ACCOUNTS RECEIVABLE WITHIN DYNAMICS 365 FOR OPERATIONS
MODULE 1: CONFIGURING THE ACCOUNTS RECEIVABLE CONTROLS

Configuring a Customer Write-Off Journal Name

How to do it...

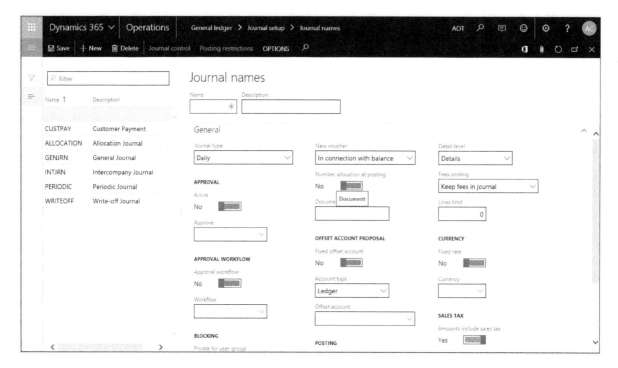

This will create a new **Journal name** record for us to start configuring.

DYNAMICS COMPANIONS
BARE BONES CONFIGURATION GUIDES

CONFIGURING ACCOUNTS RECEIVABLE WITHIN DYNAMICS 365 FOR OPERATIONS
MODULE 1: CONFIGURING THE ACCOUNTS RECEIVABLE CONTROLS

Configuring a Customer Write-Off Journal Name

How to do it...

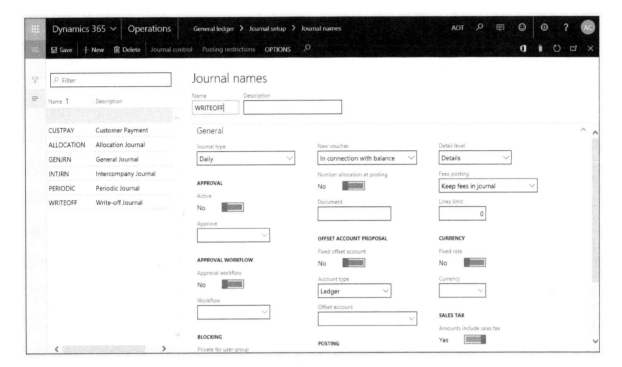

Now we will want to start configuring our **Write-Off** Journal name.

Start off by setting the **Name** for the Journal name to **WRITEOFF.**

dyn c
www.dynamicscompanions.com
Dynamics Companions

- 37 -

www.blindsquirrelpublishing.com
© 2017 Blind Squirrel Publishing, LLC, All Rights Reserved

BLIND SQUIRREL
PUBLISHING

DYNAMICS COMPANIONS
BARE BONES CONFIGURATION GUIDES

CONFIGURING ACCOUNTS RECEIVABLE WITHIN DYNAMICS 365 FOR OPERATIONS
MODULE 1: CONFIGURING THE ACCOUNTS RECEIVABLE CONTROLS

Configuring a Customer Write-Off Journal Name

How to do it...

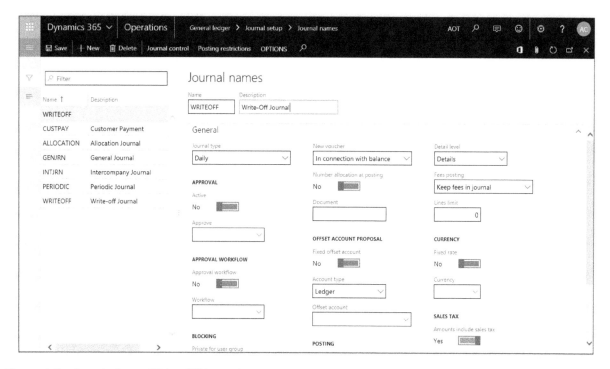

Then set the Description to Write-Off Journal.

www.dynamicscompanions.com
Dynamics Companions

- 38 -

www.blindsquirrelpublishing.com
© 2017 Blind Squirrel Publishing, LLC , All Rights Reserved

BLIND SQUIRREL
PUBLISHING

DYNAMICS COMPANIONS
BARE BONES CONFIGURATION GUIDES

CONFIGURING ACCOUNTS RECEIVABLE WITHIN DYNAMICS 365 FOR OPERATIONS
MODULE 1: CONFIGURING THE ACCOUNTS RECEIVABLE CONTROLS

Configuring a Customer Write-Off Journal Name

How to do it...

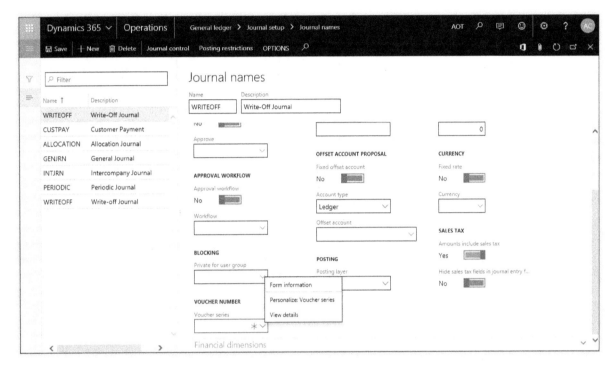

Next we will want to create a new **Number sequence** for the Write-Off Journal.

To do this, right-mouse-click on the **Voucher Series** field and select the **View details** menu item.

www.dynamicscompanions.com
Dynamics Companions

- 39 -

www.blindsquirrelpublishing.com
© 2017 Blind Squirrel Publishing, LLC, All Rights Reserved

BLIND SQUIRREL
PUBLISHING

DYNAMICS COMPANIONS
BARE BONES CONFIGURATION GUIDES

CONFIGURING ACCOUNTS RECEIVABLE WITHIN DYNAMICS 365 FOR OPERATIONS
MODULE 1: CONFIGURING THE ACCOUNTS RECEIVABLE CONTROLS

Configuring a Customer Write-Off Journal Name

How to do it...

This will open up the **Number sequence** maintenance form for us.

All we need to do here is click on the **Generate** menu item within the **New** group to the **Number sequence** action panel.

dync
www.dynamicscompanions.com
Dynamics Companions

- 40 -

www.blindsquirrelpublishing.com
© 2017 Blind Squirrel Publishing, LLC, All Rights Reserved

BLIND SQUIRREL
PUBLISHING

DYNAMICS COMPANIONS
BARE BONES CONFIGURATION GUIDES

CONFIGURING ACCOUNTS RECEIVABLE WITHIN DYNAMICS 365 FOR OPERATIONS
MODULE 1: CONFIGURING THE ACCOUNTS RECEIVABLE CONTROLS

Configuring a Customer Write-Off Journal Name

How to do it...

This will create a new **Number sequence** record for us.

dync
www.dynamicscompanions.com
Dynamics Companions

- 41 -

www.blindsquirrelpublishing.com
© 2017 Blind Squirrel Publishing, LLC , All Rights Reserved

BLIND SQUIRREL
PUBLISHING

DYNAMICS COMPANIONS
BARE BONES CONFIGURATION GUIDES

CONFIGURING ACCOUNTS RECEIVABLE WITHIN DYNAMICS 365 FOR OPERATIONS
MODULE 1: CONFIGURING THE ACCOUNTS RECEIVABLE CONTROLS

Configuring a Customer Write-Off Journal Name

How to do it...

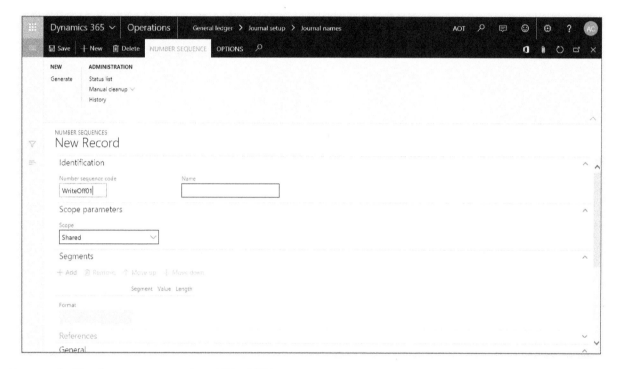

Now set the Number sequence code to *WriteOff01*.

dyn

www.dynamicscompanions.com
Dynamics Companions

- 42 -

www.blindsquirrelpublishing.com
© 2017 Blind Squirrel Publishing, LLC , All Rights Reserved

BLIND SQUIRREL
PUBLISHING

DYNAMICS COMPANIONS
BARE BONES CONFIGURATION GUIDES

CONFIGURING ACCOUNTS RECEIVABLE WITHIN DYNAMICS 365 FOR OPERATIONS
MODULE 1: CONFIGURING THE ACCOUNTS RECEIVABLE CONTROLS

Configuring a Customer Write-Off Journal Name

How to do it...

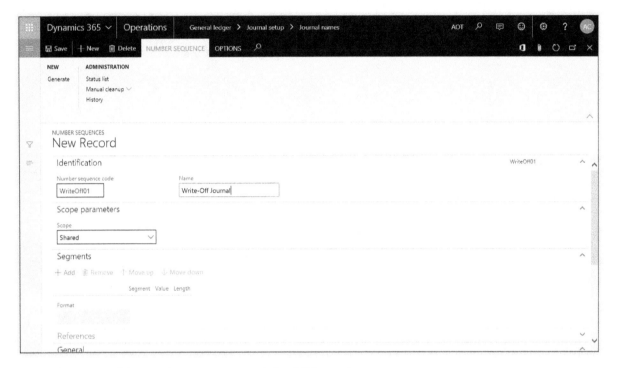

Then set the **Name** of the number sequence to *Write-Off Journal*.

dyn c
www.dynamicscompanions.com
Dynamics Companions

- 43 -

www.blindsquirrelpublishing.com
© 2017 Blind Squirrel Publishing, LLC, All Rights Reserved

BLIND SQUIRREL
PUBLISHING

DYNAMICS COMPANIONS
BARE BONES CONFIGURATION GUIDES

CONFIGURING ACCOUNTS RECEIVABLE WITHIN DYNAMICS 365 FOR OPERATIONS
MODULE 1: CONFIGURING THE ACCOUNTS RECEIVABLE CONTROLS

Configuring a Customer Write-Off Journal Name

How to do it...

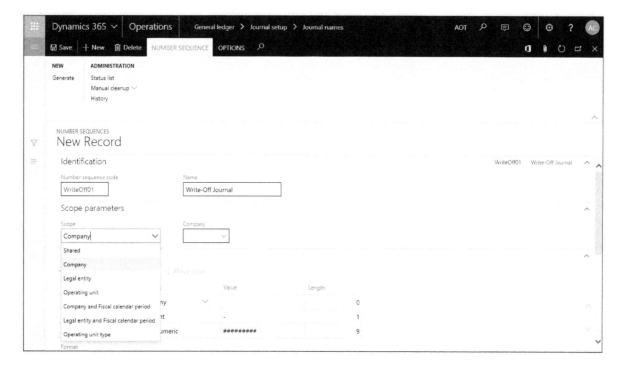

We will want this Number sequence to be associated with a particular Company, so we will want to click on the **Scope** dropdown list and select the ***Company*** option from the list.

dyn
www.dynamicscompanions.com
Dynamics Companions

- 44 -

www.blindsquirrelpublishing.com
© 2017 Blind Squirrel Publishing, LLC , All Rights Reserved

BLIND SQUIRREL
PUBLISHING

DYNAMICS COMPANIONS
BARE BONES CONFIGURATION GUIDES

CONFIGURING ACCOUNTS RECEIVABLE WITHIN DYNAMICS 365 FOR OPERATIONS
MODULE 1: CONFIGURING THE ACCOUNTS RECEIVABLE CONTROLS

Configuring a Customer Write-Off Journal Name

How to do it...

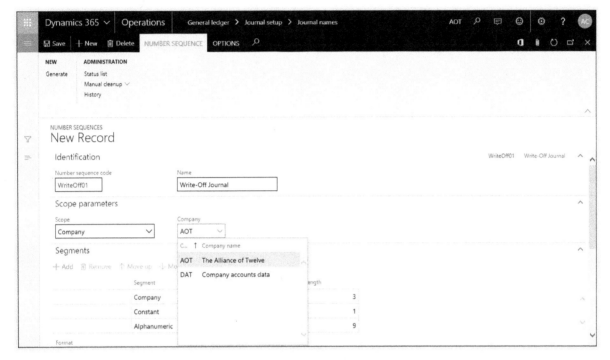

Now that we have set the Scope to Company, we can now click on the **Company** dropdown list and select the company that we want to associate the number sequence to.

In this example we will select the **AOT** Company.

dync

www.dynamicscompanions.com
Dynamics Companions

- 45 -

www.blindsquirrelpublishing.com
© 2017 Blind Squirrel Publishing, LLC , All Rights Reserved

BLIND SQUIRREL
PUBLISHING

DYNAMICS COMPANIONS
BARE BONES CONFIGURATION GUIDES

CONFIGURING ACCOUNTS RECEIVABLE WITHIN DYNAMICS 365 FOR OPERATIONS
MODULE 1: CONFIGURING THE ACCOUNTS RECEIVABLE CONTROLS

Configuring a Customer Write-Off Journal Name

How to do it...

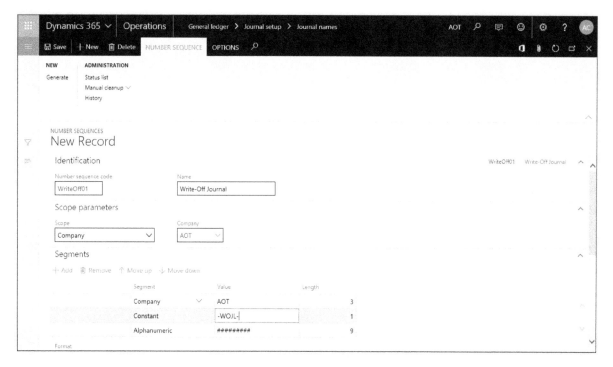

Now we will tweak the **Segment** structure a little just like we did with the other Journal Name.

The **Company** constant has already been added for us, but to make the Write-Off Journals a little easier to see we can add a unique **Constant** value that we will use just for this journal.

In this example we will set the **Constant** field to **–WOJL-** which will allow us to recognize that these postings are customer payments.

dyn

www.dynamicscompanions.com
Dynamics Companions

- 46 -

www.blindsquirrelpublishing.com
© 2017 Blind Squirrel Publishing, LLC , All Rights Reserved

BLIND SQUIRREL
PUBLISHING

DYNAMICS COMPANIONS
BARE BONES CONFIGURATION GUIDES

CONFIGURING ACCOUNTS RECEIVABLE WITHIN DYNAMICS 365 FOR OPERATIONS
MODULE 1: CONFIGURING THE ACCOUNTS RECEIVABLE CONTROLS

Configuring a Customer Write-Off Journal Name

How to do it...

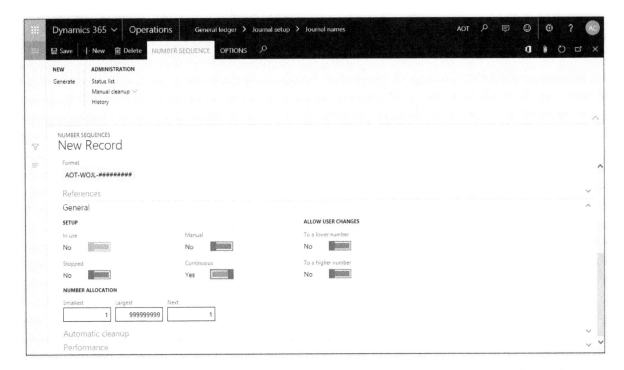

Finally, we will want to make a slight tweak to the general number sequence settings. Then set the **Continuous** flag within the **General** tab group.

www.dynamicscompanions.com
Dynamics Companions

- 47 -

www.blindsquirrelpublishing.com
© 2017 Blind Squirrel Publishing, LLC, All Rights Reserved

BLIND SQUIRREL
PUBLISHING

DYNAMICS COMPANIONS
BARE BONES CONFIGURATION GUIDES

CONFIGURING ACCOUNTS RECEIVABLE WITHIN DYNAMICS 365 FOR OPERATIONS
MODULE 1: CONFIGURING THE ACCOUNTS RECEIVABLE CONTROLS

Configuring a Customer Write-Off Journal Name

How to do it...

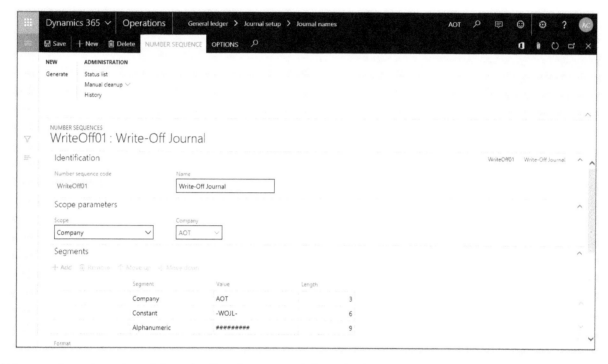

When you have done that, click on the **Close** button to exit from the form.

www.dynamicscompanions.com
Dynamics Companions

- 48 -

www.blindsquirrelpublishing.com
© 2017 Blind Squirrel Publishing, LLC, All Rights Reserved

BLIND SQUIRREL
PUBLISHING

DYNAMICS COMPANIONS
BARE BONES CONFIGURATION GUIDES

CONFIGURING ACCOUNTS RECEIVABLE WITHIN DYNAMICS 365 FOR OPERATIONS
MODULE 1: CONFIGURING THE ACCOUNTS RECEIVABLE CONTROLS

Configuring a Customer Write-Off Journal Name

How to do it...

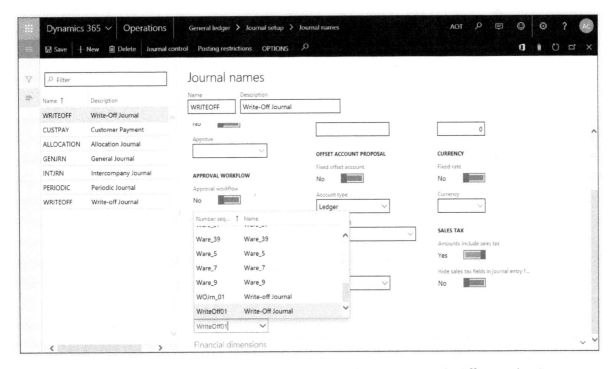

When you return to the Journal Names form you will be able to select your new **WriteOff01** Number Sequence from the **Voucher Series** dropdown list.

www.dynamicscompanions.com
Dynamics Companions

- 49 -

www.blindsquirrelpublishing.com
© 2017 Blind Squirrel Publishing, LLC, All Rights Reserved

BLIND SQUIRREL
PUBLISHING

DYNAMICS COMPANIONS
BARE BONES CONFIGURATION GUIDES

CONFIGURING ACCOUNTS RECEIVABLE WITHIN DYNAMICS 365 FOR OPERATIONS
MODULE 1: CONFIGURING THE ACCOUNTS RECEIVABLE CONTROLS

Configuring a Customer Write-Off Journal Name

How to do it...

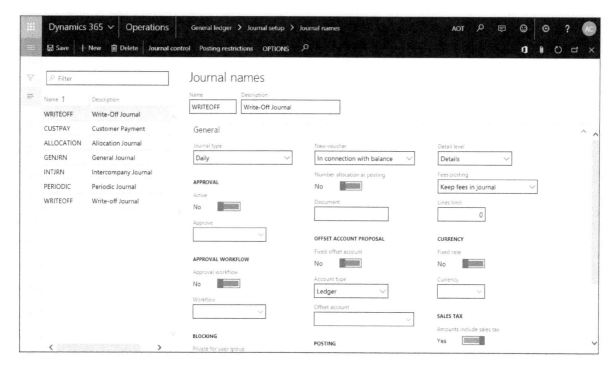

After we have done that we have set up of our new Write-Off Journal name.

www.dynamicscompanions.com
Dynamics Companions

- 50 -

www.blindsquirrelpublishing.com
© 2017 Blind Squirrel Publishing, LLC , All Rights Reserved

BLIND SQUIRREL
PUBLISHING

DYNAMICS COMPANIONS
BARE BONES CONFIGURATION GUIDES

CONFIGURING ACCOUNTS RECEIVABLE WITHIN DYNAMICS 365 FOR OPERATIONS
MODULE 1: CONFIGURING THE ACCOUNTS RECEIVABLE CONTROLS

Configuring a Customer Write-Off Journal Name

Example Data

Field Name	Value
Name	WRITEOFF
Description	Write-Off Journal
Journal Type	Daily
Voucher Series	WriteOff01

Journal Name: WRITEOFF – Write-Off Journal

Field Name	Value
Number Sequence Code	WriteOff01
Name	Write-Off Journal
Scope	Company
Company	AOT
Segment.Company	AOT
Segment.Constant	-WOJL-
Segment.Alphanumeric	########
Continuous	True

Number Sequence: GenJrnWriteOff01 – Write-Off Journal

dynco
www.dynamicscompanions.com
Dynamics Companions

- 51 -

www.blindsquirrelpublishing.com
© 2017 Blind Squirrel Publishing, LLC, All Rights Reserved

BLIND SQUIRREL
PUBLISHING

DYNAMICS COMPANIONS
BARE BONES CONFIGURATION GUIDES

CONFIGURING ACCOUNTS RECEIVABLE WITHIN DYNAMICS 365 FOR OPERATIONS
MODULE 1: CONFIGURING THE ACCOUNTS RECEIVABLE CONTROLS

Configuring a Customer Write-Off Journal Name

Review

Now you have a new journal that we can use to process customer Write-Offs.

I think our work here is done.

DYNAMICS COMPANIONS
BARE BONES CONFIGURATION GUIDES

CONFIGURING ACCOUNTS RECEIVABLE WITHIN DYNAMICS 365 FOR OPERATIONS
MODULE 1: CONFIGURING THE ACCOUNTS RECEIVABLE CONTROLS

Configuring a General Customer Posting Profile

The next setup task that we will need to perform is to configure a set of default **Customer Posting Profiles** for the Receivables area. These are used to default in common posting accounts and configurations for all, or groups of customers. The first one that we will create will be a general one that we can use for all of our customer transactions.

How to do it...

To do this, open up the navigation panel, expand out the **Modules** group, and click on **Accounts Receivable** module to see all of the menu items that are available. Then click on the **Customer posting profiles** menu item within the **Journal Setup** menu group.

Alternatively, you can search for the **Customer posting profiles** form by clicking on the search icon in the header of the form (or press **ALT+G**) and then type in **customer posting** into the search box. Then you will be able to select the **Customer posting profiles** maintenance form from the dropdown list.

When the **Customer Posting Profiles** maintenance form is displayed, click on the **New** button in the menu bar.

This will create a new Posting profile record for us to start configuring.

To start off we will want to give our posting profile a **Posting Profile** code.

For this record we will set the **Posting profile** to **GEN**.

And then we can give our **Posting Profile** a more readable **Description.**

For example, here we set the **Description** to *General Posting Profile*.

Now that we have configured the profile, we will want to start adding in all of the default posting values that we want to use.

To do this we will want to click on the **+ Add** button within the **Setup** section of the form to create a new profile record for us.

For the posting profile details, we want to specify the scope of the defaults that we are about to define.

To do this we will want to click on the **Account Code** dropdown list within the **Posting Profile** and select the scope of the rule.

Here we can select from a few different options. The **All** option will apply this posting profile setup to all of the customers. The **Group** option will allow you to create a posting profile for a group of customers. And the **Table** option will allow you to create a posting profile specific to an individual customer.

In this case we want to set this up to be the global defaults for all customers unless overridden by a more specific rule, so we will set the **Account code** to the **All** option.

Now we will want to select a main account from the **Summary Account** field dropdown.

www.dynamicscompanions.com
Dynamics Companions

- 53 -

www.blindsquirrelpublishing.com
© 2017 Blind Squirrel Publishing, LLC , All Rights Reserved

BLIND SQUIRREL
PUBLISHING

DYNAMICS COMPANIONS
BARE BONES CONFIGURATION GUIDES

CONFIGURING ACCOUNTS RECEIVABLE WITHIN DYNAMICS 365 FOR OPERATIONS
MODULE 1: CONFIGURING THE ACCOUNTS RECEIVABLE CONTROLS

In this example, we will set the **Summary Account** to *130100* for the *Accounts Receivable – Domestic* account.

www.dynamicscompanions.com
Dynamics Companions

- 54 -

www.blindsquirrelpublishing.com
© 2017 Blind Squirrel Publishing, LLC , All Rights Reserved

BLIND SQUIRREL
PUBLISHING

DYNAMICS COMPANIONS
BARE BONES CONFIGURATION GUIDES

CONFIGURING ACCOUNTS RECEIVABLE WITHIN DYNAMICS 365 FOR OPERATIONS
MODULE 1: CONFIGURING THE ACCOUNTS RECEIVABLE CONTROLS

Configuring a General Customer Posting Profile

How to do it...

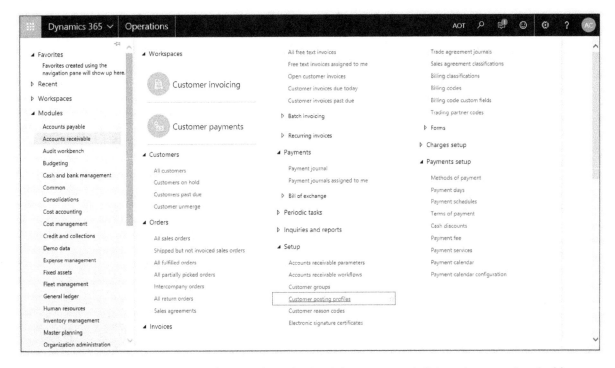

To do this, open up the navigation panel, expand out the **Modules** group, and click on **Accounts Receivable** module to see all of the menu items that are available. Then click on the **Customer posting profiles** menu item within the **Journal Setup** menu group.

dyn
www.dynamicscompanions.com
Dynamics Companions

- 55 -

www.blindsquirrelpublishing.com
© 2017 Blind Squirrel Publishing, LLC, All Rights Reserved

BLIND SQUIRREL
PUBLISHING

DYNAMICS COMPANIONS
BARE BONES CONFIGURATION GUIDES

CONFIGURING ACCOUNTS RECEIVABLE WITHIN DYNAMICS 365 FOR OPERATIONS
MODULE 1: CONFIGURING THE ACCOUNTS RECEIVABLE CONTROLS

Configuring a General Customer Posting Profile

How to do it...

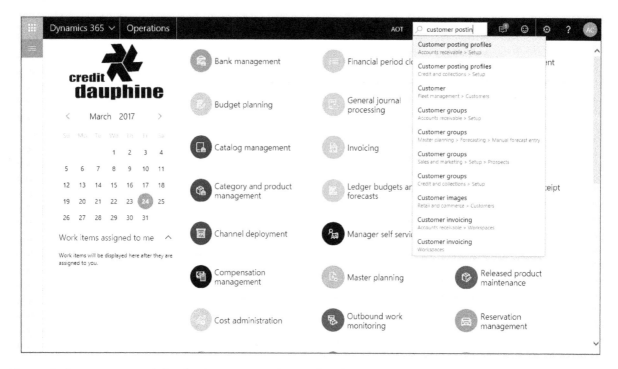

Alternatively, you can search for the **Customer posting profiles** form by clicking on the search icon in the header of the form (or press **ALT+G**) and then type in **customer posting** into the search box. Then you will be able to select the **Customer posting profiles** maintenance form from the dropdown list.

dync
www.dynamicscompanions.com
Dynamics Companions

- 56 -

www.blindsquirrelpublishing.com
© 2017 Blind Squirrel Publishing, LLC , All Rights Reserved

BLIND SQUIRREL
PUBLISHING

DYNAMICS COMPANIONS
BARE BONES CONFIGURATION GUIDES

CONFIGURING ACCOUNTS RECEIVABLE WITHIN DYNAMICS 365 FOR OPERATIONS
MODULE 1: CONFIGURING THE ACCOUNTS RECEIVABLE CONTROLS

Configuring a General Customer Posting Profile

How to do it...

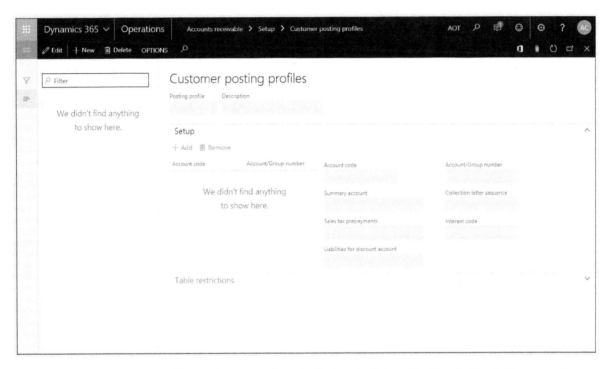

When the **Customer Posting Profiles** maintenance form is displayed, click on the **New** button in the menu bar.

dync
www.dynamicscompanions.com
Dynamics Companions

- 57 -

www.blindsquirrelpublishing.com
© 2017 Blind Squirrel Publishing, LLC , All Rights Reserved

BLIND SQUIRREL
PUBLISHING

DYNAMICS COMPANIONS
BARE BONES CONFIGURATION GUIDES

CONFIGURING ACCOUNTS RECEIVABLE WITHIN DYNAMICS 365 FOR OPERATIONS
MODULE 1: CONFIGURING THE ACCOUNTS RECEIVABLE CONTROLS

Configuring a General Customer Posting Profile

How to do it...

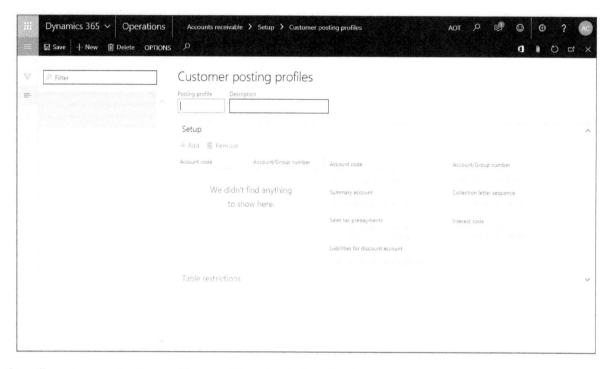

This will create a new Posting profile record for us to start configuring.

dync

www.dynamicscompanions.com
Dynamics Companions

- 58 -

www.blindsquirrelpublishing.com
© 2017 Blind Squirrel Publishing, LLC, All Rights Reserved

BLIND SQUIRREL
PUBLISHING

DYNAMICS COMPANIONS
BARE BONES CONFIGURATION GUIDES

CONFIGURING ACCOUNTS RECEIVABLE WITHIN DYNAMICS 365 FOR OPERATIONS
MODULE 1: CONFIGURING THE ACCOUNTS RECEIVABLE CONTROLS

Configuring a General Customer Posting Profile

How to do it...

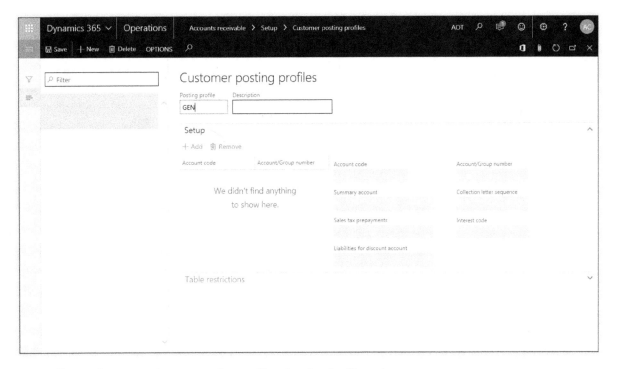

To start off we will want to give our posting profile a **Posting Profile** code.

For this record we will set the **Posting profile** to **GEN**.

dyn c

www.dynamicscompanions.com
Dynamics Companions

- 59 -

www.blindsquirrelpublishing.com
© 2017 Blind Squirrel Publishing, LLC, All Rights Reserved

BLIND SQUIRREL
PUBLISHING

DYNAMICS COMPANIONS
BARE BONES CONFIGURATION GUIDES

CONFIGURING ACCOUNTS RECEIVABLE WITHIN DYNAMICS 365 FOR OPERATIONS
MODULE 1: CONFIGURING THE ACCOUNTS RECEIVABLE CONTROLS

Configuring a General Customer Posting Profile

How to do it...

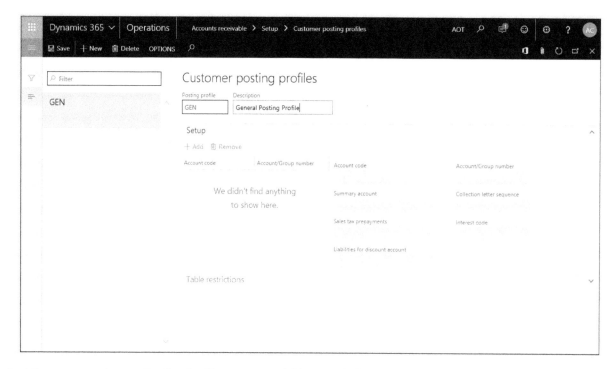

And then we can give our **Posting Profile** a more readable **Description.**

For example, here we set the **Description** to *General Posting Profile*.

DYNAMICS COMPANIONS
BARE BONES CONFIGURATION GUIDES

CONFIGURING ACCOUNTS RECEIVABLE WITHIN DYNAMICS 365 FOR OPERATIONS
MODULE 1: CONFIGURING THE ACCOUNTS RECEIVABLE CONTROLS

Configuring a General Customer Posting Profile

How to do it...

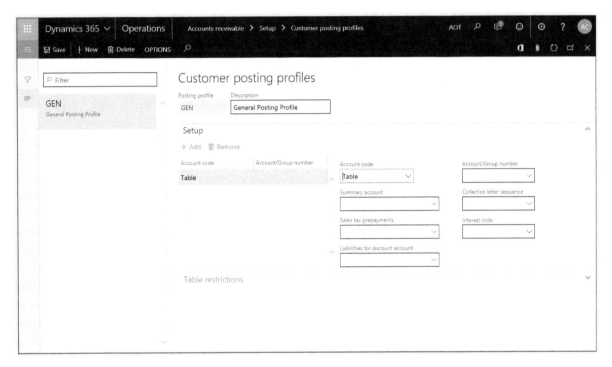

Now that we have configured the profile, we will want to start adding in all of the default posting values that we want to use.

To do this we will want to click on the **+ Add** button within the **Setup** section of the form to create a new profile record for us.

www.dynamicscompanions.com
Dynamics Companions

- 61 -

www.blindsquirrelpublishing.com
© 2017 Blind Squirrel Publishing, LLC, All Rights Reserved

BLIND SQUIRREL
PUBLISHING

DYNAMICS COMPANIONS
BARE BONES CONFIGURATION GUIDES

CONFIGURING ACCOUNTS RECEIVABLE WITHIN DYNAMICS 365 FOR OPERATIONS
MODULE 1: CONFIGURING THE ACCOUNTS RECEIVABLE CONTROLS

Configuring a General Customer Posting Profile

How to do it...

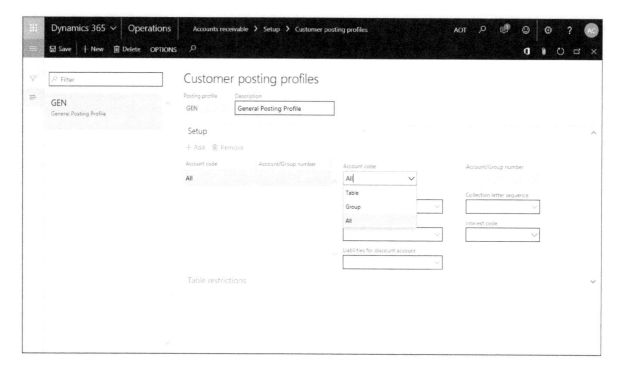

For the posting profile details, we want to specify the scope of the defaults that we are about to define.

To do this we will want to click on the **Account Code** dropdown list within the **Posting Profile** and select the scope of the rule.

Here we can select from a few different options. The **All** option will apply this posting profile setup to all of the customers. The **Group** option will allow you to create a posting profile for a group of customers. And the **Table** option will allow you to create a posting profile specific to an individual customer.

In this case we want to set this up to be the global defaults for all customers unless overridden by a more specific rule, so we will set the **Account code** to the **All** option.

dyn

www.dynamicscompanions.com
Dynamics Companions

- 62 -

www.blindsquirrelpublishing.com
© 2017 Blind Squirrel Publishing, LLC, All Rights Reserved

BLIND SQUIRREL
PUBLISHING

DYNAMICS COMPANIONS
BARE BONES CONFIGURATION GUIDES

CONFIGURING ACCOUNTS RECEIVABLE WITHIN DYNAMICS 365 FOR OPERATIONS
MODULE 1: CONFIGURING THE ACCOUNTS RECEIVABLE CONTROLS

Configuring a General Customer Posting Profile

How to do it...

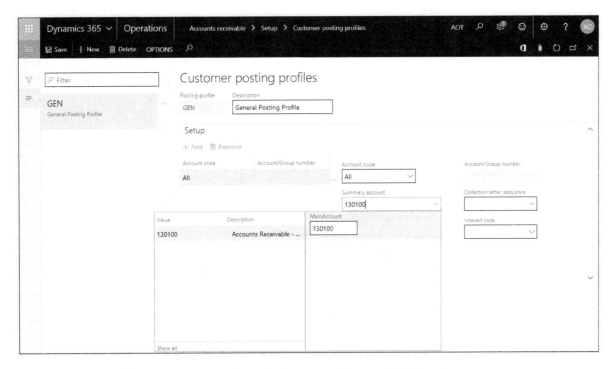

Now we will want to select a main account from the **Summary Account** field dropdown.

In this example, we will set the **Summary Account** to *130100* for the *Accounts Receivable – Domestic* account.

dync
www.dynamicscompanions.com
Dynamics Companions

- 63 -

www.blindsquirrelpublishing.com
© 2017 Blind Squirrel Publishing, LLC, All Rights Reserved

BLIND SQUIRREL
PUBLISHING

DYNAMICS COMPANIONS
BARE BONES CONFIGURATION GUIDES

CONFIGURING ACCOUNTS RECEIVABLE WITHIN DYNAMICS 365 FOR OPERATIONS
MODULE 1: CONFIGURING THE ACCOUNTS RECEIVABLE CONTROLS

Configuring a General Customer Posting Profile

Example Data

Field Name	Value
Posting Profile	GEN
Description	General Posting Profile
Account Code	All
Summary Account	130100

Posting Profile: GEN – General Posting Profile

www.dynamicscompanions.com
Dynamics Companions

- 64 -

www.blindsquirrelpublishing.com
© 2017 Blind Squirrel Publishing, LLC, All Rights Reserved

BLIND SQUIRREL
PUBLISHING

DYNAMICS COMPANIONS
BARE BONES CONFIGURATION GUIDES

CONFIGURING ACCOUNTS RECEIVABLE WITHIN DYNAMICS 365 FOR OPERATIONS
MODULE 1: CONFIGURING THE ACCOUNTS RECEIVABLE CONTROLS

Configuring a General Customer Posting Profile

Summary

Now we have a new posting profile that we can use on our customers. Later on we will show you where you will tell the system that it is the default option. So stay tuned.

DYNAMICS COMPANIONS
BARE BONES CONFIGURATION GUIDES

CONFIGURING ACCOUNTS RECEIVABLE WITHIN DYNAMICS 365 FOR OPERATIONS
MODULE 1: CONFIGURING THE ACCOUNTS RECEIVABLE CONTROLS

Configuring a Prepayment Customer Posting Profile

In addition to having a General Posting Profile, we can set up other Posting Profiles for some other types of Accounts Receivable transactions. Another example that we will want to configure is a Posting Profile for Prepayments.

How to do it...

To do this, return back to the **Customer posting profiles** maintenance form and click on the **+ New** button to create a new Customer posting profile record.

For this posting profile, set the **Posting profile** code to **PRE**.

And then set the **Description** for this posting profile to **Prepayments**.

Then click on the **+ Add** button within the **Setup** section of the form to create a new Posting Profile line.

We want this **Posting** Profile to also be associated with all customers by default, so click on the **Account Code** dropdown list and select the **All** option**.**

Set the **Summary Account** to a holding account for the pre-payments.

For this posting profile we will set the **Summary account** to *212160* for the *Customer Deposits* account.

For this Posting profile we will want to add a little bit more information. If you are going to be tracking sales tax, we will want to specify a **Main Account** for the **Sales Tax Prepayments** field.

In this example, we will set the **Sales tax prepayments** field to *221850* which is the *Other Taxes Payable* account.

When you have done that you can just click the **Close** button and exit from the form.

www.dynamicscompanions.com
Dynamics Companions

- 66 -

www.blindsquirrelpublishing.com
© 2017 Blind Squirrel Publishing, LLC, All Rights Reserved

BLIND SQUIRREL
PUBLISHING

DYNAMICS COMPANIONS
BARE BONES CONFIGURATION GUIDES

CONFIGURING ACCOUNTS RECEIVABLE WITHIN DYNAMICS 365 FOR OPERATIONS
MODULE 1: CONFIGURING THE ACCOUNTS RECEIVABLE CONTROLS

Configuring a Prepayment Customer Posting Profile

How to do it...

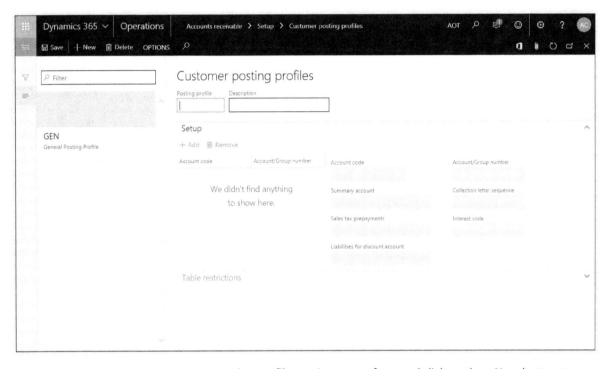

To do this, return back to the **Customer posting profiles** maintenance form and click on the **+ New** button to create a new Customer posting profile record.

dyn c
www.dynamicscompanions.com
Dynamics Companions

- 67 -

www.blindsquirrelpublishing.com
© 2017 Blind Squirrel Publishing, LLC, All Rights Reserved

BLIND SQUIRREL
PUBLISHING

DYNAMICS COMPANIONS
BARE BONES CONFIGURATION GUIDES

CONFIGURING ACCOUNTS RECEIVABLE WITHIN DYNAMICS 365 FOR OPERATIONS
MODULE 1: CONFIGURING THE ACCOUNTS RECEIVABLE CONTROLS

Configuring a Prepayment Customer Posting Profile

How to do it...

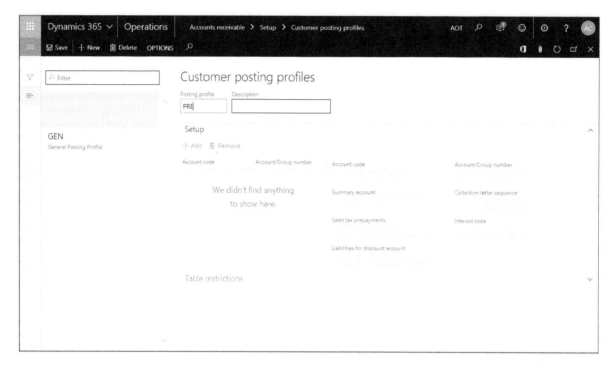

For this posting profile, set the **Posting profile** code to **PRE**.

dyn

www.dynamicscompanions.com
Dynamics Companions

- 68 -

www.blindsquirrelpublishing.com
© 2017 Blind Squirrel Publishing, LLC , All Rights Reserved

BLIND SQUIRREL
PUBLISHING

DYNAMICS COMPANIONS
BARE BONES CONFIGURATION GUIDES

CONFIGURING ACCOUNTS RECEIVABLE WITHIN DYNAMICS 365 FOR OPERATIONS
MODULE 1: CONFIGURING THE ACCOUNTS RECEIVABLE CONTROLS

Configuring a Prepayment Customer Posting Profile

How to do it...

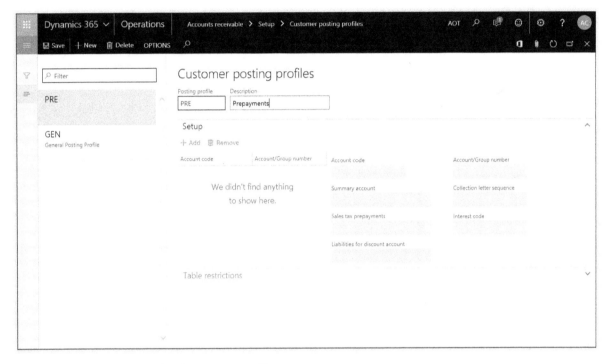

And then set the **Description** for this posting profile to **Prepayments**.

dync
www.dynamicscompanions.com
Dynamics Companions

- 69 -

www.blindsquirrelpublishing.com
© 2017 Blind Squirrel Publishing, LLC, All Rights Reserved

BLIND SQUIRREL
PUBLISHING

DYNAMICS COMPANIONS
BARE BONES CONFIGURATION GUIDES

CONFIGURING ACCOUNTS RECEIVABLE WITHIN DYNAMICS 365 FOR OPERATIONS
MODULE 1: CONFIGURING THE ACCOUNTS RECEIVABLE CONTROLS

Configuring a Prepayment Customer Posting Profile

How to do it...

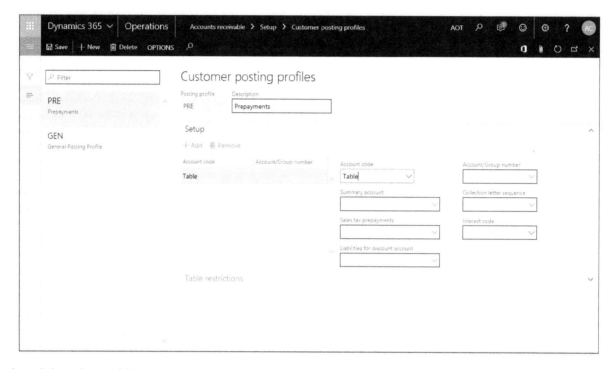

Then click on the **+ Add** button within the **Setup** section of the form to create a new Posting Profile line.

dyn

www.dynamicscompanions.com
Dynamics Companions

- 70 -

www.blindsquirrelpublishing.com
© 2017 Blind Squirrel Publishing, LLC , All Rights Reserved

BLIND SQUIRREL
PUBLISHING

DYNAMICS COMPANIONS
BARE BONES CONFIGURATION GUIDES

CONFIGURING ACCOUNTS RECEIVABLE WITHIN DYNAMICS 365 FOR OPERATIONS
MODULE 1: CONFIGURING THE ACCOUNTS RECEIVABLE CONTROLS

Configuring a Prepayment Customer Posting Profile

How to do it...

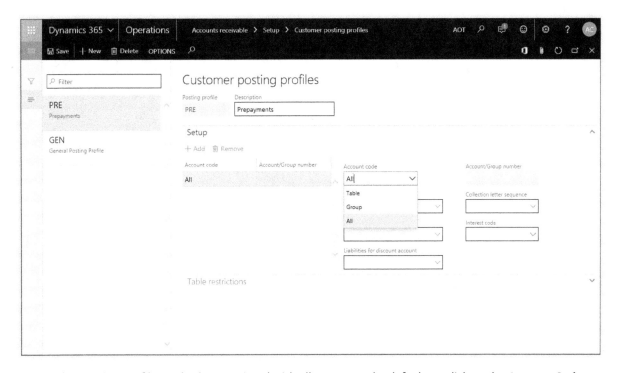

We want this **Posting** Profile to also be associated with all customers by default, so click on the **Account Code** dropdown list and select the **All** option.

dyn c
www.dynamicscompanions.com
Dynamics Companions

- 71 -

www.blindsquirrelpublishing.com
© 2017 Blind Squirrel Publishing, LLC, All Rights Reserved

BLIND SQUIRREL
PUBLISHING

DYNAMICS COMPANIONS
BARE BONES CONFIGURATION GUIDES

CONFIGURING ACCOUNTS RECEIVABLE WITHIN DYNAMICS 365 FOR OPERATIONS
MODULE 1: CONFIGURING THE ACCOUNTS RECEIVABLE CONTROLS

Configuring a Prepayment Customer Posting Profile

How to do it...

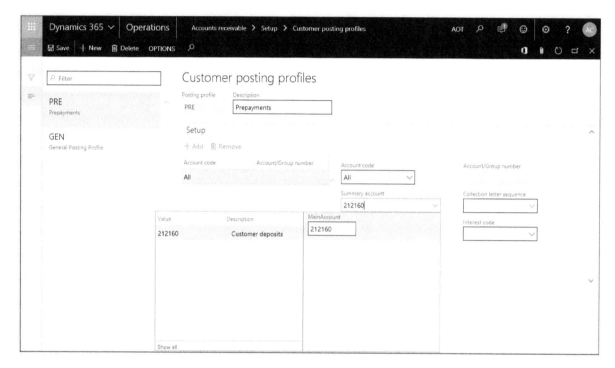

Set the **Summary Account** to a holding account for the pre-payments.

For this posting profile we will set the **Summary account** to *212160* for the *Customer Deposits* account.

dyn©
www.dynamicscompanions.com
Dynamics Companions

- 72 -

www.blindsquirrelpublishing.com
© 2017 Blind Squirrel Publishing, LLC, All Rights Reserved

BLIND SQUIRREL
PUBLISHING

DYNAMICS COMPANIONS
BARE BONES CONFIGURATION GUIDES

CONFIGURING ACCOUNTS RECEIVABLE WITHIN DYNAMICS 365 FOR OPERATIONS
MODULE 1: CONFIGURING THE ACCOUNTS RECEIVABLE CONTROLS

Configuring a Prepayment Customer Posting Profile

How to do it...

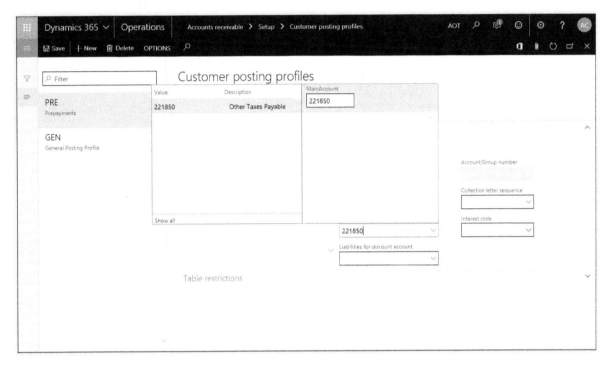

For this Posting profile we will want to add a little bit more information. If you are going to be tracking sales tax, we will want to specify a **Main Account** for the **Sales Tax Prepayments** field.

In this example, we will set the **Sales tax prepayments** field to *221850* which is the ***Other Taxes Payable*** account.

dync
www.dynamicscompanions.com
Dynamics Companions

- 73 -

www.blindsquirrelpublishing.com
© 2017 Blind Squirrel Publishing, LLC, All Rights Reserved

BLIND SQUIRREL
PUBLISHING

DYNAMICS COMPANIONS
BARE BONES CONFIGURATION GUIDES

CONFIGURING ACCOUNTS RECEIVABLE WITHIN DYNAMICS 365 FOR OPERATIONS
MODULE 1: CONFIGURING THE ACCOUNTS RECEIVABLE CONTROLS

Configuring a Prepayment Customer Posting Profile

How to do it...

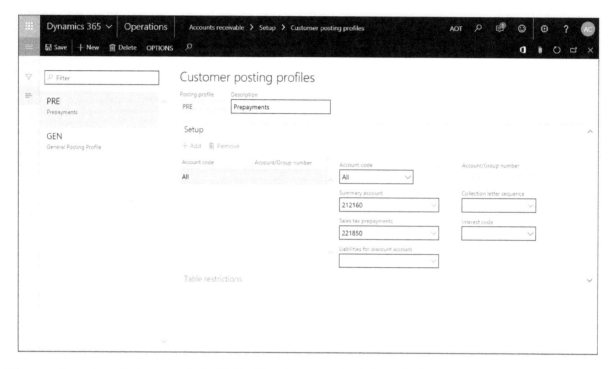

When you have done that you can just click the **Close** button and exit from the form.

dync

www.dynamicscompanions.com
Dynamics Companions

- 74 -

www.blindsquirrelpublishing.com
© 2017 Blind Squirrel Publishing, LLC , All Rights Reserved

BLIND SQUIRREL
PUBLISHING

DYNAMICS COMPANIONS
BARE BONES CONFIGURATION GUIDES

CONFIGURING ACCOUNTS RECEIVABLE WITHIN DYNAMICS 365 FOR OPERATIONS
MODULE 1: CONFIGURING THE ACCOUNTS RECEIVABLE CONTROLS

Configuring a Prepayment Customer Posting Profile

Field Name	Value
Posting Profile	PRE
Description	Prepayments
Account Code	All
Summary Account	212160
Sales tax prepayments	221850

Posting Profile: PRE – Prepayments

dyn c

www.dynamicscompanions.com
Dynamics Companions

- 75 -

www.blindsquirrelpublishing.com
© 2017 Blind Squirrel Publishing, LLC, All Rights Reserved

BLIND SQUIRREL
PUBLISHING

DYNAMICS COMPANIONS
BARE BONES CONFIGURATION GUIDES

CONFIGURING ACCOUNTS RECEIVABLE WITHIN DYNAMICS 365 FOR OPERATIONS
MODULE 1: CONFIGURING THE ACCOUNTS RECEIVABLE CONTROLS

Configuring a Prepayment Customer Posting Profile

Summary

Having the posting profiles configured is important within Dynamics 365. If you don't have them set up, then later on when you start trying to post transactions, the system will complain that it doesn't know where to post some of the transactions to.

You don't have to worry about that happening now.

DYNAMICS COMPANIONS
BARE BONES CONFIGURATION GUIDES

CONFIGURING ACCOUNTS RECEIVABLE WITHIN DYNAMICS 365 FOR OPERATIONS
MODULE 1: CONFIGURING THE ACCOUNTS RECEIVABLE CONTROLS

Configuring a Cash Terms of Payment

Now we can start configuring some of the codes and controls to manage your cash receipts. The best place to start with this is to configure your **Cash Terms of Payment** so that you can assign them to your customer accounts later.

How to do it...

To do this, open up the navigation panel, expand out the **Modules** group, and click on **Accounts Receivable** module to see all of the menu items that are available. Then click on the **Terms of Payment** menu item within the **Payments setup** menu group.

Alternatively, you can search for the **Terms of payment** form by clicking on the search icon in the header of the form (or press **ALT+G)** and then type in **terms of pay** into the search box. Then you will be able to select the **Terms of payment** maintenance form from the dropdown list.

This will open up the **Terms of payment** maintenance form for us.

To create a new **Terms of** payment record, all we need to do is click on the **+ New** button within the menu bar.

Now we can assign our new record a **Terms of payment** code.

In this exercise we will create a **Cash** payment term so we will set the **Terms of Payment** to **CASH.**

Next we will want to set the **Description** for the **Terms of Payment** to something a little friendlier.

In this example we will set the **Description** to **Cash**.

Next we will want to click on the **Payment Method** dropdown list and select the type of terms that we want to assign to this record.

For this example, we will be receiving the payment immediately, so we will set the **Payment Method** to the **COD** (Cash on delivery) option.

Also, we will want to mark this as a cash payment by checking the **Cash Payment** option flag.

Finally, within the **Ledger Posting** field group, select the main account that you want to post to from the **Cash** field dropdown list.

For this example, we will set the **Cash** field to *110110* to point to the *Bank account – USD* account.

After we have done that we are done with the first of our **Terms of Payment** records.

www.dynamicscompanions.com
Dynamics Companions

- 77 -

www.blindsquirrelpublishing.com
© 2017 Blind Squirrel Publishing, LLC , All Rights Reserved

BLIND SQUIRREL
PUBLISHING

DYNAMICS COMPANIONS
BARE BONES CONFIGURATION GUIDES

CONFIGURING ACCOUNTS RECEIVABLE WITHIN DYNAMICS 365 FOR OPERATIONS
MODULE 1: CONFIGURING THE ACCOUNTS RECEIVABLE CONTROLS

Configuring a Cash Terms of Payment

How to do it...

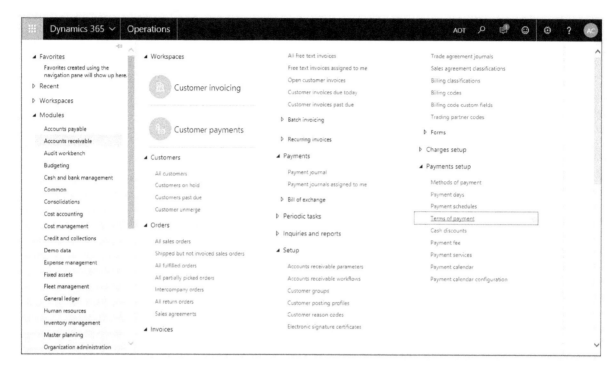

To do this, open up the navigation panel, expand out the **Modules** group, and click on **Accounts Receivable** module to see all of the menu items that are available. Then click on the **Terms of Payment** menu item within the **Payments setup** menu group.

dyn

www.dynamicscompanions.com
Dynamics Companions

- 78 -

www.blindsquirrelpublishing.com
© 2017 Blind Squirrel Publishing, LLC, All Rights Reserved

BLIND SQUIRREL
PUBLISHING

DYNAMICS COMPANIONS
BARE BONES CONFIGURATION GUIDES

CONFIGURING ACCOUNTS RECEIVABLE WITHIN DYNAMICS 365 FOR OPERATIONS
MODULE 1: CONFIGURING THE ACCOUNTS RECEIVABLE CONTROLS

Configuring a Cash Terms of Payment

How to do it...

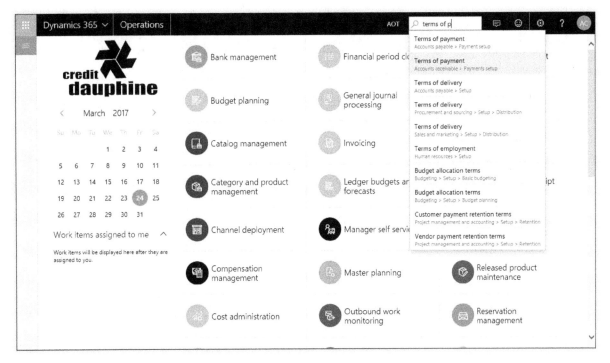

Alternatively, you can search for the **Terms of payment** form by clicking on the search icon in the header of the form (or press **ALT+G)** and then type in **terms of pay** into the search box. Then you will be able to select the **Terms of payment** maintenance form from the dropdown list.

www.dynamicscompanions.com
Dynamics Companions

- 79 -

www.blindsquirrelpublishing.com
© 2017 Blind Squirrel Publishing, LLC, All Rights Reserved

BLIND SQUIRREL
PUBLISHING

DYNAMICS COMPANIONS
BARE BONES CONFIGURATION GUIDES

CONFIGURING ACCOUNTS RECEIVABLE WITHIN DYNAMICS 365 FOR OPERATIONS
MODULE 1: CONFIGURING THE ACCOUNTS RECEIVABLE CONTROLS

Configuring a Cash Terms of Payment

How to do it...

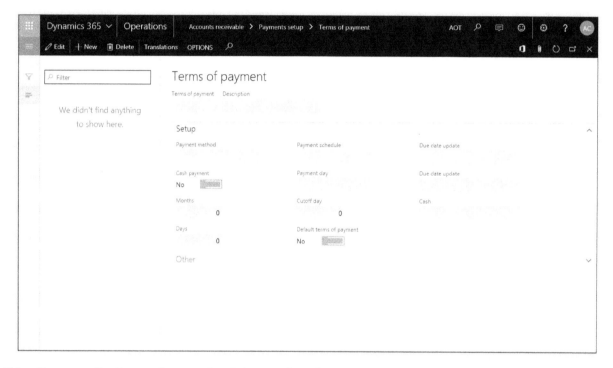

This will open up the **Terms of payment** maintenance form for us.

dyn c

www.dynamicscompanions.com
Dynamics Companions

- 80 -

www.blindsquirrelpublishing.com
© 2017 Blind Squirrel Publishing, LLC, All Rights Reserved

BLIND SQUIRREL
PUBLISHING

DYNAMICS COMPANIONS
BARE BONES CONFIGURATION GUIDES

CONFIGURING ACCOUNTS RECEIVABLE WITHIN DYNAMICS 365 FOR OPERATIONS
MODULE 1: CONFIGURING THE ACCOUNTS RECEIVABLE CONTROLS

Configuring a Cash Terms of Payment

How to do it...

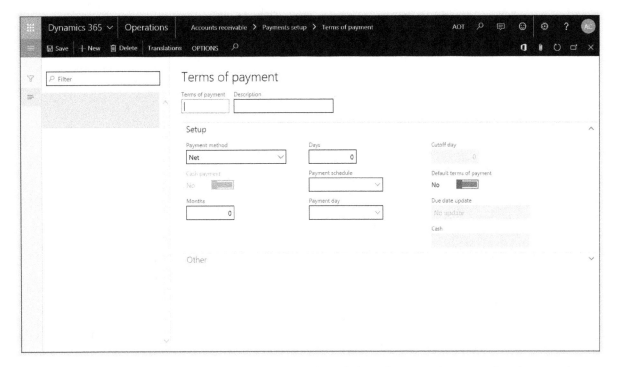

To create a new **Terms of** payment record, all we need to do is click on the **+ New** button within the menu bar.

www.dynamicscompanions.com
Dynamics Companions

- 81 -

www.blindsquirrelpublishing.com
© 2017 Blind Squirrel Publishing, LLC , All Rights Reserved

BLIND SQUIRREL
PUBLISHING

DYNAMICS COMPANIONS
BARE BONES CONFIGURATION GUIDES

CONFIGURING ACCOUNTS RECEIVABLE WITHIN DYNAMICS 365 FOR OPERATIONS
MODULE 1: CONFIGURING THE ACCOUNTS RECEIVABLE CONTROLS

Configuring a Cash Terms of Payment

How to do it...

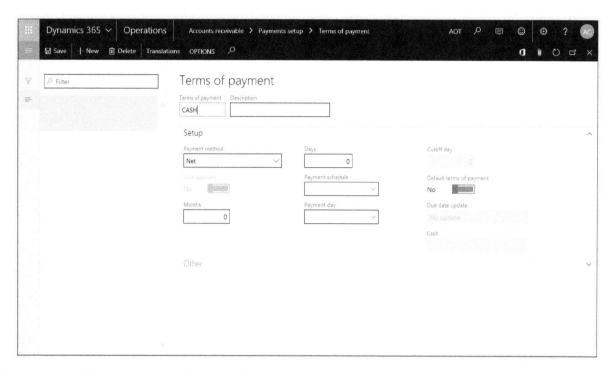

Now we can assign our new record a **Terms of payment** code.

In this exercise we will create a **Cash** payment term so we will set the **Terms of Payment** to **CASH.**

dync
www.dynamicscompanions.com
Dynamics Companions

- 82 -

www.blindsquirrelpublishing.com
© 2017 Blind Squirrel Publishing, LLC , All Rights Reserved

BLIND SQUIRREL
PUBLISHING

DYNAMICS COMPANIONS
BARE BONES CONFIGURATION GUIDES

CONFIGURING ACCOUNTS RECEIVABLE WITHIN DYNAMICS 365 FOR OPERATIONS
MODULE 1: CONFIGURING THE ACCOUNTS RECEIVABLE CONTROLS

Configuring a Cash Terms of Payment

How to do it...

Next we will want to set the **Description** for the **Terms of Payment** to something a little friendlier.

In this example we will set the **Description** to **Cash**.

DYNAMICS COMPANIONS
BARE BONES CONFIGURATION GUIDES

CONFIGURING ACCOUNTS RECEIVABLE WITHIN DYNAMICS 365 FOR OPERATIONS
MODULE 1: CONFIGURING THE ACCOUNTS RECEIVABLE CONTROLS

Configuring a Cash Terms of Payment

How to do it...

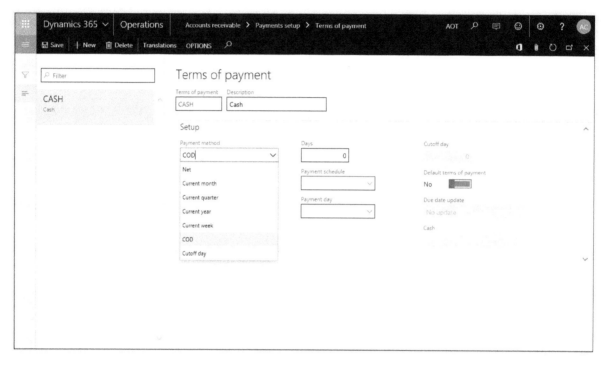

Next we will want to click on the **Payment Method** dropdown list and select the type of terms that we want to assign to this record.

For this example, we will be receiving the payment immediately, so we will set the **Payment Method** to the **COD** (Cash on delivery) option.

dyn c
www.dynamicscompanions.com
Dynamics Companions

- 84 -

www.blindsquirrelpublishing.com
© 2017 Blind Squirrel Publishing, LLC , All Rights Reserved

BLIND SQUIRREL
PUBLISHING

DYNAMICS COMPANIONS
BARE BONES CONFIGURATION GUIDES

CONFIGURING ACCOUNTS RECEIVABLE WITHIN DYNAMICS 365 FOR OPERATIONS
MODULE 1: CONFIGURING THE ACCOUNTS RECEIVABLE CONTROLS

Configuring a Cash Terms of Payment

How to do it...

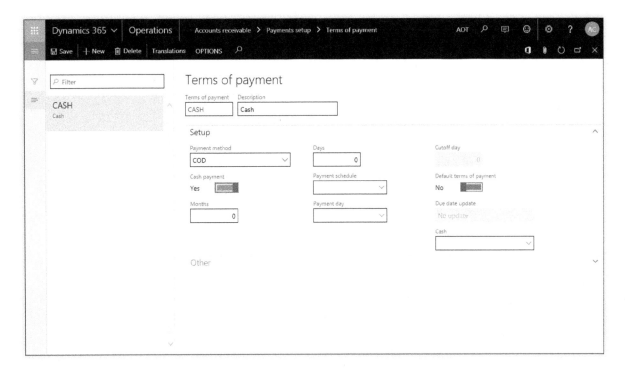

Also, we will want to mark this as a cash payment by checking the **Cash Payment** option flag.

dyn c
www.dynamicscompanions.com
Dynamics Companions

- 85 -

www.blindsquirrelpublishing.com
© 2017 Blind Squirrel Publishing, LLC , All Rights Reserved

BLIND SQUIRREL
PUBLISHING

DYNAMICS COMPANIONS
BARE BONES CONFIGURATION GUIDES

CONFIGURING ACCOUNTS RECEIVABLE WITHIN DYNAMICS 365 FOR OPERATIONS
MODULE 1: CONFIGURING THE ACCOUNTS RECEIVABLE CONTROLS

Configuring a Cash Terms of Payment

How to do it...

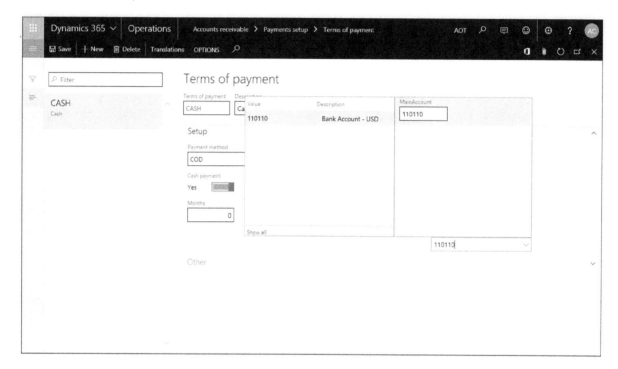

Finally, within the **Ledger Posting** field group, select the main account that you want to post to from the **Cash** field dropdown list.

For this example, we will set the **Cash** field to *110110* to point to the *Bank account – USD* account.

dyn

www.dynamicscompanions.com
Dynamics Companions

- 86 -

www.blindsquirrelpublishing.com
© 2017 Blind Squirrel Publishing, LLC, All Rights Reserved

BLIND SQUIRREL
PUBLISHING

DYNAMICS COMPANIONS
BARE BONES CONFIGURATION GUIDES

CONFIGURING ACCOUNTS RECEIVABLE WITHIN DYNAMICS 365 FOR OPERATIONS
MODULE 1: CONFIGURING THE ACCOUNTS RECEIVABLE CONTROLS

Configuring a Cash Terms of Payment

How to do it...

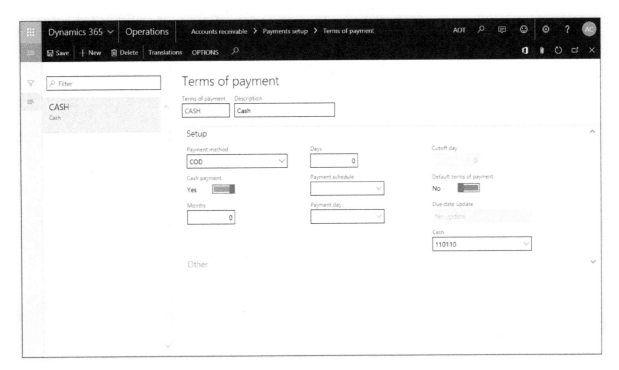

After we have done that we are done with the first of our **Terms of Payment** records.

dyn c
www.dynamicscompanions.com
Dynamics Companions

- 87 -

www.blindsquirrelpublishing.com
© 2017 Blind Squirrel Publishing, LLC, All Rights Reserved

BLIND SQUIRREL
PUBLISHING

DYNAMICS COMPANIONS
BARE BONES CONFIGURATION GUIDES

CONFIGURING ACCOUNTS RECEIVABLE WITHIN DYNAMICS 365 FOR OPERATIONS
MODULE 1: CONFIGURING THE ACCOUNTS RECEIVABLE CONTROLS

Configuring a Cash Terms of Payment

Example Data

Field Name	Value
Terms of payment	CASH
Description	Cash
Payment method	COD
Cash Payment	True
Cash	110110

Terms of Payment: CASH – Cash

www.dynamicscompanions.com
Dynamics Companions

- 88 -

www.blindsquirrelpublishing.com
© 2017 Blind Squirrel Publishing, LLC , All Rights Reserved

BLIND SQUIRREL
PUBLISHING

DYNAMICS COMPANIONS
BARE BONES CONFIGURATION GUIDES

CONFIGURING ACCOUNTS RECEIVABLE WITHIN DYNAMICS 365 FOR OPERATIONS
MODULE 1: CONFIGURING THE ACCOUNTS RECEIVABLE CONTROLS

Configuring a Cash Terms of Payment

Summary

How easy was that. Now we have a way that we can tell the customer that he needs to pay in cash.

DYNAMICS COMPANIONS
BARE BONES CONFIGURATION GUIDES

CONFIGURING ACCOUNTS RECEIVABLE WITHIN DYNAMICS 365 FOR OPERATIONS
MODULE 1: CONFIGURING THE ACCOUNTS RECEIVABLE CONTROLS

Configuring a Cash on Delivery Terms of Payment

Another variation of the Cash Terms of Payment that we may want to configure is **Cash on Delivery**. This is going to be similar to the previous Terms of Payment code that we set up, but not quite the same.

How to do it...

Start off by returning back to the **Terms of payment** maintenance form and click on the **+ New** button in the menu bar to create a new record.

Then give your new record a **Terms of Payment** code.

Here we will set the **Terms on payment** code to **COD**.

Then give your Terms of payment record a **Description.**

For example, set the **Description** to *Cash on Delivery*.

And then click on the **Payment Method** dropdown list and select the type of terms for this record.

Here we will want to set the **Payment Method** to the **COD** (Cash on delivery) as well.

For this type of **Terms of delivery** we do not need to check the **Cash Payment** flag.

And now we are done.

www.dynamicscompanions.com
Dynamics Companions

- 90 -

www.blindsquirrelpublishing.com
© 2017 Blind Squirrel Publishing, LLC , All Rights Reserved

BLIND SQUIRREL
PUBLISHING

DYNAMICS COMPANIONS
BARE BONES CONFIGURATION GUIDES

CONFIGURING ACCOUNTS RECEIVABLE WITHIN DYNAMICS 365 FOR OPERATIONS
MODULE 1: CONFIGURING THE ACCOUNTS RECEIVABLE CONTROLS

Configuring a Cash on Delivery Terms of Payment

How to do it...

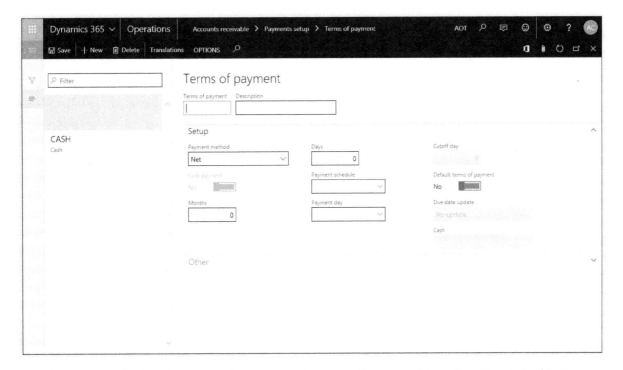

Start off by returning back to the **Terms of payment** maintenance form and click on the **+ New** button in the menu bar to create a new record.

dyn

www.dynamicscompanions.com
Dynamics Companions

- 91 -

www.blindsquirrelpublishing.com
© 2017 Blind Squirrel Publishing, LLC , All Rights Reserved

BLIND SQUIRREL
PUBLISHING

DYNAMICS COMPANIONS
BARE BONES CONFIGURATION GUIDES

CONFIGURING ACCOUNTS RECEIVABLE WITHIN DYNAMICS 365 FOR OPERATIONS
MODULE 1: CONFIGURING THE ACCOUNTS RECEIVABLE CONTROLS

Configuring a Cash on Delivery Terms of Payment

How to do it...

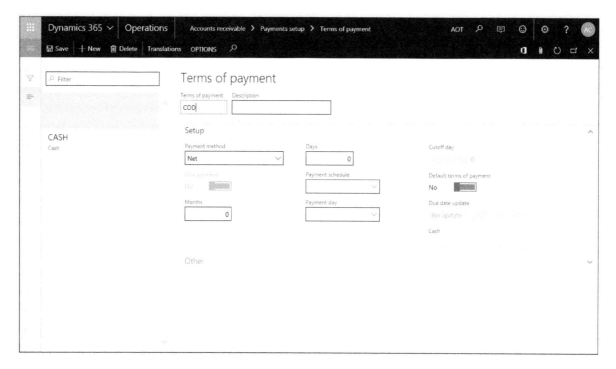

Then give your new record a **Terms of Payment** code.

Here we will set the **Terms on payment** code to **COD**.

dyn
www.dynamicscompanions.com
Dynamics Companions
- 92 -
www.blindsquirrelpublishing.com
© 2017 Blind Squirrel Publishing, LLC, All Rights Reserved
BLIND SQUIRREL
PUBLISHING

DYNAMICS COMPANIONS
BARE BONES CONFIGURATION GUIDES

CONFIGURING ACCOUNTS RECEIVABLE WITHIN DYNAMICS 365 FOR OPERATIONS
MODULE 1: CONFIGURING THE ACCOUNTS RECEIVABLE CONTROLS

Configuring a Cash on Delivery Terms of Payment

How to do it...

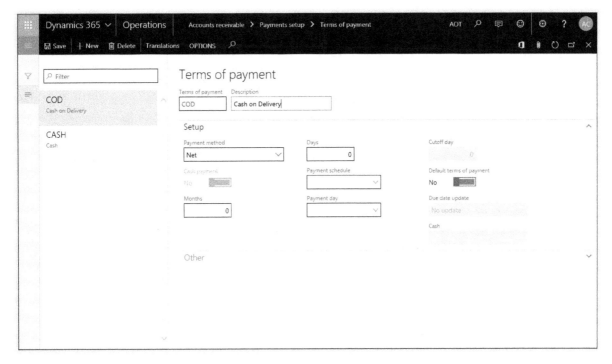

Then give your Terms of payment record a **Description.**

For example, set the **Description** to ***Cash on Delivery***.

www.dynamicscompanions.com
Dynamics Companions

- 93 -

www.blindsquirrelpublishing.com
© 2017 Blind Squirrel Publishing, LLC , All Rights Reserved

BLIND SQUIRREL
PUBLISHING

DYNAMICS COMPANIONS
BARE BONES CONFIGURATION GUIDES

CONFIGURING ACCOUNTS RECEIVABLE WITHIN DYNAMICS 365 FOR OPERATIONS
MODULE 1: CONFIGURING THE ACCOUNTS RECEIVABLE CONTROLS

Configuring a Cash on Delivery Terms of Payment

How to do it...

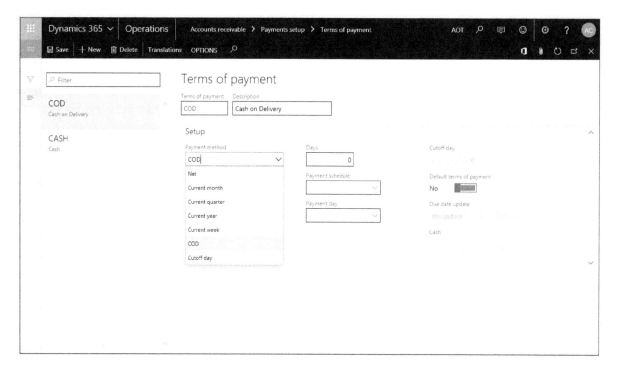

And then click on the **Payment Method** dropdown list and select the type of terms for this record.

Here we will want to set the **Payment Method** to the **COD** (Cash on delivery) as well.

dyn c

www.dynamicscompanions.com
Dynamics Companions

- 94 -

www.blindsquirrelpublishing.com
© 2017 Blind Squirrel Publishing, LLC , All Rights Reserved

BLIND SQUIRREL
PUBLISHING

DYNAMICS COMPANIONS
BARE BONES CONFIGURATION GUIDES

CONFIGURING ACCOUNTS RECEIVABLE WITHIN DYNAMICS 365 FOR OPERATIONS
MODULE 1: CONFIGURING THE ACCOUNTS RECEIVABLE CONTROLS

Configuring a Cash on Delivery Terms of Payment

How to do it...

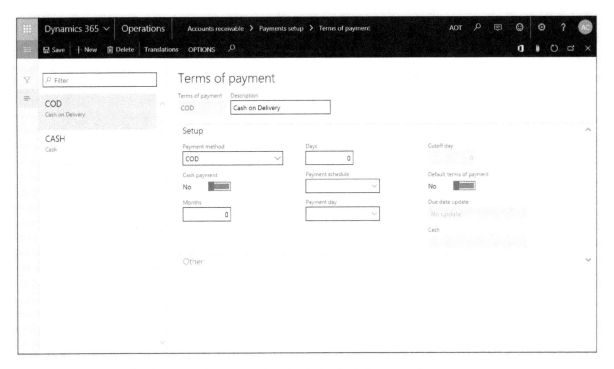

For this type of **Terms of delivery** we do not need to check the **Cash Payment** flag.

And now we are done.

dyn

www.dynamicscompanions.com
Dynamics Companions

- 95 -

www.blindsquirrelpublishing.com
© 2017 Blind Squirrel Publishing, LLC, All Rights Reserved

BLIND SQUIRREL
PUBLISHING

DYNAMICS COMPANIONS
BARE BONES CONFIGURATION GUIDES

CONFIGURING ACCOUNTS RECEIVABLE WITHIN DYNAMICS 365 FOR OPERATIONS
MODULE 1: CONFIGURING THE ACCOUNTS RECEIVABLE CONTROLS

Configuring a Cash on Delivery Terms of Payment

Example Data

Field Name	Value
Terms of payment	COD
Description	Cash on Delivery
Payment method	COD

Terms of Payment: COD – Cash on Delivery

dyn

www.dynamicscompanions.com
Dynamics Companions

- 96 -

www.blindsquirrelpublishing.com
© 2017 Blind Squirrel Publishing, LLC, All Rights Reserved

BLIND SQUIRREL
PUBLISHING

DYNAMICS COMPANIONS
BARE BONES CONFIGURATION GUIDES

CONFIGURING ACCOUNTS RECEIVABLE WITHIN DYNAMICS 365 FOR OPERATIONS
MODULE 1: CONFIGURING THE ACCOUNTS RECEIVABLE CONTROLS

Configuring a Cash on Delivery Terms of Payment

Summary

Now we have a couple of Cash Payment terms configured we now have a way of telling if we are receiving our cash payments right away or when we deliver the products and services.

DYNAMICS COMPANIONS
BARE BONES CONFIGURATION GUIDES

CONFIGURING ACCOUNTS RECEIVABLE WITHIN DYNAMICS 365 FOR OPERATIONS
MODULE 1: CONFIGURING THE ACCOUNTS RECEIVABLE CONTROLS

Configuring Net Day Payment Terms

Another type of **Payment Term** that you may want to configure is a **Net Days Payment** to pay on or before the date.

How to do it...

To do this, return to the **Terms of payment** maintenance form and click on the **+ New** button in the menu bar to create a new record.

Then set the **Terms of payment** code that we want to use to identify this record.

Here we will set the **Terms of payment** to *NET30*.

And then give your record a more descriptive **Description.**

For example, here we set the **Description** to *Net 30 Days*.

Now we will need to click on the **Payment method** dropdown list and select the method that we want to use to calculate this **Term of payment**.

For this record we will want to set the **Payment Method** to the **Net** option.

This will allow us to specify the timeframe that we want the payment within.

Now we will be able to specify either the number of **Months** or **Days** that we want to be paid within.

For this **Term of payment,** we want to be paid within 30 days. So within the **Days** field, set the number of days to **30**.

Let's create a couple more variations of this **Term of payment** with different timeframes.

Click on the **+ New** button in the menu bar to create a new record, set the **Terms of payment** code to *NET15*, then the **Description** to *Net 15 Days*, select the **Payment method** of *Net* and then set the **Days** to *15*.

Now we have a way to specify that we want to be paid within 15 days.

Click on the **+ New** button in the menu bar to create a new record, set the **Terms of payment** code to *NET10*, then the **Description** to *Net 10 Days*, select the **Payment method** of *Net* and then set the **Days** to *10*.

Now we have a way to specify that we want to be paid within 10 days.

Let's click on the **+ New** button in the menu bar to create one last record, set the **Terms of payment** code to *NET1*, then the **Description** to *Net 1 Days*, select the **Payment method** of *Net* and then set the **Days** to *1*.

Now we have a way to specify that we want to be paid within 1 day for those customers that we want to be paid almost immediately.

After we have done that I think we are done. So we can exit from the form.

dyn

www.dynamicscompanions.com
Dynamics Companions

- 98 -

www.blindsquirrelpublishing.com
© 2017 Blind Squirrel Publishing, LLC , All Rights Reserved

BLIND SQUIRREL
PUBLISHING

DYNAMICS COMPANIONS
BARE BONES CONFIGURATION GUIDES

CONFIGURING ACCOUNTS RECEIVABLE WITHIN DYNAMICS 365 FOR OPERATIONS
MODULE 1: CONFIGURING THE ACCOUNTS RECEIVABLE CONTROLS

Configuring Net Day Payment Terms

How to do it...

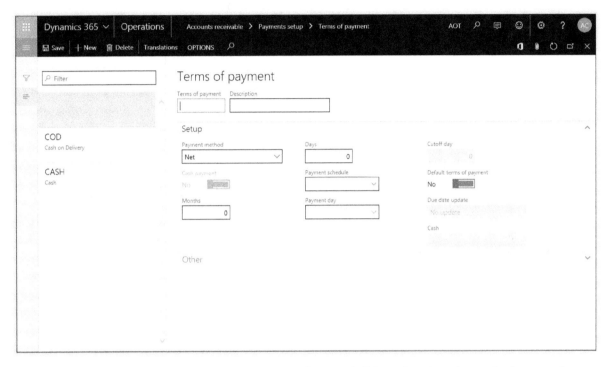

To do this, return to the **Terms of payment** maintenance form and click on the **+ New** button in the menu bar to create a new record.

www.dynamicscompanions.com
Dynamics Companions

- 99 -

www.blindsquirrelpublishing.com
© 2017 Blind Squirrel Publishing, LLC, All Rights Reserved

BLIND SQUIRREL
PUBLISHING

DYNAMICS COMPANIONS
BARE BONES CONFIGURATION GUIDES

CONFIGURING ACCOUNTS RECEIVABLE WITHIN DYNAMICS 365 FOR OPERATIONS
MODULE 1: CONFIGURING THE ACCOUNTS RECEIVABLE CONTROLS

Configuring Net Day Payment Terms

How to do it...

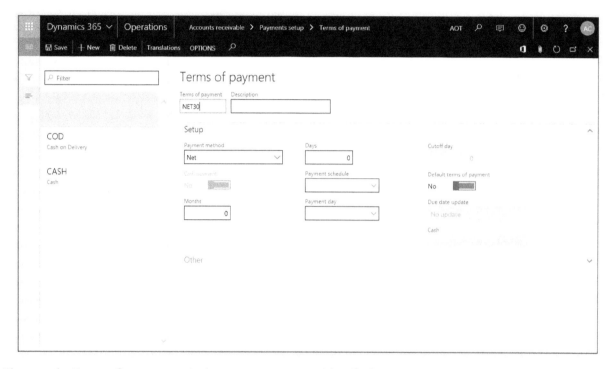

Then set the **Terms of payment** code that we want to use to identify this record.

Here we will set the **Terms of payment** to *NET30*.

dynᴄ
www.dynamicscompanions.com
Dynamics Companions

- 100 -

www.blindsquirrelpublishing.com
© 2017 Blind Squirrel Publishing, LLC, All Rights Reserved

BLIND SQUIRREL
PUBLISHING

DYNAMICS COMPANIONS
BARE BONES CONFIGURATION GUIDES

CONFIGURING ACCOUNTS RECEIVABLE WITHIN DYNAMICS 365 FOR OPERATIONS
MODULE 1: CONFIGURING THE ACCOUNTS RECEIVABLE CONTROLS

Configuring Net Day Payment Terms

How to do it...

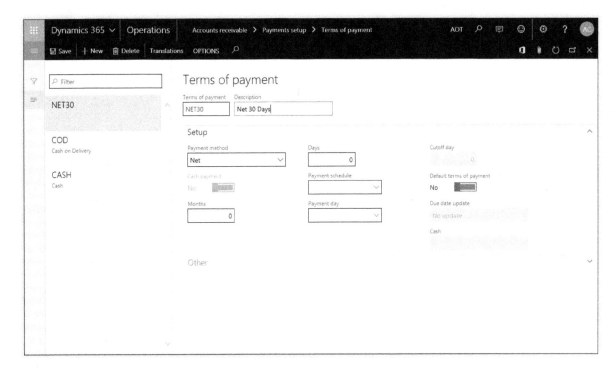

And then give your record a more descriptive **Description.**

For example, here we set the **Description** to *Net 30 Days*.

dyn c
www.dynamicscompanions.com
Dynamics Companions

- 101 -

www.blindsquirrelpublishing.com
© 2017 Blind Squirrel Publishing, LLC, All Rights Reserved

BLIND SQUIRREL
PUBLISHING

DYNAMICS COMPANIONS
BARE BONES CONFIGURATION GUIDES

CONFIGURING ACCOUNTS RECEIVABLE WITHIN DYNAMICS 365 FOR OPERATIONS
MODULE 1: CONFIGURING THE ACCOUNTS RECEIVABLE CONTROLS

Configuring Net Day Payment Terms

How to do it...

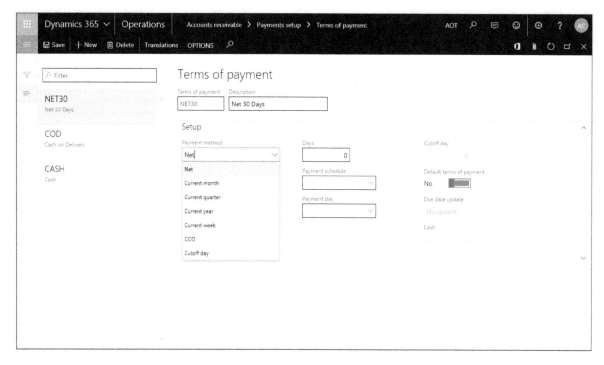

Now we will need to click on the **Payment method** dropdown list and select the method that we want to use to calculate this **Term of payment**.

For this record we will want to set the **Payment Method** to the **Net** option.

This will allow us to specify the timeframe that we want the payment within.

dyn
www.dynamicscompanions.com
Dynamics Companions

- 102 -

www.blindsquirrelpublishing.com
© 2017 Blind Squirrel Publishing, LLC, All Rights Reserved

BLIND SQUIRREL
PUBLISHING

DYNAMICS COMPANIONS
BARE BONES CONFIGURATION GUIDES

CONFIGURING ACCOUNTS RECEIVABLE WITHIN DYNAMICS 365 FOR OPERATIONS
MODULE 1: CONFIGURING THE ACCOUNTS RECEIVABLE CONTROLS

Configuring Net Day Payment Terms

How to do it...

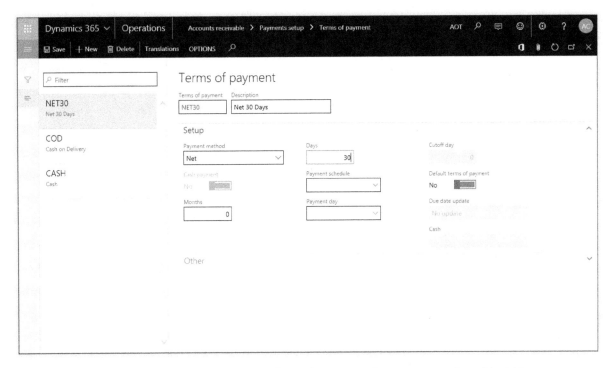

Now we will be able to specify either the number of **Months** or **Days** that we want to be paid within.

For this **Term of payment,** we want to be paid within 30 days. So within the **Days** field, set the number of days to **30**.

dyn c
www.dynamicscompanions.com
Dynamics Companions

- 103 -

www.blindsquirrelpublishing.com
© 2017 Blind Squirrel Publishing, LLC, All Rights Reserved

BLIND SQUIRREL
PUBLISHING

DYNAMICS COMPANIONS
BARE BONES CONFIGURATION GUIDES

CONFIGURING ACCOUNTS RECEIVABLE WITHIN DYNAMICS 365 FOR OPERATIONS
MODULE 1: CONFIGURING THE ACCOUNTS RECEIVABLE CONTROLS

Configuring Net Day Payment Terms

How to do it...

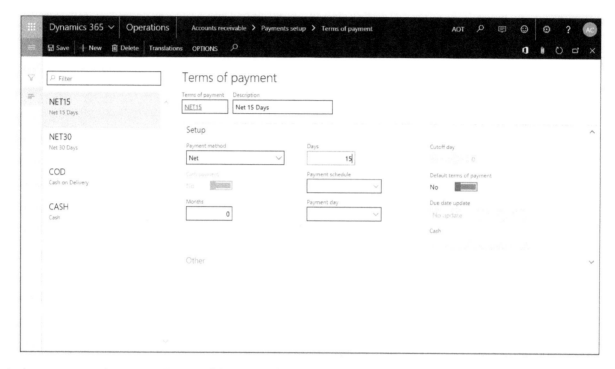

Let's create a couple more variations of this **Term of payment** with different timeframes.

Click on the **+ New** button in the menu bar to create a new record, set the **Terms of payment** code to **NET15**, then the **Description** to **Net 15 Days**, select the **Payment method** of **Net** and then set the **Days** to **15**.

Now we have a way to specify that we want to be paid within 15 days.

dync

www.dynamicscompanions.com
Dynamics Companions

- 104 -

www.blindsquirrelpublishing.com
© 2017 Blind Squirrel Publishing, LLC, All Rights Reserved

BLIND SQUIRREL
PUBLISHING

DYNAMICS COMPANIONS
BARE BONES CONFIGURATION GUIDES

CONFIGURING ACCOUNTS RECEIVABLE WITHIN DYNAMICS 365 FOR OPERATIONS
MODULE 1: CONFIGURING THE ACCOUNTS RECEIVABLE CONTROLS

Configuring Net Day Payment Terms

How to do it...

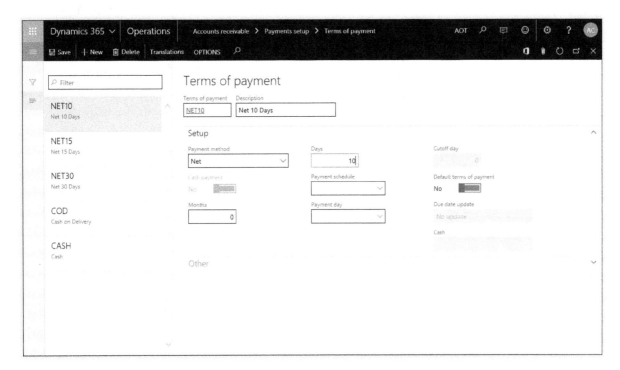

Click on the **+ New** button in the menu bar to create a new record, set the **Terms of payment** code to *NET10*, then the **Description** to *Net 10 Days*, select the **Payment method** of *Net* and then set the **Days** to *10*.

Now we have a way to specify that we want to be paid within 10 days.

dyn c
www.dynamicscompanions.com
Dynamics Companions

- 105 -

www.blindsquirrelpublishing.com
© 2017 Blind Squirrel Publishing, LLC , All Rights Reserved

BLIND SQUIRREL
PUBLISHING

DYNAMICS COMPANIONS
BARE BONES CONFIGURATION GUIDES

CONFIGURING ACCOUNTS RECEIVABLE WITHIN DYNAMICS 365 FOR OPERATIONS
MODULE 1: CONFIGURING THE ACCOUNTS RECEIVABLE CONTROLS

Configuring Net Day Payment Terms

How to do it...

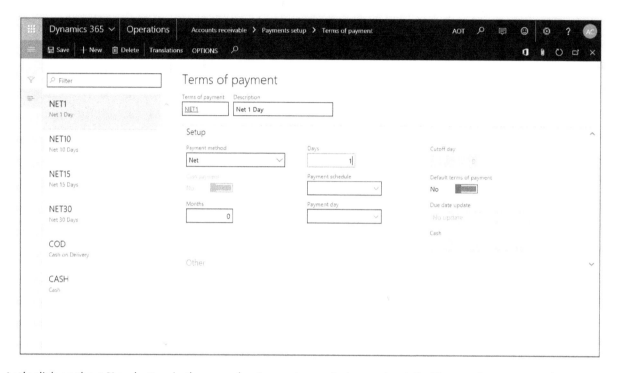

Let's click on the **+ New** button in the menu bar to create one last record, set the **Terms of payment** code to *NET1*, then the **Description** to *Net 1 Days*, select the **Payment method** of *Net* and then set the **Days** to *1*.

Now we have a way to specify that we want to be paid within 1 day for those customers that we want to be paid almost immediately.

After we have done that I think we are done. So we can exit from the form.

dyn
www.dynamicscompanions.com
Dynamics Companions

- 106 -

www.blindsquirrelpublishing.com
© 2017 Blind Squirrel Publishing, LLC , All Rights Reserved

BLIND SQUIRREL
PUBLISHING

DYNAMICS COMPANIONS
BARE BONES CONFIGURATION GUIDES

CONFIGURING ACCOUNTS RECEIVABLE WITHIN DYNAMICS 365 FOR OPERATIONS
MODULE 1: CONFIGURING THE ACCOUNTS RECEIVABLE CONTROLS

Configuring Net Day Payment Terms

Example Data

Field Name	Value
Terms of payment	NET30
Description	Net 30 Days
Payment method	Net
Days	30

Terms of Payment: NET30 – Net 30 Days

Field Name	Value
Terms of payment	NET15
Description	Net 15 Days
Payment method	Net
Days	15

Terms of Payment: NET15 – Net 15 Days

Field Name	Value
Terms of payment	NET10
Description	Net 10 Days
Payment method	Net
Days	10

Terms of Payment: NET10 – Net 10 Days

Field Name	Value
Terms of payment	NET1
Description	Net 1 Day
Payment method	Net
Days	1

Terms of Payment: NET1 – Net 1 Day

DYNAMICS COMPANIONS
BARE BONES CONFIGURATION GUIDES

CONFIGURING ACCOUNTS RECEIVABLE WITHIN DYNAMICS 365 FOR OPERATIONS
MODULE 1: CONFIGURING THE ACCOUNTS RECEIVABLE CONTROLS

Configuring Net Day Payment Terms

Summary

Now we have set up our Net Days payment terms we will be able to set customers up to pay on account, but we will also track when they are supposed to pay as well to make sure that we get our money in a timely manner.

DYNAMICS COMPANIONS
BARE BONES CONFIGURATION GUIDES

CONFIGURING ACCOUNTS RECEIVABLE WITHIN DYNAMICS 365 FOR OPERATIONS
MODULE 1: CONFIGURING THE ACCOUNTS RECEIVABLE CONTROLS

Configuring Net Day of Month Term of Payment

Another type of **Term of payment** that you may want to offer to your customers is the option to pay on a certain day of the month. This requires a little additional configuration, but is still not a big deal.

How to do it...

To do this, open up the navigation panel, expand out the **Modules** group, and click on **Accounts receivable** module to see all of the menu items that are available. Then click on the **Payment days** menu item within the **Payment setup** menu group.

Alternatively, you can search for the **Payment days** form by clicking on the search icon in the header of the form (or press **ALT+G**) and then type in **payment days** into the search box. Then you will be able to select the **Payment days** maintenance form from the dropdown list.

This will open up the **Payment days** maintenance form for us where we can start configuring the codes to specify the day of the month that we want to be paid.

To start creating our **Payment days** record, click on the **+ New** button in the menu bar.

Next we will want to dive our record a **Payment day** code.

For this example, we are creating a configuration for the 15th day of the month, so we will set the **Payment day** code to **15DOM**.

And then give the new record a more readable Description.

Here we wet the **Description** to *15th Day of The Month*.

Then within the **Payment Day Lines** table, click on the **Week/Month** dropdown list and select the timeframe that we want to select for the Payment Days.

We can wither select **Week** which would allow us to specify a week day that we want to be paid on, or **Month** which will allow us to specify the day of the month that we want to be paid on.

For this example, select the **Month** option from the dropdown list.

Now that we have done that, the **Day of Month** field will become enabled and we can set the day that we expect payment.

In this case we will set the **Day of month** to **15**.

Before we leave this form, we will create another variation of this record, but in this case we will make it so that our payment date is the 20th of the month.

To do this, click on the **+ New** button in the menu bar to create a new record. Then set the **Payment day** code to **20DOM**, the **Description** to *20th Day of the Month*, click on the **Week/Month** dropdown list and select the **Month** option and then set the **Day of month** to *20*.

When you are done, just exit from the form.

Now that we have our **Payment days** configured, we can start using them within our **Terms of payment** configurations.

www.dynamicscompanions.com
Dynamics Companions

- 109 -

www.blindsquirrelpublishing.com
© 2017 Blind Squirrel Publishing, LLC, All Rights Reserved

BLIND SQUIRREL
PUBLISHING

DYNAMICS COMPANIONS
BARE BONES CONFIGURATION GUIDES

CONFIGURING ACCOUNTS RECEIVABLE WITHIN DYNAMICS 365 FOR OPERATIONS
MODULE 1: CONFIGURING THE ACCOUNTS RECEIVABLE CONTROLS

So return back to the **Terms of payment** maintenance form, and click on the **+ New** button to create a new record.

First we will configure a **Terms of** payment record for payment on the 15th of the month using the firdt Payment days configuration that we created.

So set the **Terms of payment** code to *DOM15*.

And then set the Description to 15th Day of The Month.

For this **Terms of payment** we will do something a little different and click on the **Payment method** dropdown, select the **Current Month** option.

This will say that the payment needs to fall within the current month.

And then from the **Payment Day** dropdown field select the **15DOM** record that we just created.

Before we finish here we will want to create one more **Term of payment** for the other Payment day code that we just configured.

So, click on the **+ New** button to create a new record. Then set the **Term of payment** code to **DOM20**, set the **Description** to *20th Day of the Month*, set the **Payment method** to *Current month*, and then click on the **Payment day** and select the *20DOM code that we just created in the previous step*.

dyn

www.dynamicscompanions.com
Dynamics Companions

- 110 -

www.blindsquirrelpublishing.com
© 2017 Blind Squirrel Publishing, LLC , All Rights Reserved

BLIND SQUIRREL
PUBLISHING

DYNAMICS COMPANIONS
BARE BONES CONFIGURATION GUIDES

CONFIGURING ACCOUNTS RECEIVABLE WITHIN DYNAMICS 365 FOR OPERATIONS
MODULE 1: CONFIGURING THE ACCOUNTS RECEIVABLE CONTROLS

Configuring Net Day of Month Term of Payment

How to do it...

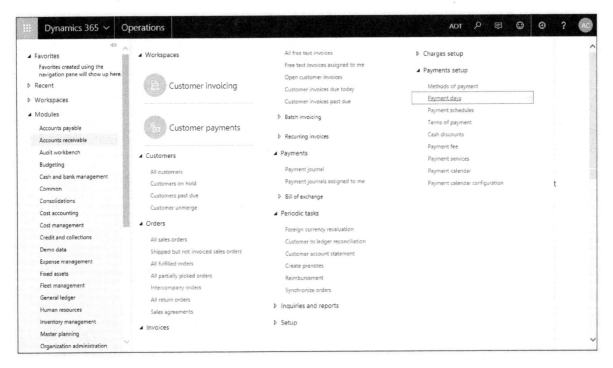

To do this, open up the navigation panel, expand out the **Modules** group, and click on **Accounts receivable** module to see all of the menu items that are available. Then click on the **Payment days** menu item within the **Payment setup** menu group.

www.dynamicscompanions.com
Dynamics Companions

- 111 -

www.blindsquirrelpublishing.com
© 2017 Blind Squirrel Publishing, LLC, All Rights Reserved

BLIND SQUIRREL
PUBLISHING

DYNAMICS COMPANIONS
BARE BONES CONFIGURATION GUIDES

CONFIGURING ACCOUNTS RECEIVABLE WITHIN DYNAMICS 365 FOR OPERATIONS
MODULE 1: CONFIGURING THE ACCOUNTS RECEIVABLE CONTROLS

Configuring Net Day of Month Term of Payment

How to do it...

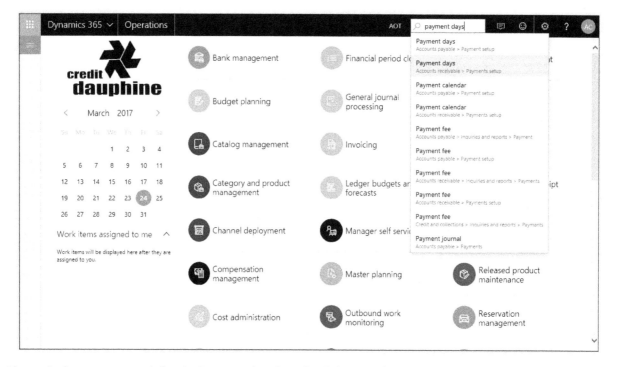

Alternatively, you can search for the **Payment days** form by clicking on the search icon in the header of the form (or press **ALT+G**) and then type in **payment days** into the search box. Then you will be able to select the **Payment days** maintenance form from the dropdown list.

dyn᠎c
www.dynamicscompanions.com
Dynamics Companions

- 112 -

www.blindsquirrelpublishing.com
© 2017 Blind Squirrel Publishing, LLC, All Rights Reserved

BLIND SQUIRREL
PUBLISHING

DYNAMICS COMPANIONS
BARE BONES CONFIGURATION GUIDES

CONFIGURING ACCOUNTS RECEIVABLE WITHIN DYNAMICS 365 FOR OPERATIONS
MODULE 1: CONFIGURING THE ACCOUNTS RECEIVABLE CONTROLS

Configuring Net Day of Month Term of Payment

How to do it...

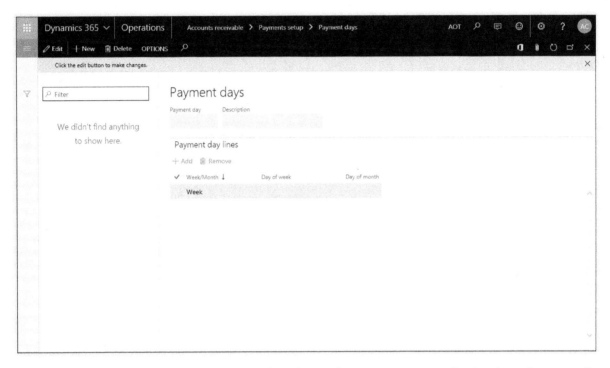

This will open up the **Payment days** maintenance form for us where we can start configuring the codes to specify the day of the month that we want to be paid.

www.dynamicscompanions.com
Dynamics Companions

- 113 -

www.blindsquirrelpublishing.com
© 2017 Blind Squirrel Publishing, LLC, All Rights Reserved

BLIND SQUIRREL
PUBLISHING

DYNAMICS COMPANIONS
BARE BONES CONFIGURATION GUIDES

CONFIGURING ACCOUNTS RECEIVABLE WITHIN DYNAMICS 365 FOR OPERATIONS
MODULE 1: CONFIGURING THE ACCOUNTS RECEIVABLE CONTROLS

Configuring Net Day of Month Term of Payment

How to do it...

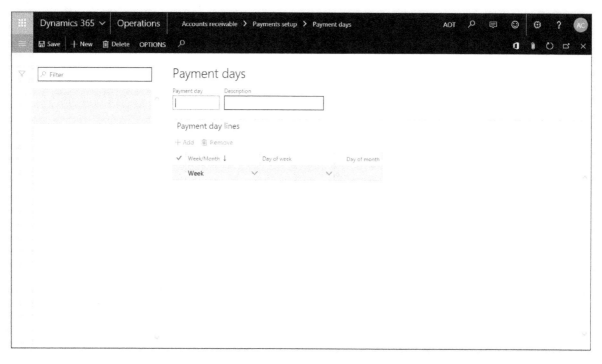

To start creating our **Payment days** record, click on the **+ New** button in the menu bar.

www.dynamicscompanions.com
Dynamics Companions

- 114 -

www.blindsquirrelpublishing.com
© 2017 Blind Squirrel Publishing, LLC , All Rights Reserved

BLIND SQUIRREL
PUBLISHING

DYNAMICS COMPANIONS
BARE BONES CONFIGURATION GUIDES

CONFIGURING ACCOUNTS RECEIVABLE WITHIN DYNAMICS 365 FOR OPERATIONS
MODULE 1: CONFIGURING THE ACCOUNTS RECEIVABLE CONTROLS

Configuring Net Day of Month Term of Payment

How to do it...

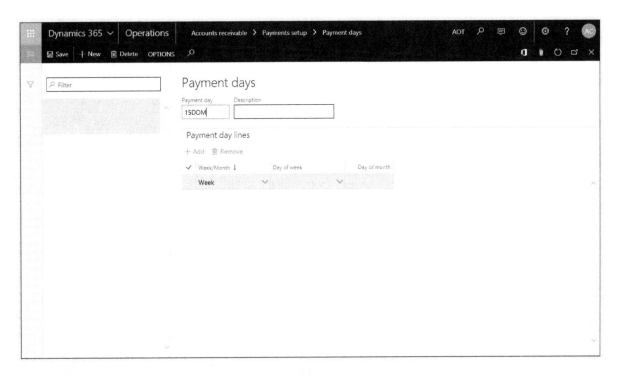

Next we will want to dive our record a **Payment day** code.

For this example, we are creating a configuration for the 15th day of the month, so we will set the **Payment day** code to **15DOM**.

DYNAMICS COMPANIONS
BARE BONES CONFIGURATION GUIDES

CONFIGURING ACCOUNTS RECEIVABLE WITHIN DYNAMICS 365 FOR OPERATIONS
MODULE 1: CONFIGURING THE ACCOUNTS RECEIVABLE CONTROLS

Configuring Net Day of Month Term of Payment

How to do it...

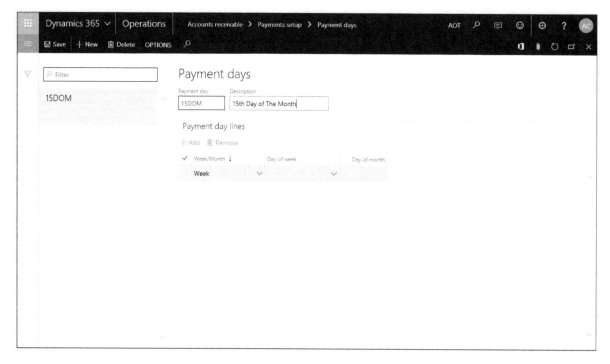

And then give the new record a more readable Description.

Here we wet the **Description** to *15th Day of The Month*.

dyn

www.dynamicscompanions.com
Dynamics Companions

- 116 -

www.blindsquirrelpublishing.com
© 2017 Blind Squirrel Publishing, LLC , All Rights Reserved

BLIND SQUIRREL
PUBLISHING

DYNAMICS COMPANIONS
BARE BONES CONFIGURATION GUIDES

CONFIGURING ACCOUNTS RECEIVABLE WITHIN DYNAMICS 365 FOR OPERATIONS
MODULE 1: CONFIGURING THE ACCOUNTS RECEIVABLE CONTROLS

Configuring Net Day of Month Term of Payment

How to do it...

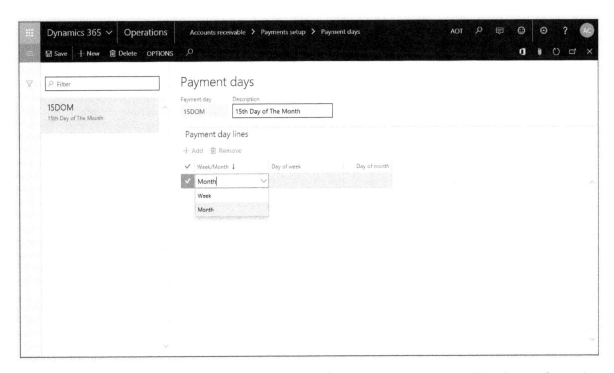

Then within the **Payment Day Lines** table, click on the **Week/Month** dropdown list and select the timeframe that we want to select for the Payment Days.

We can wither select **Week** which would allow us to specify a week day that we want to be paid on, or **Month** which will allow us to specify the day of the month that we want to be paid on.

For this example, select the **Month** option from the dropdown list.

dync
www.dynamicscompanions.com
Dynamics Companions

- 117 -

www.blindsquirrelpublishing.com
© 2017 Blind Squirrel Publishing, LLC, All Rights Reserved

BLIND SQUIRREL
PUBLISHING

DYNAMICS COMPANIONS
BARE BONES CONFIGURATION GUIDES

CONFIGURING ACCOUNTS RECEIVABLE WITHIN DYNAMICS 365 FOR OPERATIONS
MODULE 1: CONFIGURING THE ACCOUNTS RECEIVABLE CONTROLS

Configuring Net Day of Month Term of Payment

How to do it...

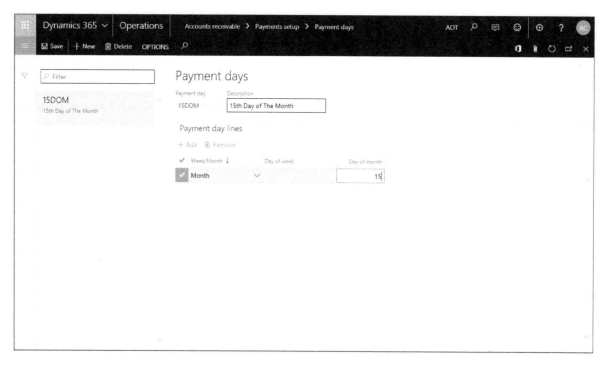

Now that we have done that, the **Day of Month** field will become enabled and we can set the day that we expect payment.

In this case we will set the **Day of month** to **15**.

www.dynamicscompanions.com
Dynamics Companions

- 118 -

www.blindsquirrelpublishing.com
© 2017 Blind Squirrel Publishing, LLC, All Rights Reserved

BLIND SQUIRREL
PUBLISHING

DYNAMICS COMPANIONS
BARE BONES CONFIGURATION GUIDES

CONFIGURING ACCOUNTS RECEIVABLE WITHIN DYNAMICS 365 FOR OPERATIONS
MODULE 1: CONFIGURING THE ACCOUNTS RECEIVABLE CONTROLS

Configuring Net Day of Month Term of Payment

How to do it...

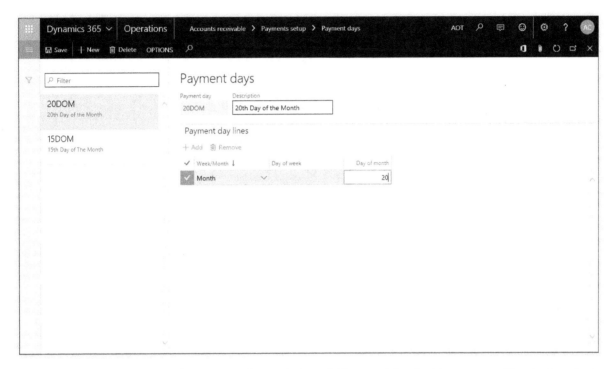

Before we leave this form, we will create another variation of this record, but in this case we will make it so that our payment date is the 20th of the month.

To do this, click on the **+ New** button in the menu bar to create a new record. Then set the **Payment day** code to **20DOM**, the **Description** to *20th Day of the Month*, click on the **Week/Month** dropdown list and select the **Month** option and then set the **Day of month** to *20*.

When you are done, just exit from the form.

dyn c

www.dynamicscompanions.com
Dynamics Companions

- 119 -

www.blindsquirrelpublishing.com
© 2017 Blind Squirrel Publishing, LLC, All Rights Reserved

BLIND SQUIRREL
PUBLISHING

DYNAMICS COMPANIONS
BARE BONES CONFIGURATION GUIDES

CONFIGURING ACCOUNTS RECEIVABLE WITHIN DYNAMICS 365 FOR OPERATIONS
MODULE 1: CONFIGURING THE ACCOUNTS RECEIVABLE CONTROLS

Configuring Net Day of Month Term of Payment

How to do it...

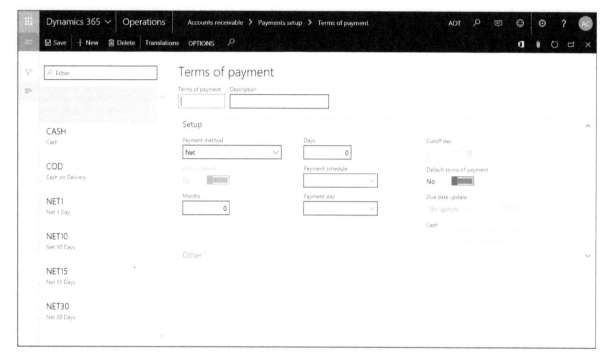

Now that we have our **Payment days** configured, we can start using them within our **Terms of payment** configurations.

So return back to the **Terms of payment** maintenance form, and click on the **+ New** button to create a new record.

dyn

www.dynamicscompanions.com
Dynamics Companions

- 120 -

www.blindsquirrelpublishing.com
© 2017 Blind Squirrel Publishing, LLC , All Rights Reserved

BLIND SQUIRREL
PUBLISHING

DYNAMICS COMPANIONS
BARE BONES CONFIGURATION GUIDES

CONFIGURING ACCOUNTS RECEIVABLE WITHIN DYNAMICS 365 FOR OPERATIONS
MODULE 1: CONFIGURING THE ACCOUNTS RECEIVABLE CONTROLS

Configuring Net Day of Month Term of Payment

How to do it...

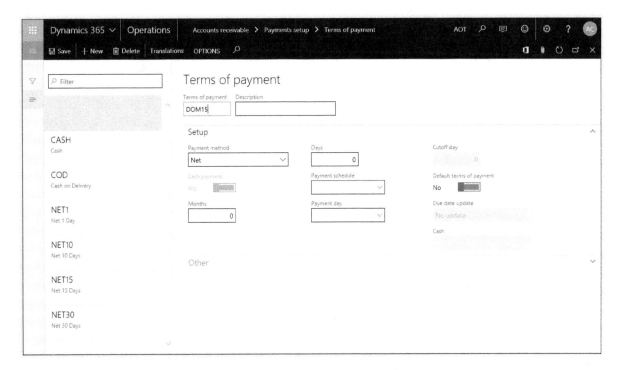

First we will configure a **Terms of** payment record for payment on the 15th of the month using the firdt Payment days configuration that we created.

So set the **Terms of payment** code to *DOM15*.

dyn c
www.dynamicscompanions.com
Dynamics Companions

- 121 -

www.blindsquirrelpublishing.com
© 2017 Blind Squirrel Publishing, LLC , All Rights Reserved

BLIND SQUIRREL
PUBLISHING

DYNAMICS COMPANIONS
BARE BONES CONFIGURATION GUIDES

CONFIGURING ACCOUNTS RECEIVABLE WITHIN DYNAMICS 365 FOR OPERATIONS
MODULE 1: CONFIGURING THE ACCOUNTS RECEIVABLE CONTROLS

Configuring Net Day of Month Term of Payment

How to do it...

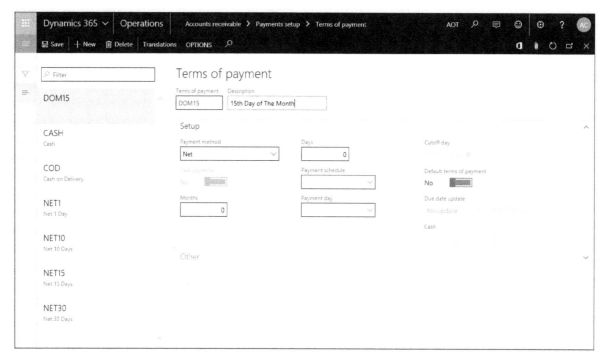

And then set the Description to 15th Day of The Month.

www.dynamicscompanions.com
Dynamics Companions

- 122 -

www.blindsquirrelpublishing.com
© 2017 Blind Squirrel Publishing, LLC, All Rights Reserved

BLIND SQUIRREL
PUBLISHING

DYNAMICS COMPANIONS
BARE BONES CONFIGURATION GUIDES

CONFIGURING ACCOUNTS RECEIVABLE WITHIN DYNAMICS 365 FOR OPERATIONS
MODULE 1: CONFIGURING THE ACCOUNTS RECEIVABLE CONTROLS

Configuring Net Day of Month Term of Payment

How to do it...

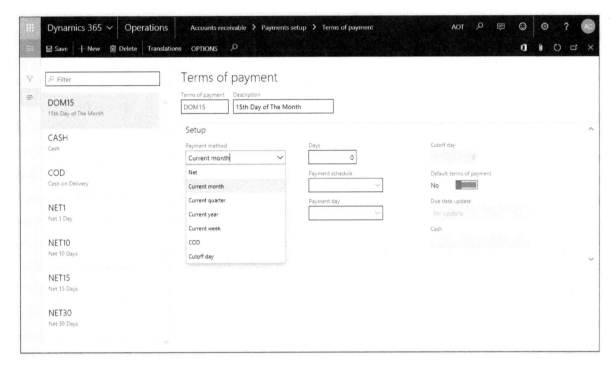

For this **Terms of payment** we will do something a little different and click on the **Payment method** dropdown, select the **Current Month** option.

This will say that the payment needs to fall within the current month.

dyn c
www.dynamicscompanions.com
Dynamics Companions

- 123 -

www.blindsquirrelpublishing.com
© 2017 Blind Squirrel Publishing, LLC, All Rights Reserved

BLIND SQUIRREL
PUBLISHING

DYNAMICS COMPANIONS
BARE BONES CONFIGURATION GUIDES

CONFIGURING ACCOUNTS RECEIVABLE WITHIN DYNAMICS 365 FOR OPERATIONS
MODULE 1: CONFIGURING THE ACCOUNTS RECEIVABLE CONTROLS

Configuring Net Day of Month Term of Payment

How to do it...

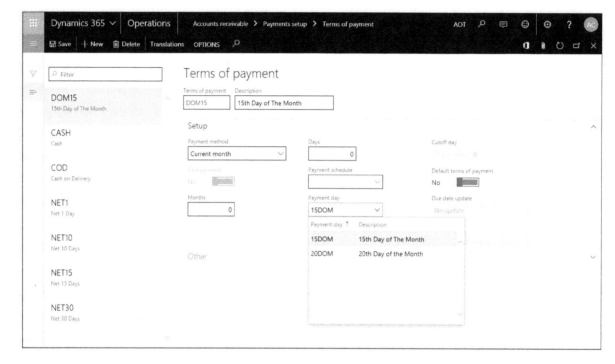

And then from the **Payment Day** dropdown field select the **15DOM** record that we just created.

dyn c   www.dynamicscompanions.com
Dynamics Companions   - 124 -

www.blindsquirrelpublishing.com
© 2017 Blind Squirrel Publishing, LLC, All Rights Reserved

BLIND SQUIRREL
PUBLISHING

DYNAMICS COMPANIONS
BARE BONES CONFIGURATION GUIDES

CONFIGURING ACCOUNTS RECEIVABLE WITHIN DYNAMICS 365 FOR OPERATIONS
MODULE 1: CONFIGURING THE ACCOUNTS RECEIVABLE CONTROLS

Configuring Net Day of Month Term of Payment

How to do it...

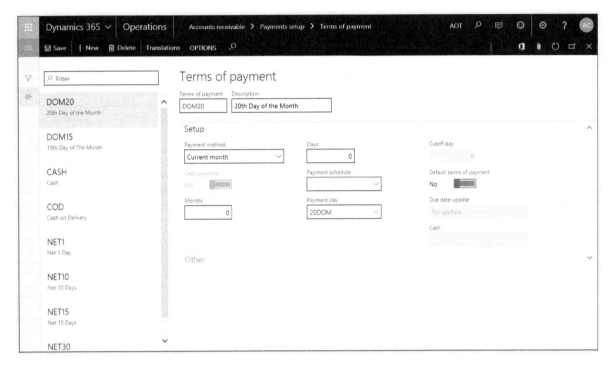

Before we finish here we will want to create one more **Term of payment** for the other Payment day code that we just configured.

So, click on the **+ New** button to create a new record. Then set the **Term of payment** code to **DOM20**, set the **Description** to *20th Day of the Month*, set the **Payment method** to *Current month*, and then click on the **Payment day** and select the *20DOM code that we just created in the previous step.*

dync
www.dynamicscompanions.com
Dynamics Companions

- 125 -

www.blindsquirrelpublishing.com
© 2017 Blind Squirrel Publishing, LLC , All Rights Reserved

BLIND SQUIRREL
PUBLISHING

DYNAMICS COMPANIONS
BARE BONES CONFIGURATION GUIDES

CONFIGURING ACCOUNTS RECEIVABLE WITHIN DYNAMICS 365 FOR OPERATIONS
MODULE 1: CONFIGURING THE ACCOUNTS RECEIVABLE CONTROLS

Configuring Net Day of Month Term of Payment

Example Data

Field Name	Value
Payment day	15DOM
Description	15th Day of The Month
Week/Month	Month
Day of month	15

Payment Days: 15DOM – 15th Day of The Month

Field Name	Value
Payment day	20DOM
Description	20th Day of The Month
Week/Month	Month
Day of month	20

Payment Days: 20DOM – 20th Day of The Month

Field Name	Value
Terms of payment	DOM15
Description	15th Day of The Month
Payment method	Current Month
Payment Day	15DOM

Terms of Payment: DOM15 – 15th Day of The Month

Field Name	Value
Terms of payment	DOM20
Description	20th Day of The Month
Payment method	Current Month
Payment Day	20DOM

Terms of Payment: DOM20 – 20th Day of The Month

www.dynamicscompanions.com
Dynamics Companions

- 126 -

www.blindsquirrelpublishing.com
© 2017 Blind Squirrel Publishing, LLC, All Rights Reserved

BLIND SQUIRREL
PUBLISHING

DYNAMICS COMPANIONS
BARE BONES CONFIGURATION GUIDES

CONFIGURING ACCOUNTS RECEIVABLE WITHIN DYNAMICS 365 FOR OPERATIONS
MODULE 1: CONFIGURING THE ACCOUNTS RECEIVABLE CONTROLS

Configuring Net Day of Month Term of Payment

Summary

The Net Day of Month Terms of Payment are a great way to give customers a consistent date that they are supposed to pay their bills on. You can set these up so that they are due in the following month as well – if you want to give your customers a little more time to pay their bills.

DYNAMICS COMPANIONS
BARE BONES CONFIGURATION GUIDES

CONFIGURING ACCOUNTS RECEIVABLE WITHIN DYNAMICS 365 FOR OPERATIONS
MODULE 1: CONFIGURING THE ACCOUNTS RECEIVABLE CONTROLS

Configuring Equal Monthly Scheduled Payment Terms

Payment terms don't have to be just a lump sum payment; you can also configure payment schedules with multiple payment dates. The first type of payment schedule that you may want to configure is a monthly payment for a set number of months.

How to do it...

To do this, open up the navigation panel, expand out the **Modules** group, and click on **Accounts Receivable** module to see all of the menu items that are available. Then click on the **Payment schedule** menu item within the **Payment setup** menu group.

Alternatively, you can search for the **Payment schedule** form by clicking on the search icon in the header of the form (or press **ALT+G**) and then type in **payment sche** into the search box. Then you will be able to select the **Payment schedule** maintenance form from the dropdown list.

This will open up the **Payment schedules** maintenance form where we can start defining more elaborate ways to receive payments.

To create a new **Payment schedule** record. click on the **+ New** button within the menu bar.

Then give your new record a **Payment schedule** code.

In this example we will be creating a payment schedule that has equal payments over 9 months, so we will set the **Payment schedule** code to *9MONTH*.

Then give your new Payment schedule a more understandable **Description.**

Here we set the **Description** to **Equal Payments Over 9 Months**.

Now we will want to click on the **Allocation** field dropdown and select the way that we want to allocate out all of the payments.

The **Total** option will specify that the total amount outstanding is due when the invoice is due.

The **Fixed amount** option will allow us to specify that a specific, fixed amount is due for each payment on the calculated payment dates.

The **Fixed quantity** option will allow us to specify that the payment of the total amount is divided into a fixed quantity of payments, due at a specifies schedule.

The **Specified** option will allow us to say that a specified amount is due on each specified payment date, and also define the payment schedule lines and amounts.

For this example, we will set the **Allocation** field to the **Fixed Quantity** option to tell the system that you want to have equal payments over a set number of intervals.

Now we will want to set the **Payment per** field to either **Days, Months, or** Years depending on the payment interval that we want to use.

For this option we will set the **Payment pe**r to **Months**.

Then we will want to set the **Change** field to the interval that we want to payments to recur in.

www.dynamicscompanions.com
Dynamics Companions

- 128 -

www.blindsquirrelpublishing.com
© 2017 Blind Squirrel Publishing, LLC , All Rights Reserved

BLIND SQUIRREL
PUBLISHING

DYNAMICS COMPANIONS
BARE BONES CONFIGURATION GUIDES

CONFIGURING ACCOUNTS RECEIVABLE WITHIN DYNAMICS 365 FOR OPERATIONS
MODULE 1: CONFIGURING THE ACCOUNTS RECEIVABLE CONTROLS

In this example, we will set the **Change** to *1* which will tell the system that we want to have payments every month.

Finally we will want to set the **Number of Payments** that you want to have within the schedule.

In this case, we set the **Number of payments** to **9**.

After you have done this you can add additional payment schedule variations, and when you are done exit from the form.

Now we will want to return to the **Terms of Payments** maintenance form to set up a record that will take advantage of the payment schedule that we just created.

When we are there we can click the **+ New** button in the menu bar to create a new record.

For this example, we will want to set the **Terms of payment** code to *SCH9M*.

And then set the Description to Equal Payments Scheduled over 9 Months.

We will then want to click on the **Payment method** dropdown list and select the **Net** option.

To take advantage of the schedule that we configured, all we need to do is click on the **Payment Schedule** field dropdown list and select the new *9MONTH* monthly schedule that we just created.

After you have done that we can exit from the form.

DYNAMICS COMPANIONS
BARE BONES CONFIGURATION GUIDES

CONFIGURING ACCOUNTS RECEIVABLE WITHIN DYNAMICS 365 FOR OPERATIONS
MODULE 1: CONFIGURING THE ACCOUNTS RECEIVABLE CONTROLS

Configuring Equal Monthly Scheduled Payment Terms

How to do it...

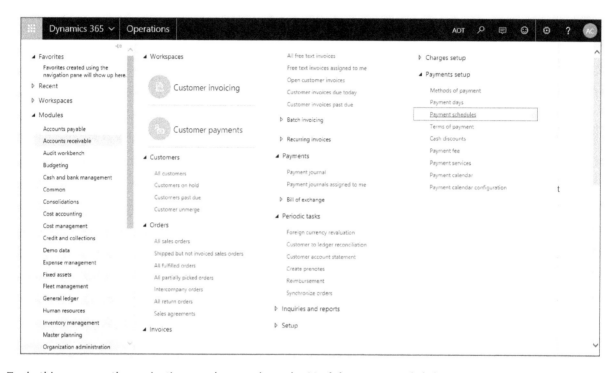

To do this, open up the navigation panel, expand out the **Modules** group, and click on **Accounts Receivable** module to see all of the menu items that are available. Then click on the **Payment schedule** menu item within the **Payment setup** menu group.

dyn
www.dynamicscompanions.com
Dynamics Companions

- 130 -

www.blindsquirrelpublishing.com
© 2017 Blind Squirrel Publishing, LLC, All Rights Reserved

BLIND SQUIRREL
PUBLISHING

DYNAMICS COMPANIONS
BARE BONES CONFIGURATION GUIDES

CONFIGURING ACCOUNTS RECEIVABLE WITHIN DYNAMICS 365 FOR OPERATIONS
MODULE 1: CONFIGURING THE ACCOUNTS RECEIVABLE CONTROLS

Configuring Equal Monthly Scheduled Payment Terms

How to do it...

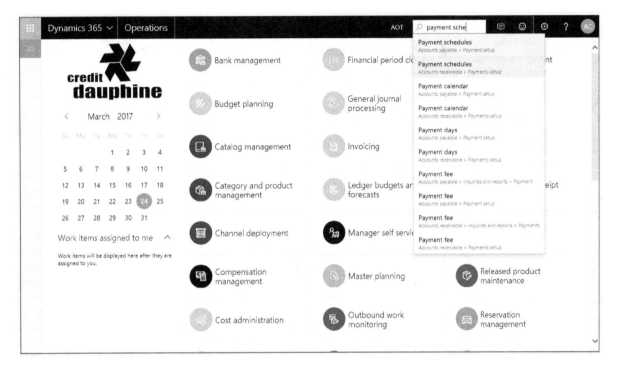

Alternatively, you can search for the **Payment schedule** form by clicking on the search icon in the header of the form (or press **ALT+G**) and then type in **payment sche** into the search box. Then you will be able to select the **Payment schedule** maintenance form from the dropdown list.

dyn c
www.dynamicscompanions.com
Dynamics Companions

- 131 -

www.blindsquirrelpublishing.com
© 2017 Blind Squirrel Publishing, LLC, All Rights Reserved

 BLIND SQUIRREL
PUBLISHING

DYNAMICS COMPANIONS
BARE BONES CONFIGURATION GUIDES

CONFIGURING ACCOUNTS RECEIVABLE WITHIN DYNAMICS 365 FOR OPERATIONS
MODULE 1: CONFIGURING THE ACCOUNTS RECEIVABLE CONTROLS

Configuring Equal Monthly Scheduled Payment Terms

How to do it...

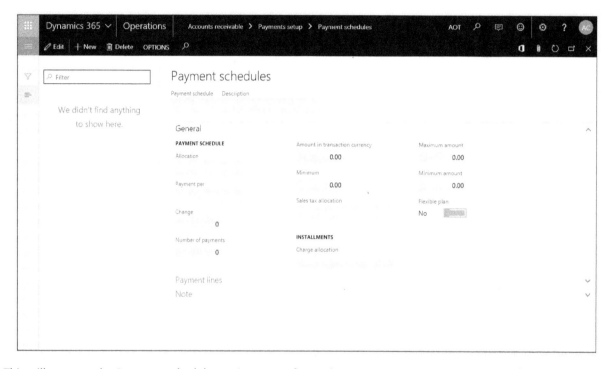

This will open up the **Payment schedules** maintenance form where we can start defining more elaborate ways to receive payments.

dyn

www.dynamicscompanions.com
Dynamics Companions

- 132 -

www.blindsquirrelpublishing.com
© 2017 Blind Squirrel Publishing, LLC , All Rights Reserved

BLIND SQUIRREL
PUBLISHING

DYNAMICS COMPANIONS
BARE BONES CONFIGURATION GUIDES

CONFIGURING ACCOUNTS RECEIVABLE WITHIN DYNAMICS 365 FOR OPERATIONS
MODULE 1: CONFIGURING THE ACCOUNTS RECEIVABLE CONTROLS

Configuring Equal Monthly Scheduled Payment Terms

How to do it...

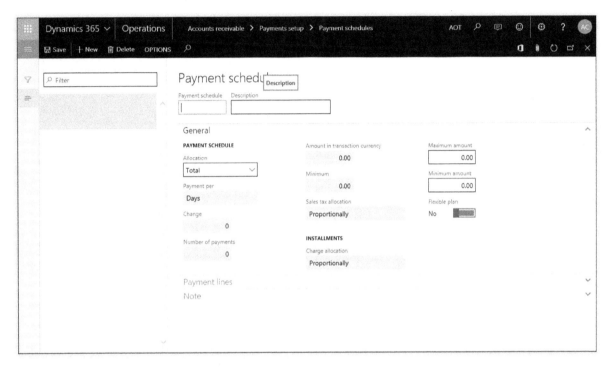

To create a new **Payment schedule** record. click on the **+ New** button within the menu bar.

www.dynamicscompanions.com
Dynamics Companions

- 133 -

www.blindsquirrelpublishing.com
© 2017 Blind Squirrel Publishing, LLC , All Rights Reserved

BLIND SQUIRREL
PUBLISHING

DYNAMICS COMPANIONS
BARE BONES CONFIGURATION GUIDES

CONFIGURING ACCOUNTS RECEIVABLE WITHIN DYNAMICS 365 FOR OPERATIONS
MODULE 1: CONFIGURING THE ACCOUNTS RECEIVABLE CONTROLS

Configuring Equal Monthly Scheduled Payment Terms

How to do it...

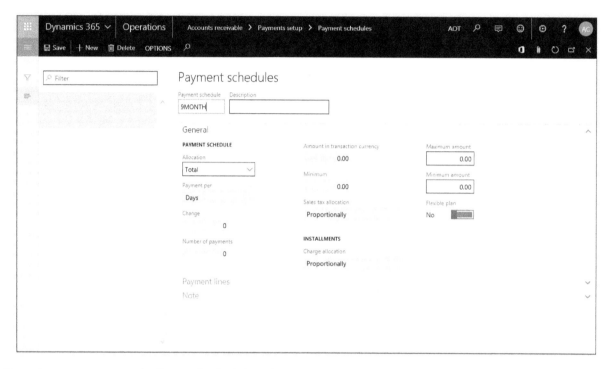

Then give your new record a **Payment schedule** code.

In this example we will be creating a payment schedule that has equal payments over 9 months, so we will set the **Payment schedule** code to *9MONTH*.

dyn c   www.dynamicscompanions.com
Dynamics Companions

- 134 -

www.blindsquirrelpublishing.com
© 2017 Blind Squirrel Publishing, LLC, All Rights Reserved

BLIND SQUIRREL
PUBLISHING

DYNAMICS COMPANIONS
BARE BONES CONFIGURATION GUIDES

CONFIGURING ACCOUNTS RECEIVABLE WITHIN DYNAMICS 365 FOR OPERATIONS
MODULE 1: CONFIGURING THE ACCOUNTS RECEIVABLE CONTROLS

Configuring Equal Monthly Scheduled Payment Terms

How to do it...

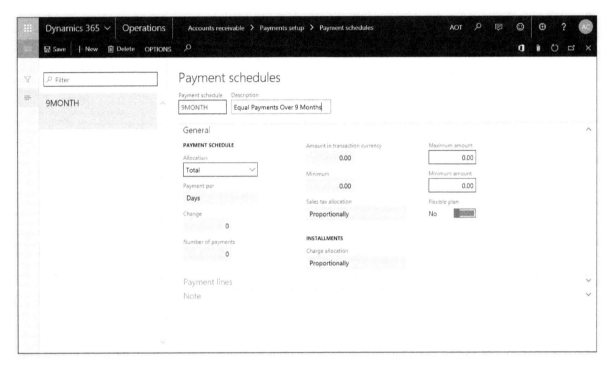

Then give your new Payment schedule a more understandable **Description.**

Here we set the **Description** to **Equal Payments Over 9 Months**.

dyn c
www.dynamicscompanions.com
Dynamics Companions

- 135 -

www.blindsquirrelpublishing.com
© 2017 Blind Squirrel Publishing, LLC, All Rights Reserved

BLIND SQUIRREL
PUBLISHING

DYNAMICS COMPANIONS
BARE BONES CONFIGURATION GUIDES

CONFIGURING ACCOUNTS RECEIVABLE WITHIN DYNAMICS 365 FOR OPERATIONS
MODULE 1: CONFIGURING THE ACCOUNTS RECEIVABLE CONTROLS

Configuring Equal Monthly Scheduled Payment Terms

How to do it...

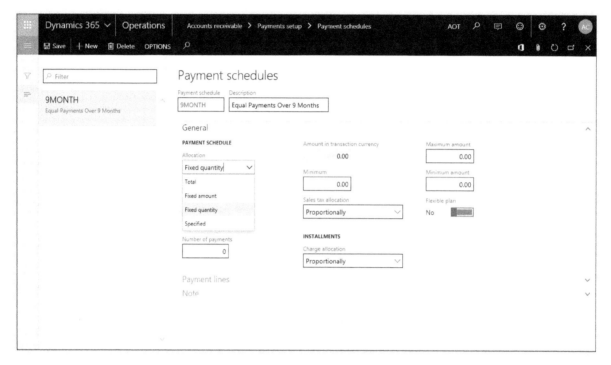

Now we will want to click on the **Allocation** field dropdown and select the way that we want to allocate out all of the payments.

The **Total** option will specify that the total amount outstanding is due when the invoice is due.

The **Fixed amount** option will allow us to specify that a specific, fixed amount is due for each payment on the calculated payment dates.

The **Fixed quantity** option will allow us to specify that the payment of the total amount is divided into a fixed quantity of payments, due at a specifies schedule.

The **Specified** option will allow us to say that a specified amount is due on each specified payment date, and also define the payment schedule lines and amounts.

For this example, we will set the **Allocation** field to the **Fixed Quantity** option to tell the system that you want to have equal payments over a set number of intervals.

dync   www.dynamicscompanions.com
Dynamics Companions

- 136 -

www.blindsquirrelpublishing.com
© 2017 Blind Squirrel Publishing, LLC, All Rights Reserved

BLIND SQUIRREL
PUBLISHING

DYNAMICS COMPANIONS
BARE BONES CONFIGURATION GUIDES

CONFIGURING ACCOUNTS RECEIVABLE WITHIN DYNAMICS 365 FOR OPERATIONS
MODULE 1: CONFIGURING THE ACCOUNTS RECEIVABLE CONTROLS

Configuring Equal Monthly Scheduled Payment Terms

How to do it...

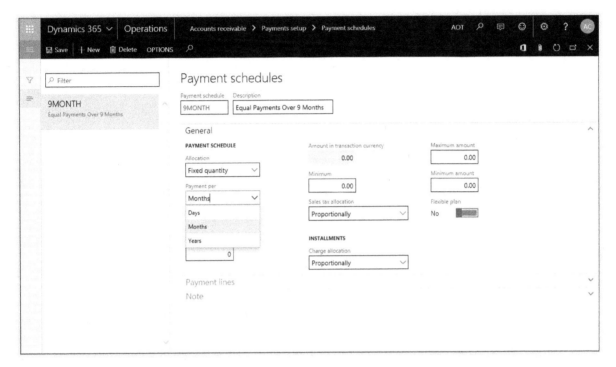

Now we will want to set the **Payment per** field to either **Days, Months, or** Years depending on the payment interval that we want to use.

For this option we will set the **Payment pe**r to **Months**.

dync
www.dynamicscompanions.com
Dynamics Companions

- 137 -

www.blindsquirrelpublishing.com
© 2017 Blind Squirrel Publishing, LLC, All Rights Reserved

BLIND SQUIRREL
PUBLISHING

DYNAMICS COMPANIONS
BARE BONES CONFIGURATION GUIDES

CONFIGURING ACCOUNTS RECEIVABLE WITHIN DYNAMICS 365 FOR OPERATIONS
MODULE 1: CONFIGURING THE ACCOUNTS RECEIVABLE CONTROLS

Configuring Equal Monthly Scheduled Payment Terms

How to do it...

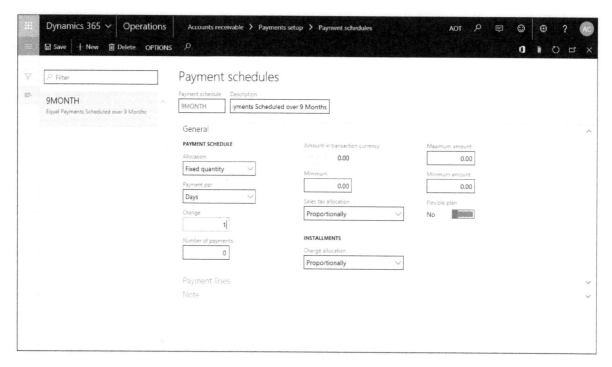

Then we will want to set the **Change** field to the interval that we want to payments to recur in.

In this example, we will set the **Change** to *1* which will tell the system that we want to have payments every month.

dyn

www.dynamicscompanions.com
Dynamics Companions

- 138 -

www.blindsquirrelpublishing.com
© 2017 Blind Squirrel Publishing, LLC, All Rights Reserved

BLIND SQUIRREL
PUBLISHING

DYNAMICS COMPANIONS
BARE BONES CONFIGURATION GUIDES

CONFIGURING ACCOUNTS RECEIVABLE WITHIN DYNAMICS 365 FOR OPERATIONS
MODULE 1: CONFIGURING THE ACCOUNTS RECEIVABLE CONTROLS

Configuring Equal Monthly Scheduled Payment Terms

How to do it...

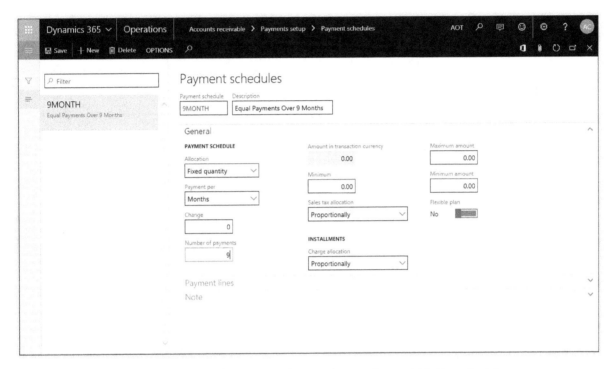

Finally we will want to set the **Number of Payments** that you want to have within the schedule.

In this case, we set the **Number of payments** to **9**.

After you have done this you can add additional payment schedule variations, and when you are done exit from the form.

dyn c

www.dynamicscompanions.com
Dynamics Companions

- 139 -

www.blindsquirrelpublishing.com
© 2017 Blind Squirrel Publishing, LLC, All Rights Reserved

BLIND SQUIRREL
PUBLISHING

DYNAMICS COMPANIONS
BARE BONES CONFIGURATION GUIDES

CONFIGURING ACCOUNTS RECEIVABLE WITHIN DYNAMICS 365 FOR OPERATIONS
MODULE 1: CONFIGURING THE ACCOUNTS RECEIVABLE CONTROLS

Configuring Equal Monthly Scheduled Payment Terms

How to do it...

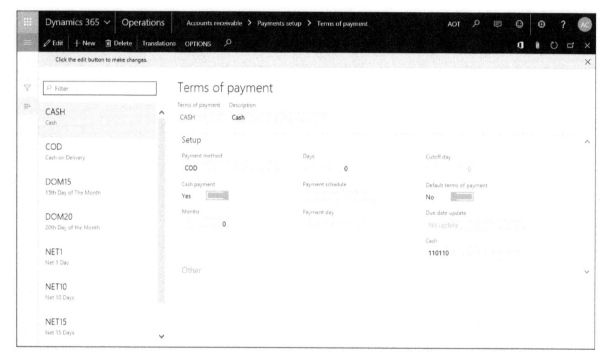

Now we will want to return to the **Terms of Payments** maintenance form to set up a record that will take advantage of the payment schedule that we just created.

When we are there we can click the **+ New** button in the menu bar to create a new record.

dyn

www.dynamicscompanions.com
Dynamics Companions

- 140 -

www.blindsquirrelpublishing.com
© 2017 Blind Squirrel Publishing, LLC , All Rights Reserved

BLIND SQUIRREL
PUBLISHING

DYNAMICS COMPANIONS
BARE BONES CONFIGURATION GUIDES

CONFIGURING ACCOUNTS RECEIVABLE WITHIN DYNAMICS 365 FOR OPERATIONS
MODULE 1: CONFIGURING THE ACCOUNTS RECEIVABLE CONTROLS

Configuring Equal Monthly Scheduled Payment Terms

How to do it...

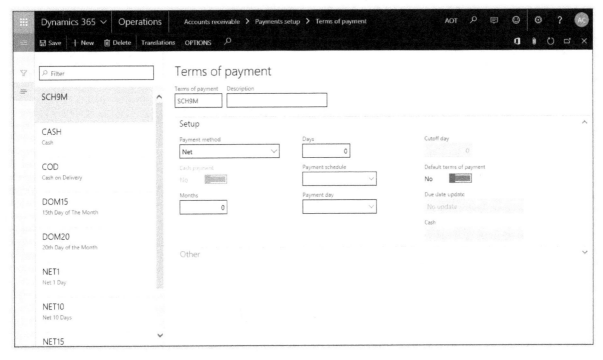

For this example, we will want to set the **Terms of payment** code to *SCH9M*.

dyn
www.dynamicscompanions.com
Dynamics Companions

- 141 -

www.blindsquirrelpublishing.com
© 2017 Blind Squirrel Publishing, LLC, All Rights Reserved

BLIND SQUIRREL
PUBLISHING

DYNAMICS COMPANIONS
BARE BONES CONFIGURATION GUIDES

CONFIGURING ACCOUNTS RECEIVABLE WITHIN DYNAMICS 365 FOR OPERATIONS
MODULE 1: CONFIGURING THE ACCOUNTS RECEIVABLE CONTROLS

Configuring Equal Monthly Scheduled Payment Terms

How to do it...

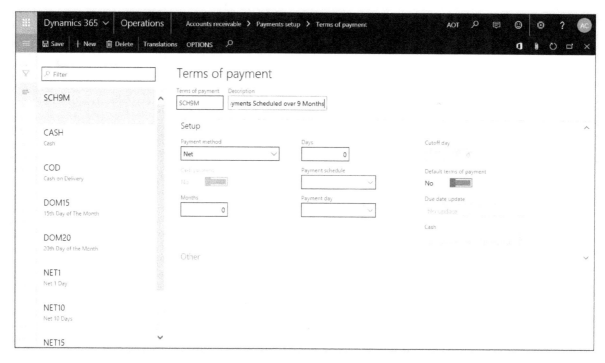

And then set the Description to Equal Payments Scheduled over 9 Months.

dyn

www.dynamicscompanions.com
Dynamics Companions

- 142 -

www.blindsquirrelpublishing.com
© 2017 Blind Squirrel Publishing, LLC , All Rights Reserved

BLIND SQUIRREL
PUBLISHING

DYNAMICS COMPANIONS
BARE BONES CONFIGURATION GUIDES

CONFIGURING ACCOUNTS RECEIVABLE WITHIN DYNAMICS 365 FOR OPERATIONS
MODULE 1: CONFIGURING THE ACCOUNTS RECEIVABLE CONTROLS

Configuring Equal Monthly Scheduled Payment Terms

How to do it...

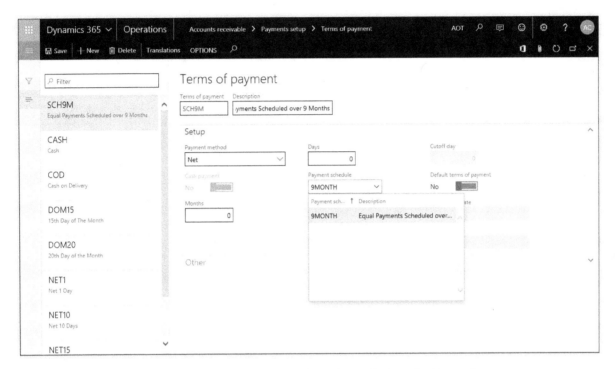

We will then want to click on the **Payment method** dropdown list and select the **Net** option.

To take advantage of the schedule that we configured, all we need to do is click on the **Payment Schedule** field dropdown list and select the new *9MONTH* monthly schedule that we just created.

After you have done that we can exit from the form.

dync
www.dynamicscompanions.com
Dynamics Companions

- 143 -

www.blindsquirrelpublishing.com
© 2017 Blind Squirrel Publishing, LLC, All Rights Reserved

BLIND SQUIRREL
PUBLISHING

DYNAMICS COMPANIONS
BARE BONES CONFIGURATION GUIDES

CONFIGURING ACCOUNTS RECEIVABLE WITHIN DYNAMICS 365 FOR OPERATIONS
MODULE 1: CONFIGURING THE ACCOUNTS RECEIVABLE CONTROLS

Configuring Equal Monthly Scheduled Payment Terms

Example Data

Field Name	Value
Payment schedule	9MONTH
Description	Equal Payments Over 9 Months
Allocation	Fixed Quantity
Payment Type	Months
Number of Payments	9

Payment Schedule: 9MONTH – Equal Payments Over 9 Months

Field Name	Value
Terms of payment	SCH9M
Description	Equal Payments Scheduled over 9 Months
Payment method	Net
Payment schedule	9MONTH

Terms of Payment: SCH9M – Equal Payments Scheduled over 9 Months

dyn

www.dynamicscompanions.com
Dynamics Companions

- 144 -

www.blindsquirrelpublishing.com
© 2017 Blind Squirrel Publishing, LLC, All Rights Reserved

BLIND SQUIRREL
PUBLISHING

DYNAMICS COMPANIONS
BARE BONES CONFIGURATION GUIDES

CONFIGURING ACCOUNTS RECEIVABLE WITHIN DYNAMICS 365 FOR OPERATIONS
MODULE 1: CONFIGURING THE ACCOUNTS RECEIVABLE CONTROLS

Configuring Equal Monthly Scheduled Payment Terms

Summary

For larger purchased, you may want to use the Fixed Payment Schedule option for your customers. These payment terms will even break down the payment lines on the customer's invoice if you like.

DYNAMICS COMPANIONS
BARE BONES CONFIGURATION GUIDES

CONFIGURING ACCOUNTS RECEIVABLE WITHIN DYNAMICS 365 FOR OPERATIONS
MODULE 1: CONFIGURING THE ACCOUNTS RECEIVABLE CONTROLS

Configuring Proportional Monthly Scheduled Payment Terms

Another variation of the monthly payment schedule that you can create within Dynamics 365 is a proportional payment schedule with varying payment percentages by month. With this you could require a lump sum up front, or have balloon payments structured at the end of the payments.

How to do it...

To do this, open up the navigation panel, expand out the **Modules** group, and click on **Accounts receivable** module to see all of the menu items that are available. Then click on the **Payment schedules** menu item within the **Payment setup** menu group.

Alternatively, you can search for the **Payment schedules** form by clicking on the search icon in the header of the form (or press **ALT+G**) and then type in **payment sche** into the search box. Then you will be able to select the **Payment schedules** maintenance form from the dropdown list.

This will open up the **Payment schedules** form and we will see the other schedule that we just created.

To create a new **Payment schedule** record. click on the **+ New** button within the menu bar.

Then give your new record a **Payment schedule** code.

In this example we will be creating a payment schedule that has equal payments over 9 months, so we will set the **Payment schedule** code to *6MDECL*.

Then give your new Payment schedule a more understandable **Description.**

Here we set the **Description** to **Declining Payments Over 6 Months**.

Then from the **Allocation** dropdown list select the **Specified** option.

Set the **Payment per** field to **Months** to identify that we are going to have monthly payments.

Now collapse the **General group** so that you can see the **Payment Lines** tab group.

Click on the **+ Add** button in the **Payment Lines** table to create a new payment line record.

Now we will want to start specifying the payment lines and the periods that they are associated with.

For this first line, set the **Number of period** to 1 to create a record for the first month.

Then set the **Percent or Amount** field to be the percentage of payment that is due in that first month.

Here we set the **Percent or Amount** to *40* to specify that 40% is due in the first month.

Now we will add the remaining lines to the Payment schedule by repeating the process for all the other months that you require payments along with the percentage amount. Make sure that they add up to 100% so that you are not giving away money.

Click on the **+ Add** button to create a new record and then set the **Number of period** to *2* and the **Percent or amount** to *20*.

Click on the **+ Add** button to create a new record and then set the **Number of period** to *3* and the **Percent or amount** to *10*.

www.dynamicscompanions.com
Dynamics Companions

- 146 -

www.blindsquirrelpublishing.com
© 2017 Blind Squirrel Publishing, LLC , All Rights Reserved

BLIND SQUIRREL
PUBLISHING

DYNAMICS COMPANIONS
BARE BONES CONFIGURATION GUIDES

CONFIGURING ACCOUNTS RECEIVABLE WITHIN DYNAMICS 365 FOR OPERATIONS
MODULE 1: CONFIGURING THE ACCOUNTS RECEIVABLE CONTROLS

Click on the **+ Add** button to create a new record and then set the **Number of period** to *4* and the **Percent or amount** to *10*.

Click on the **+ Add** button to create a new record and then set the **Number of period** to *5* and the **Percent or amount** to *10*.

And click on the **+ Add** button one last time to create a new record and then set the **Number of period** to *6* and the **Percent or amount** to *10*.

When you are done, we can exit from the form.

Now we will want to return to the **Terms of Payments** maintenance form to set up a record that will take advantage of the payment schedule that we just created.

When we are there we can click the **+ New** button in the menu bar to create a new record.

For this example, we will want to set the **Terms of payment** code to *SCH6M*.

And then set the Description to Declining Payments Scheduled over 6 Months.

Set the **Payment Method** to be **Net** and then from the **Payment Schedule** field, select the new proportional monthly schedule that you just created.

After you have done that we are done and we can exit from the form.

www.dynamicscompanions.com
Dynamics Companions

- 147 -

www.blindsquirrelpublishing.com
© 2017 Blind Squirrel Publishing, LLC, All Rights Reserved

BLIND SQUIRREL
PUBLISHING

DYNAMICS COMPANIONS
BARE BONES CONFIGURATION GUIDES

CONFIGURING ACCOUNTS RECEIVABLE WITHIN DYNAMICS 365 FOR OPERATIONS
MODULE 1: CONFIGURING THE ACCOUNTS RECEIVABLE CONTROLS

Configuring Proportional Monthly Scheduled Payment Terms

How to do it...

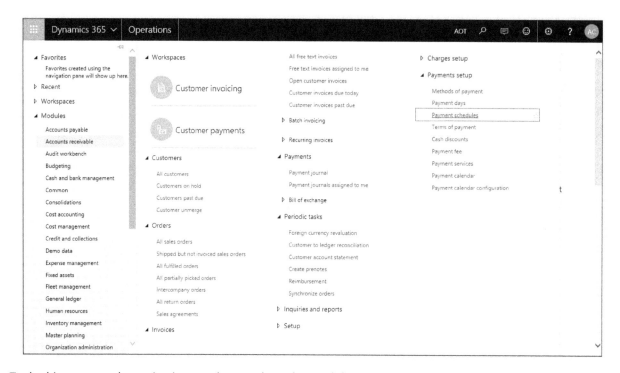

To do this, open up the navigation panel, expand out the **Modules** group, and click on **Accounts receivable** module to see all of the menu items that are available. Then click on the **Payment schedules** menu item within the **Payment setup** menu group.

dyn ©

www.dynamicscompanions.com
Dynamics Companions

- 148 -

www.blindsquirrelpublishing.com
© 2017 Blind Squirrel Publishing, LLC , All Rights Reserved

BLIND SQUIRREL
PUBLISHING

DYNAMICS COMPANIONS
BARE BONES CONFIGURATION GUIDES

CONFIGURING ACCOUNTS RECEIVABLE WITHIN DYNAMICS 365 FOR OPERATIONS
MODULE 1: CONFIGURING THE ACCOUNTS RECEIVABLE CONTROLS

Configuring Proportional Monthly Scheduled Payment Terms

How to do it...

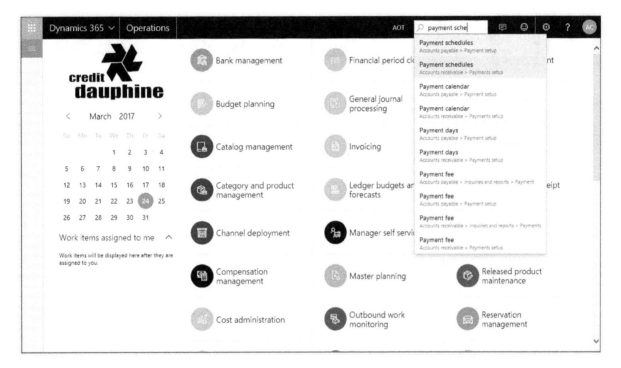

Alternatively, you can search for the **Payment schedules** form by clicking on the search icon in the header of the form (or press **ALT+G**) and then type in **payment sche** into the search box. Then you will be able to select the **Payment schedules** maintenance form from the dropdown list.

dyn c
www.dynamicscompanions.com
Dynamics Companions

- 149 -

www.blindsquirrelpublishing.com
© 2017 Blind Squirrel Publishing, LLC, All Rights Reserved

BLIND SQUIRREL
PUBLISHING

DYNAMICS COMPANIONS
BARE BONES CONFIGURATION GUIDES

CONFIGURING ACCOUNTS RECEIVABLE WITHIN DYNAMICS 365 FOR OPERATIONS
MODULE 1: CONFIGURING THE ACCOUNTS RECEIVABLE CONTROLS

Configuring Proportional Monthly Scheduled Payment Terms

How to do it...

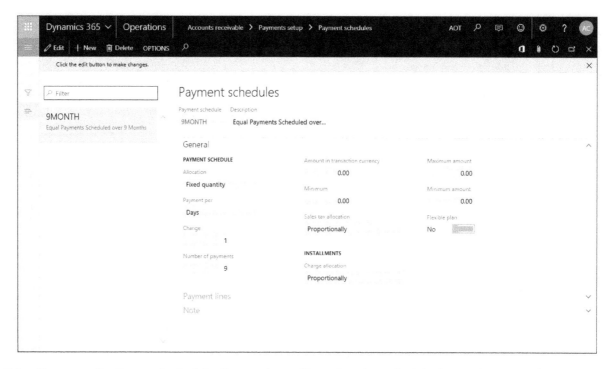

This will open up the **Payment schedules** form and we will see the other schedule that we just created.

www.dynamicscompanions.com
Dynamics Companions

- 150 -

www.blindsquirrelpublishing.com
© 2017 Blind Squirrel Publishing, LLC, All Rights Reserved

BLIND SQUIRREL
PUBLISHING

DYNAMICS COMPANIONS
BARE BONES CONFIGURATION GUIDES

CONFIGURING ACCOUNTS RECEIVABLE WITHIN DYNAMICS 365 FOR OPERATIONS
MODULE 1: CONFIGURING THE ACCOUNTS RECEIVABLE CONTROLS

Configuring Proportional Monthly Scheduled Payment Terms

How to do it...

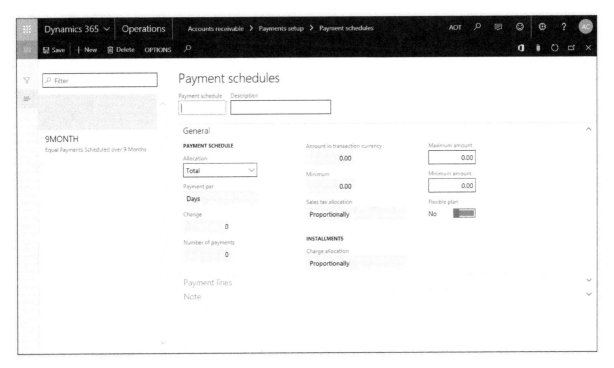

To create a new **Payment schedule** record. click on the **+ New** button within the menu bar.

dyn c

www.dynamicscompanions.com
Dynamics Companions

- 151 -

www.blindsquirrelpublishing.com
© 2017 Blind Squirrel Publishing, LLC, All Rights Reserved

BLIND SQUIRREL
PUBLISHING

DYNAMICS COMPANIONS
BARE BONES CONFIGURATION GUIDES

CONFIGURING ACCOUNTS RECEIVABLE WITHIN DYNAMICS 365 FOR OPERATIONS
MODULE 1: CONFIGURING THE ACCOUNTS RECEIVABLE CONTROLS

Configuring Proportional Monthly Scheduled Payment Terms

How to do it...

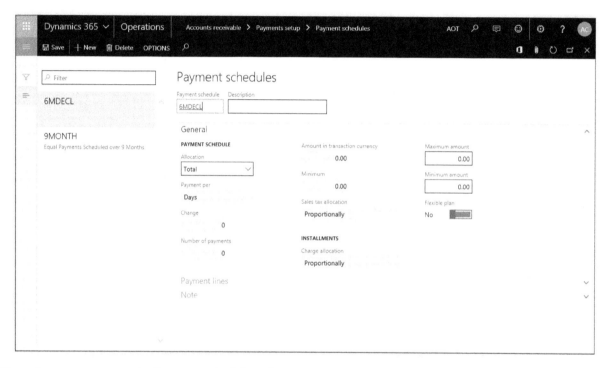

Then give your new record a **Payment schedule** code.

In this example we will be creating a payment schedule that has equal payments over 9 months, so we will set the **Payment schedule** code to *6MDECL*.

dyn

www.dynamicscompanions.com
Dynamics Companions

- 152 -

www.blindsquirrelpublishing.com
© 2017 Blind Squirrel Publishing, LLC, All Rights Reserved

BLIND SQUIRREL
PUBLISHING

DYNAMICS COMPANIONS
BARE BONES CONFIGURATION GUIDES

CONFIGURING ACCOUNTS RECEIVABLE WITHIN DYNAMICS 365 FOR OPERATIONS
MODULE 1: CONFIGURING THE ACCOUNTS RECEIVABLE CONTROLS

Configuring Proportional Monthly Scheduled Payment Terms

How to do it...

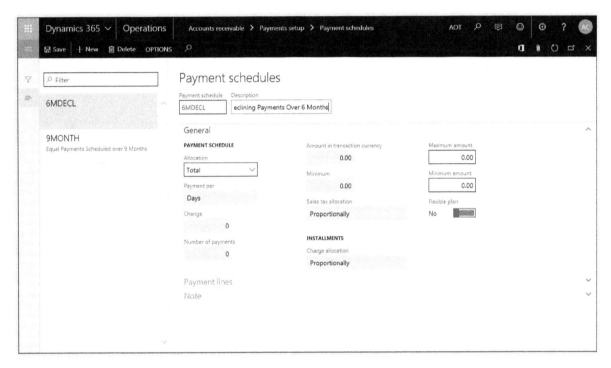

Then give your new Payment schedule a more understandable **Description.**

Here we set the **Description** to **Declining Payments Over 6 Months**.

dync
www.dynamicscompanions.com
Dynamics Companions

- 153 -

www.blindsquirrelpublishing.com
© 2017 Blind Squirrel Publishing, LLC, All Rights Reserved

BLIND SQUIRREL
PUBLISHING

DYNAMICS COMPANIONS
BARE BONES CONFIGURATION GUIDES

CONFIGURING ACCOUNTS RECEIVABLE WITHIN DYNAMICS 365 FOR OPERATIONS
MODULE 1: CONFIGURING THE ACCOUNTS RECEIVABLE CONTROLS

Configuring Proportional Monthly Scheduled Payment Terms

How to do it...

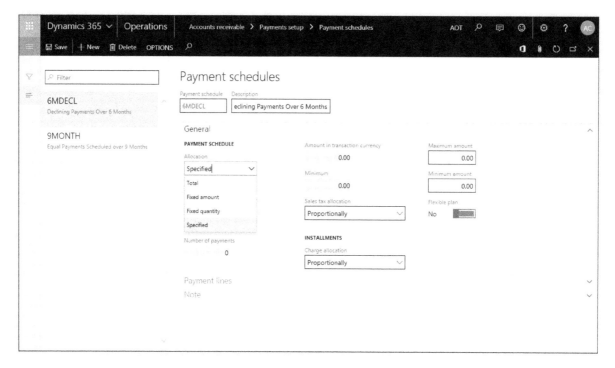

Then from the **Allocation** dropdown list select the **Specified** option.

dyn○
www.dynamicscompanions.com
Dynamics Companions

- 154 -

www.blindsquirrelpublishing.com
© 2017 Blind Squirrel Publishing, LLC, All Rights Reserved

BLIND SQUIRREL
PUBLISHING

DYNAMICS COMPANIONS
BARE BONES CONFIGURATION GUIDES

CONFIGURING ACCOUNTS RECEIVABLE WITHIN DYNAMICS 365 FOR OPERATIONS
MODULE 1: CONFIGURING THE ACCOUNTS RECEIVABLE CONTROLS

Configuring Proportional Monthly Scheduled Payment Terms

How to do it...

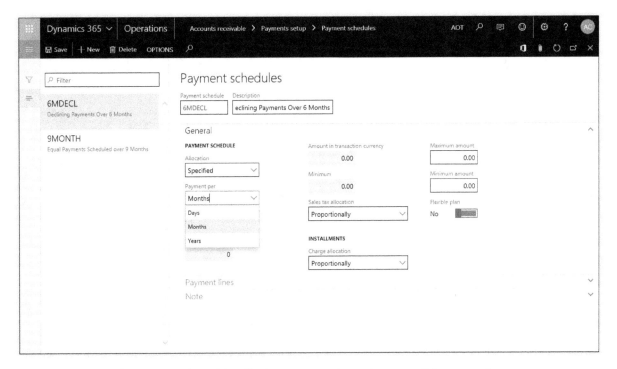

Set the **Payment per** field to **Months** to identify that we are going to have monthly payments.

dyn

www.dynamicscompanions.com
Dynamics Companions

- 155 -

www.blindsquirrelpublishing.com
© 2017 Blind Squirrel Publishing, LLC, All Rights Reserved

BLIND SQUIRREL
PUBLISHING

DYNAMICS COMPANIONS
BARE BONES CONFIGURATION GUIDES

CONFIGURING ACCOUNTS RECEIVABLE WITHIN DYNAMICS 365 FOR OPERATIONS
MODULE 1: CONFIGURING THE ACCOUNTS RECEIVABLE CONTROLS

Configuring Proportional Monthly Scheduled Payment Terms

How to do it...

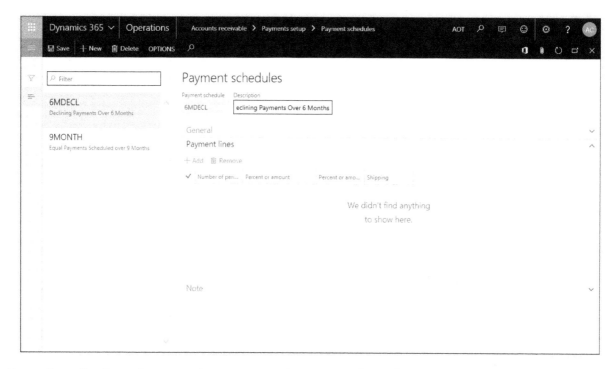

Now collapse the **General group** so that you can see the **Payment Lines** tab group.

dyn

www.dynamicscompanions.com
Dynamics Companions

- 156 -

www.blindsquirrelpublishing.com
© 2017 Blind Squirrel Publishing, LLC , All Rights Reserved

BLIND SQUIRREL
PUBLISHING

DYNAMICS COMPANIONS
BARE BONES CONFIGURATION GUIDES

CONFIGURING ACCOUNTS RECEIVABLE WITHIN DYNAMICS 365 FOR OPERATIONS
MODULE 1: CONFIGURING THE ACCOUNTS RECEIVABLE CONTROLS

Configuring Proportional Monthly Scheduled Payment Terms

How to do it...

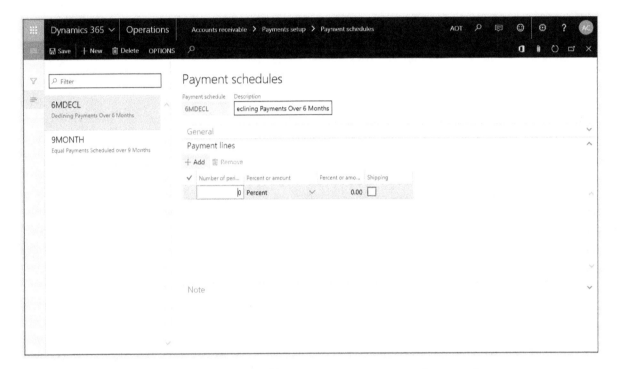

Click on the **+ Add** button in the **Payment Lines** table to create a new payment line record.

dyn c
dynamics companions

www.dynamicscompanions.com
Dynamics Companions

- 157 -

www.blindsquirrelpublishing.com
© 2017 Blind Squirrel Publishing, LLC , All Rights Reserved

BLIND SQUIRREL
PUBLISHING

DYNAMICS COMPANIONS
BARE BONES CONFIGURATION GUIDES

CONFIGURING ACCOUNTS RECEIVABLE WITHIN DYNAMICS 365 FOR OPERATIONS
MODULE 1: CONFIGURING THE ACCOUNTS RECEIVABLE CONTROLS

Configuring Proportional Monthly Scheduled Payment Terms

How to do it...

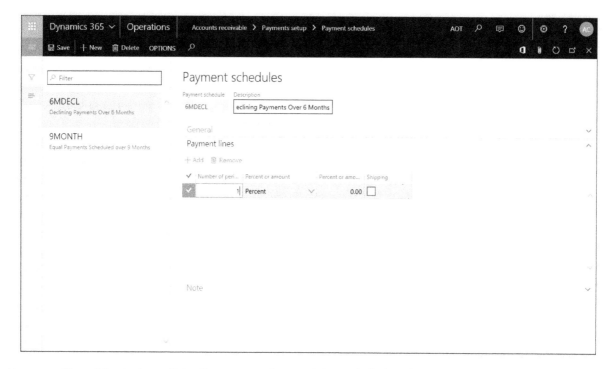

Now we will want to start specifying the payment lines and the periods that they are associated with.

For this first line, set the **Number of period** to 1 to create a record for the first month.

dyn c
www.dynamicscompanions.com
Dynamics Companions

- 158 -

www.blindsquirrelpublishing.com
© 2017 Blind Squirrel Publishing, LLC, All Rights Reserved

BLIND SQUIRREL
PUBLISHING

DYNAMICS COMPANIONS
BARE BONES CONFIGURATION GUIDES

CONFIGURING ACCOUNTS RECEIVABLE WITHIN DYNAMICS 365 FOR OPERATIONS
MODULE 1: CONFIGURING THE ACCOUNTS RECEIVABLE CONTROLS

Configuring Proportional Monthly Scheduled Payment Terms

How to do it...

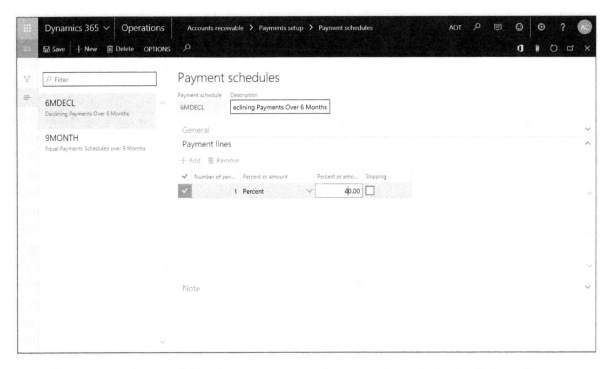

Then set the **Percent or Amount** field to be the percentage of payment that is due in that first month.

Here we set the **Percent or Amount** to *40* to specify that 40% is due in the first month.

www.dynamicscompanions.com
Dynamics Companions

- 159 -

www.blindsquirrelpublishing.com
© 2017 Blind Squirrel Publishing, LLC , All Rights Reserved

BLIND SQUIRREL
PUBLISHING

DYNAMICS COMPANIONS
BARE BONES CONFIGURATION GUIDES

CONFIGURING ACCOUNTS RECEIVABLE WITHIN DYNAMICS 365 FOR OPERATIONS
MODULE 1: CONFIGURING THE ACCOUNTS RECEIVABLE CONTROLS

Configuring Proportional Monthly Scheduled Payment Terms

How to do it...

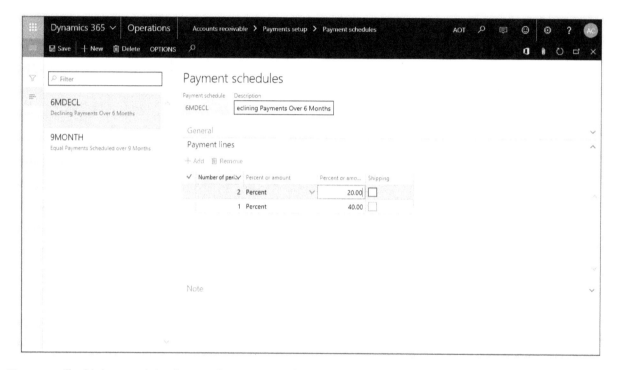

Now we will add the remaining lines to the Payment schedule by repeating the process for all the other months that you require payments along with the percentage amount. Make sure that they add up to 100% so that you are not giving away money.

Click on the **+ Add** button to create a new record and then set the **Number of period** to *2* and the **Percent or amount** to *20*.

www.dynamicscompanions.com
Dynamics Companions

- 160 -

www.blindsquirrelpublishing.com
© 2017 Blind Squirrel Publishing, LLC, All Rights Reserved

BLIND SQUIRREL
PUBLISHING

DYNAMICS COMPANIONS
BARE BONES CONFIGURATION GUIDES

CONFIGURING ACCOUNTS RECEIVABLE WITHIN DYNAMICS 365 FOR OPERATIONS
MODULE 1: CONFIGURING THE ACCOUNTS RECEIVABLE CONTROLS

Configuring Proportional Monthly Scheduled Payment Terms

How to do it...

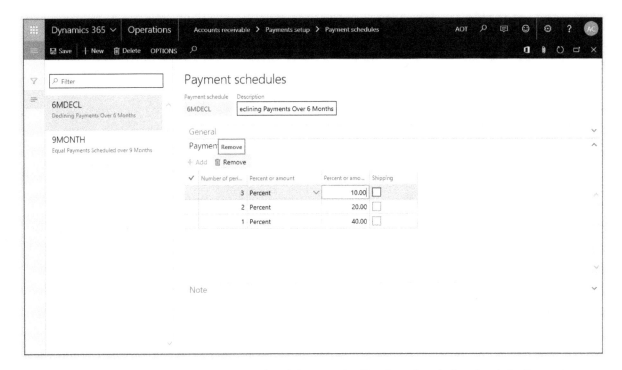

Click on the **+ Add** button to create a new record and then set the **Number of period** to *3* and the **Percent or amount** to *10*.

dync
www.dynamicscompanions.com
Dynamics Companions

- 161 -

www.blindsquirrelpublishing.com
© 2017 Blind Squirrel Publishing, LLC, All Rights Reserved

BLIND SQUIRREL
PUBLISHING

DYNAMICS COMPANIONS
BARE BONES CONFIGURATION GUIDES

CONFIGURING ACCOUNTS RECEIVABLE WITHIN DYNAMICS 365 FOR OPERATIONS
MODULE 1: CONFIGURING THE ACCOUNTS RECEIVABLE CONTROLS

Configuring Proportional Monthly Scheduled Payment Terms

How to do it...

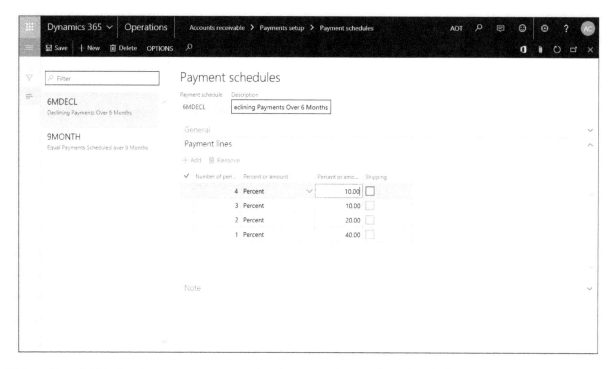

Click on the **+ Add** button to create a new record and then set the **Number of period** to *4* and the **Percent or amount** to *10*.

www.dynamicscompanions.com
Dynamics Companions

- 162 -

www.blindsquirrelpublishing.com
© 2017 Blind Squirrel Publishing, LLC , All Rights Reserved

BLIND SQUIRREL
PUBLISHING

DYNAMICS COMPANIONS
BARE BONES CONFIGURATION GUIDES

CONFIGURING ACCOUNTS RECEIVABLE WITHIN DYNAMICS 365 FOR OPERATIONS
MODULE 1: CONFIGURING THE ACCOUNTS RECEIVABLE CONTROLS

Configuring Proportional Monthly Scheduled Payment Terms

How to do it...

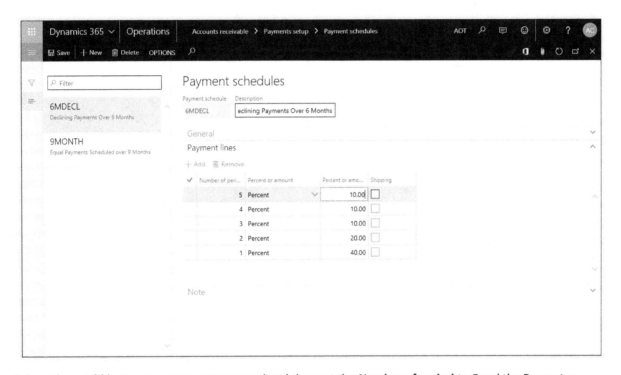

Click on the **+ Add** button to create a new record and then set the **Number of period** to *5* and the **Percent or amount** to *10*.

www.dynamicscompanions.com
Dynamics Companions

- 163 -

www.blindsquirrelpublishing.com
© 2017 Blind Squirrel Publishing, LLC, All Rights Reserved

BLIND SQUIRREL
PUBLISHING

DYNAMICS COMPANIONS
BARE BONES CONFIGURATION GUIDES

CONFIGURING ACCOUNTS RECEIVABLE WITHIN DYNAMICS 365 FOR OPERATIONS
MODULE 1: CONFIGURING THE ACCOUNTS RECEIVABLE CONTROLS

Configuring Proportional Monthly Scheduled Payment Terms

How to do it...

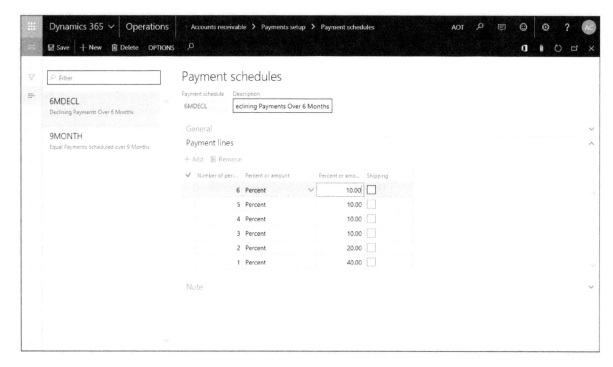

And click on the **+ Add** button one last time to create a new record and then set the **Number of period** to *6* and the **Percent or amount** to *10*.

When you are done, we can exit from the form.

dyn

www.dynamicscompanions.com
Dynamics Companions

- 164 -

www.blindsquirrelpublishing.com
© 2017 Blind Squirrel Publishing, LLC, All Rights Reserved

BLIND SQUIRREL
PUBLISHING

DYNAMICS COMPANIONS
BARE BONES CONFIGURATION GUIDES

CONFIGURING ACCOUNTS RECEIVABLE WITHIN DYNAMICS 365 FOR OPERATIONS
MODULE 1: CONFIGURING THE ACCOUNTS RECEIVABLE CONTROLS

Configuring Proportional Monthly Scheduled Payment Terms

How to do it...

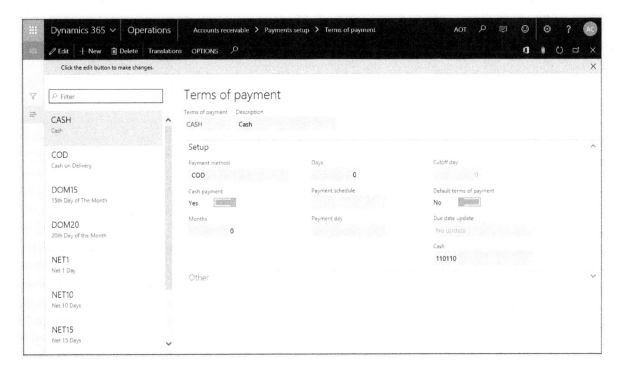

Now we will want to return to the **Terms of Payments** maintenance form to set up a record that will take advantage of the payment schedule that we just created.

dync
www.dynamicscompanions.com
Dynamics Companions

- 165 -

www.blindsquirrelpublishing.com
© 2017 Blind Squirrel Publishing, LLC, All Rights Reserved

BLIND SQUIRREL
PUBLISHING

DYNAMICS COMPANIONS
BARE BONES CONFIGURATION GUIDES

CONFIGURING ACCOUNTS RECEIVABLE WITHIN DYNAMICS 365 FOR OPERATIONS
MODULE 1: CONFIGURING THE ACCOUNTS RECEIVABLE CONTROLS

Configuring Proportional Monthly Scheduled Payment Terms

How to do it...

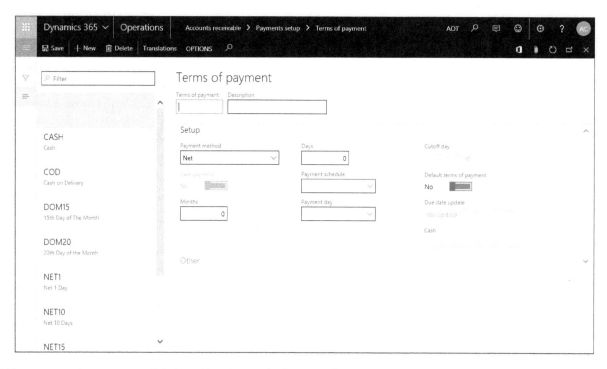

When we are there we can click the **+ New** button in the menu bar to create a new record.

www.dynamicscompanions.com
Dynamics Companions

- 166 -

www.blindsquirrelpublishing.com
© 2017 Blind Squirrel Publishing, LLC, All Rights Reserved

BLIND SQUIRREL
PUBLISHING

DYNAMICS COMPANIONS
BARE BONES CONFIGURATION GUIDES

CONFIGURING ACCOUNTS RECEIVABLE WITHIN DYNAMICS 365 FOR OPERATIONS
MODULE 1: CONFIGURING THE ACCOUNTS RECEIVABLE CONTROLS

Configuring Proportional Monthly Scheduled Payment Terms

How to do it...

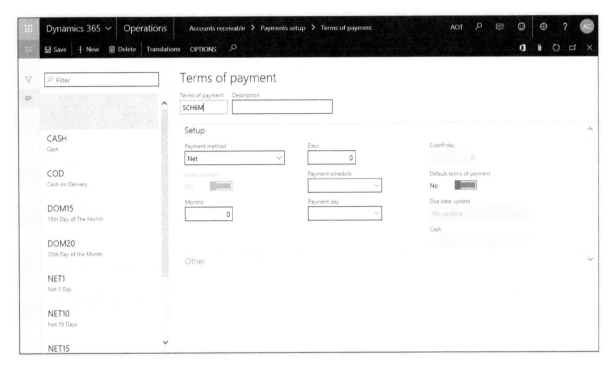

For this example, we will want to set the **Terms of payment** code to *SCH6M*.

dync
www.dynamicscompanions.com
Dynamics Companions

- 167 -

www.blindsquirrelpublishing.com
© 2017 Blind Squirrel Publishing, LLC, All Rights Reserved

BLIND SQUIRREL
PUBLISHING

DYNAMICS COMPANIONS
BARE BONES CONFIGURATION GUIDES

CONFIGURING ACCOUNTS RECEIVABLE WITHIN DYNAMICS 365 FOR OPERATIONS
MODULE 1: CONFIGURING THE ACCOUNTS RECEIVABLE CONTROLS

Configuring Proportional Monthly Scheduled Payment Terms

How to do it...

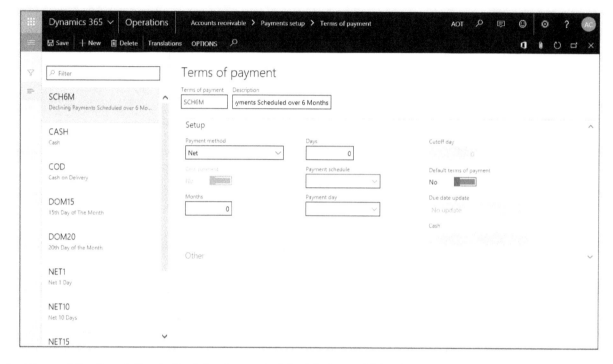

And then set the Description to Declining Payments Scheduled over 6 Months.

dync   www.dynamicscompanions.com
Dynamics Companions

- 168 -

www.blindsquirrelpublishing.com
© 2017 Blind Squirrel Publishing, LLC, All Rights Reserved

BLIND SQUIRREL
PUBLISHING

DYNAMICS COMPANIONS
BARE BONES CONFIGURATION GUIDES

CONFIGURING ACCOUNTS RECEIVABLE WITHIN DYNAMICS 365 FOR OPERATIONS
MODULE 1: CONFIGURING THE ACCOUNTS RECEIVABLE CONTROLS

Configuring Proportional Monthly Scheduled Payment Terms

How to do it...

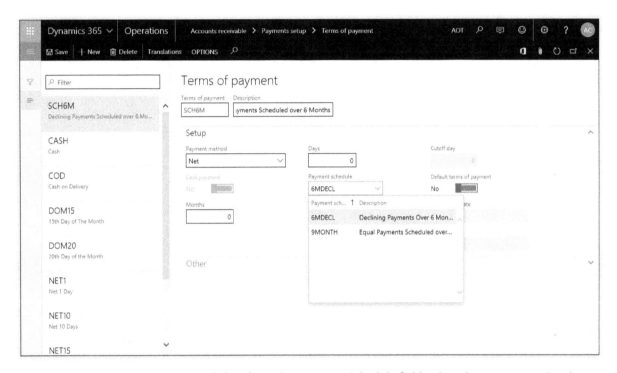

Set the **Payment Method** to be **Net** and then from the **Payment Schedule** field, select the new proportional monthly schedule that you just created.

dync
www.dynamicscompanions.com
Dynamics Companions

- 169 -

www.blindsquirrelpublishing.com
© 2017 Blind Squirrel Publishing, LLC , All Rights Reserved

BLIND SQUIRREL
PUBLISHING

DYNAMICS COMPANIONS
BARE BONES CONFIGURATION GUIDES

CONFIGURING ACCOUNTS RECEIVABLE WITHIN DYNAMICS 365 FOR OPERATIONS
MODULE 1: CONFIGURING THE ACCOUNTS RECEIVABLE CONTROLS

Configuring Proportional Monthly Scheduled Payment Terms

How to do it...

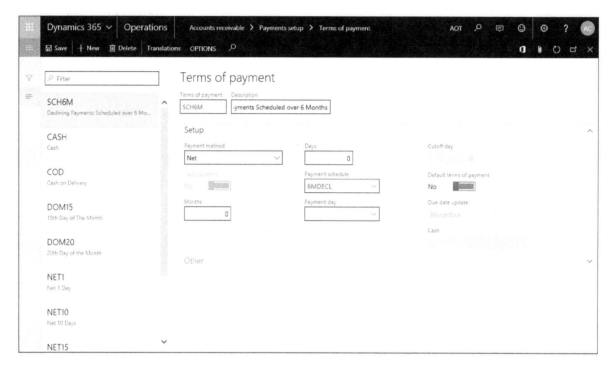

After you have done that we are done and we can exit from the form.

dyn
www.dynamicscompanions.com
Dynamics Companions

- 170 -

www.blindsquirrelpublishing.com
© 2017 Blind Squirrel Publishing, LLC, All Rights Reserved

BLIND SQUIRREL
PUBLISHING

DYNAMICS COMPANIONS
BARE BONES CONFIGURATION GUIDES

CONFIGURING ACCOUNTS RECEIVABLE WITHIN DYNAMICS 365 FOR OPERATIONS
MODULE 1: CONFIGURING THE ACCOUNTS RECEIVABLE CONTROLS

Configuring Proportional Monthly Scheduled Payment Terms

Example Data

Field Name	Value
Payment schedule	6MDECL
Description	Declining Payments Over 6 Months
Allocation	Specified
Payment Per	Months
Payment Lines 1 - Number of period	1
Payment Lines 1 – Percent or amount	40
Payment Lines 2 - Number of period	2
Payment Lines 2 - Percent or amount	20
Payment Lines 3- Number of period	3
Payment Lines 3 - Percent or amount	10
Payment Lines 4- Number of period	4
Payment Lines 4 - Percent or amount	10
Payment Lines 5- Number of period	5
Payment Lines 5 - Percent or amount	10
Payment Lines 6- Number of period	6
Payment Lines 6 - Percent or amount	10

Payment Schedule: 6MDECL – Declining Payments over 6 Months

Field Name	Value
Terms of payment	SCH6MD
Description	Declining Payments Schedule Over 6 Months
Payment method	Net
Payment schedule	6MDECL

Terms of Payment: SCH6MD – Declining Payments Schedule Over 6 Months

dyn

www.dynamicscompanions.com
Dynamics Companions

- 171 -

www.blindsquirrelpublishing.com
© 2017 Blind Squirrel Publishing, LLC, All Rights Reserved

BLIND SQUIRREL
PUBLISHING

DYNAMICS COMPANIONS
BARE BONES CONFIGURATION GUIDES

CONFIGURING ACCOUNTS RECEIVABLE WITHIN DYNAMICS 365 FOR OPERATIONS
MODULE 1: CONFIGURING THE ACCOUNTS RECEIVABLE CONTROLS

Configuring Proportional Monthly Scheduled Payment Terms

Summary

The Proportional Payment Terms are useful when you want to be a little more creative with the payment terms offered to your customers. As you can see from this example, you can structure the payments several different ways to track the payment accounts and this allows you to have deposits up front and then have smaller payments afterwards, or set up smaller initial payments and then have larger payments at the end. The options with this Payment Term structure is unlimited.

 www.dynamicscompanions.com
Dynamics Companions

- 172 -

www.blindsquirrelpublishing.com
© 2017 Blind Squirrel Publishing, LLC, All Rights Reserved

 BLIND SQUIRREL
PUBLISHING

DYNAMICS COMPANIONS
BARE BONES CONFIGURATION GUIDES

CONFIGURING ACCOUNTS RECEIVABLE WITHIN DYNAMICS 365 FOR OPERATIONS
MODULE 1: CONFIGURING THE ACCOUNTS RECEIVABLE CONTROLS

Configuring Cash Discount Codes

In addition to configuring the **Terms of Payments** you may also want to configure **Cash Discount Codes** as incentives for early payment with discount percentages.

How to do it...

To do this, open up the navigation panel, expand out the **Modules** group, and click on **Accounts Receivable** module to see all of the menu items that are available. Then click on the **Cash discounts** menu item within the **Payment setup** menu group.

Alternatively, you can search for the **Cash discounts** form by clicking on the search icon in the header of the form (or press **ALT+G**) and then type in **cash disc** into the search box. Then you will be able to select the **Cash discounts** maintenance form from the dropdown list.

This will open up the **Cash discounts** maintenance form where we can start setting up our discount codes,

To start creating our first **Cash discount** record, just click on the **New** button in the menu bar.

Then give your new record a **Cash discount** code.

The first **Cash discount** that we will create will an early payment incentive to give the customer a discount of 1% if they pay within 10 days, so we will set the **Cash discount** code to **1NET10**.

Then add a more descriptive **Description.**

For this Cash discount, we set the **Description** to **1% Net 10.**

Set the **Days** field to be the number of days that you want to encourage the customer to pay in – in our case **10**.

And then in the **Discount Percentage** field set the discount percentage that you want to give the customer.

Here we set the **Discount percentage** to **1**.

Then assign a **Main Account for Customer Discounts** to identify where the discount is going to be posted to.

In this example, we set the **Main Account for Customer Discounts** to *403300*.

These Cash Discounts codes are also used for the Accounts Payable discounts – no point in reinventing the wheel. So, while we are here we will also configure the AP settings for the discounts so that we don't need to set them up later. To do this, select the **Use Main Account for Vendor Discounts** option from the **Discount Offset Accounts** field.

And then select the **Main Account for Vendor Discounts** that you want to post the Vendor Discounts to.

For this example, we set the **Main Account for Vendor Discounts** to *520200* to point to the *Cash Discounts Taken* account.

Let's create a few more **Cash discount** codes, starting with another discount that gives the customer 1% off for paying within 30 days.

So click on the **+ New** button in the menu bar and set the **Cash discount** code to *1NET30*, set the **Description** to *1% Net 30 Days*, set the **Days** to *30*,

 www.dynamicscompanions.com
Dynamics Companions

- 173 -

www.blindsquirrelpublishing.com
© 2017 Blind Squirrel Publishing, LLC, All Rights Reserved

BLIND SQUIRREL
PUBLISHING

DYNAMICS COMPANIONS
BARE BONES CONFIGURATION GUIDES

CONFIGURING ACCOUNTS RECEIVABLE WITHIN DYNAMICS 365 FOR OPERATIONS
MODULE 1: CONFIGURING THE ACCOUNTS RECEIVABLE CONTROLS

set the **Discount percentage** to *1*, set the **Main Account for Customer discounts** to *403300*, set the **Discount offset account** to *Use Main Account for Vendor Discounts*, and then set the **Main Account for Vendor discounts** to *520200*.

Now create another **Cash discount** code, that gives the customer 2% off for paying within 10 days.

So click on the **+ New** button in the menu bar and set the **Cash discount** code to *2NET10*, set the **Description** to *2% Net 10 Days*, set the **Days** to *10*, set the **Discount percentage** to *2*, set the **Main Account for Customer discounts** to *403300*, set the **Discount offset account** to *Use Main Account for Vendor Discounts*, and then set the **Main Account for Vendor discounts** to *520200*.

And create one last **Cash discount** code, that gives the customer 3% off for paying within 10 days.

So click on the **+ New** button in the menu bar and set the **Cash discount** code to *3NET10*, set the **Description** to *3% Net 10 Days*, set the **Days** to *10*, set the **Discount percentage** to *3*, set the **Main Account for Customer discounts** to *403300*, set the **Discount offset account** to *Use Main Account for Vendor Discounts*, and then set the **Main Account for Vendor discounts** to *520200*.

You can repeat this process for any other combinations and variations of the discount terms that you want to offer to your customers, and when you a done, just to exit from the form.

dyn
www.dynamicscompanions.com
Dynamics Companions
- 174 -
www.blindsquirrelpublishing.com
© 2017 Blind Squirrel Publishing, LLC, All Rights Reserved
BLIND SQUIRREL
PUBLISHING

DYNAMICS COMPANIONS
BARE BONES CONFIGURATION GUIDES

CONFIGURING ACCOUNTS RECEIVABLE WITHIN DYNAMICS 365 FOR OPERATIONS
MODULE 1: CONFIGURING THE ACCOUNTS RECEIVABLE CONTROLS

Configuring Cash Discount Codes

How to do it...

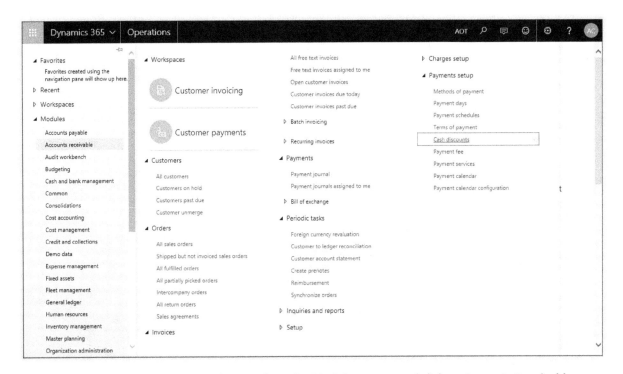

To do this, open up the navigation panel, expand out the **Modules** group, and click on **Accounts Receivable** module to see all of the menu items that are available. Then click on the **Cash discounts** menu item within the **Payment setup** menu group.

www.dynamicscompanions.com
Dynamics Companions

- 175 -

www.blindsquirrelpublishing.com
© 2017 Blind Squirrel Publishing, LLC, All Rights Reserved

BLIND SQUIRREL
PUBLISHING

DYNAMICS COMPANIONS
BARE BONES CONFIGURATION GUIDES

CONFIGURING ACCOUNTS RECEIVABLE WITHIN DYNAMICS 365 FOR OPERATIONS
MODULE 1: CONFIGURING THE ACCOUNTS RECEIVABLE CONTROLS

Configuring Cash Discount Codes

How to do it...

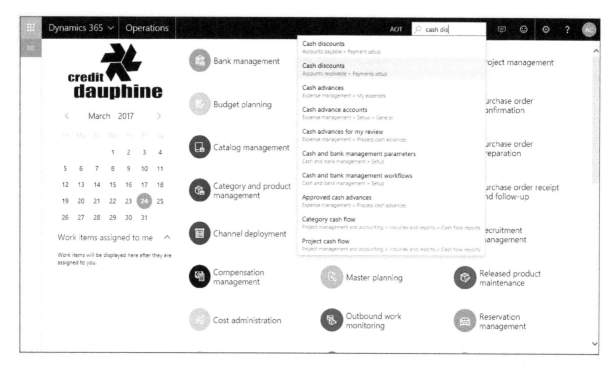

Alternatively, you can search for the **Cash discounts** form by clicking on the search icon in the header of the form (or press **ALT+G**) and then type in **cash disc** into the search box. Then you will be able to select the **Cash discounts** maintenance form from the dropdown list.

dyn⊂
www.dynamicscompanions.com
Dynamics Companions

- 176 -

www.blindsquirrelpublishing.com
© 2017 Blind Squirrel Publishing, LLC , All Rights Reserved

BLIND SQUIRREL
PUBLISHING

DYNAMICS COMPANIONS
BARE BONES CONFIGURATION GUIDES

CONFIGURING ACCOUNTS RECEIVABLE WITHIN DYNAMICS 365 FOR OPERATIONS
MODULE 1: CONFIGURING THE ACCOUNTS RECEIVABLE CONTROLS

Configuring Cash Discount Codes

How to do it...

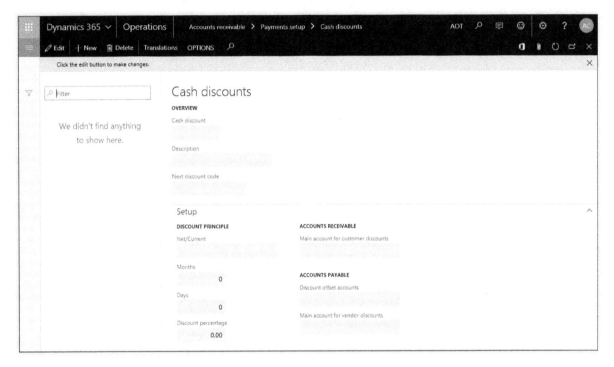

This will open up the **Cash discounts** maintenance form where we can start setting up our discount codes,

dync
www.dynamicscompanions.com
Dynamics Companions

- 177 -

www.blindsquirrelpublishing.com
© 2017 Blind Squirrel Publishing, LLC, All Rights Reserved

BLIND SQUIRREL
PUBLISHING

DYNAMICS COMPANIONS
BARE BONES CONFIGURATION GUIDES

CONFIGURING ACCOUNTS RECEIVABLE WITHIN DYNAMICS 365 FOR OPERATIONS
MODULE 1: CONFIGURING THE ACCOUNTS RECEIVABLE CONTROLS

Configuring Cash Discount Codes

How to do it...

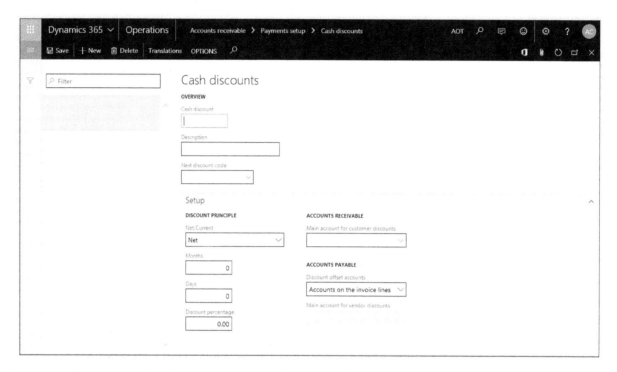

To start creating our first **Cash discount** record, just click on the **New** button in the menu bar.

www.dynamicscompanions.com
Dynamics Companions

- 178 -

www.blindsquirrelpublishing.com
© 2017 Blind Squirrel Publishing, LLC, All Rights Reserved

BLIND SQUIRREL
PUBLISHING

DYNAMICS COMPANIONS
BARE BONES CONFIGURATION GUIDES

CONFIGURING ACCOUNTS RECEIVABLE WITHIN DYNAMICS 365 FOR OPERATIONS
MODULE 1: CONFIGURING THE ACCOUNTS RECEIVABLE CONTROLS

Configuring Cash Discount Codes

How to do it...

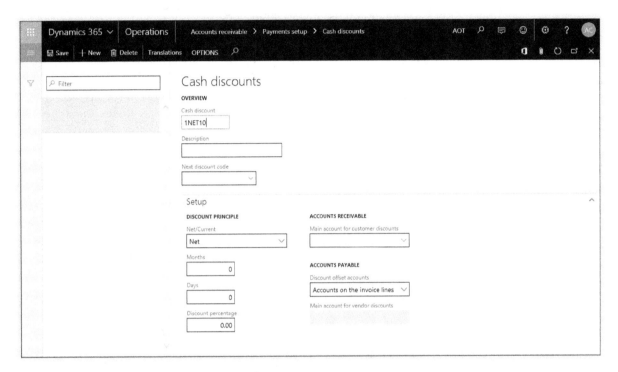

Then give your new record a **Cash discount** code.

The first **Cash discount** that we will create will an early payment incentive to give the customer a discount of 1% if they pay within 10 days, so we will set the **Cash discount** code to **1NET10**.

dyn c
www.dynamicscompanions.com
Dynamics Companions

- 179 -

www.blindsquirrelpublishing.com
© 2017 Blind Squirrel Publishing, LLC, All Rights Reserved

BLIND SQUIRREL
PUBLISHING

DYNAMICS COMPANIONS
BARE BONES CONFIGURATION GUIDES

CONFIGURING ACCOUNTS RECEIVABLE WITHIN DYNAMICS 365 FOR OPERATIONS
MODULE 1: CONFIGURING THE ACCOUNTS RECEIVABLE CONTROLS

Configuring Cash Discount Codes

How to do it...

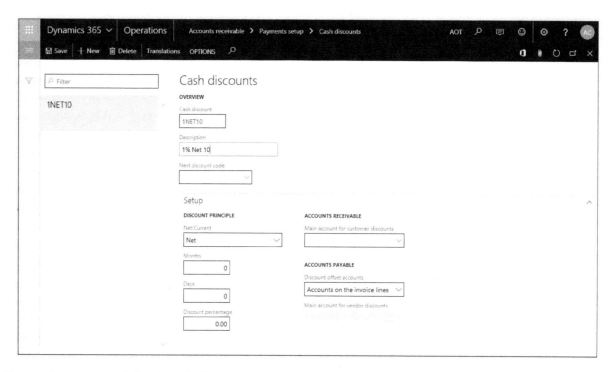

Then add a more descriptive **Description.**

For this Cash discount, we set the **Description** to **1% Net 10.**

dyn c   www.dynamicscompanions.com
Dynamics Companions

- 180 -

www.blindsquirrelpublishing.com
© 2017 Blind Squirrel Publishing, LLC , All Rights Reserved

BLIND SQUIRREL
PUBLISHING

DYNAMICS COMPANIONS
BARE BONES CONFIGURATION GUIDES

CONFIGURING ACCOUNTS RECEIVABLE WITHIN DYNAMICS 365 FOR OPERATIONS
MODULE 1: CONFIGURING THE ACCOUNTS RECEIVABLE CONTROLS

Configuring Cash Discount Codes

How to do it...

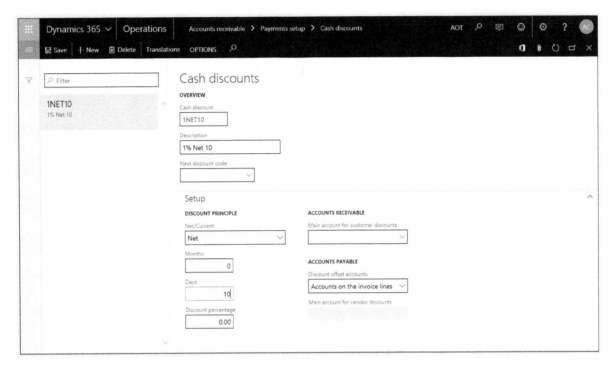

Set the **Days** field to be the number of days that you want to encourage the customer to pay in – in our case **10**.

DYNAMICS COMPANIONS
BARE BONES CONFIGURATION GUIDES

CONFIGURING ACCOUNTS RECEIVABLE WITHIN DYNAMICS 365 FOR OPERATIONS
MODULE 1: CONFIGURING THE ACCOUNTS RECEIVABLE CONTROLS

Configuring Cash Discount Codes

How to do it...

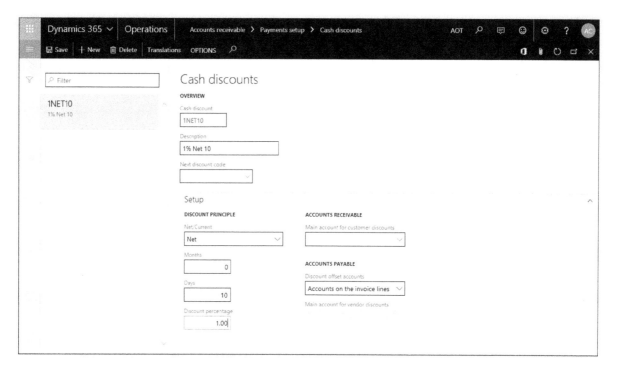

And then in the **Discount Percentage** field set the discount percentage that you want to give the customer.

Here we set the **Discount percentage** to **1**.

www.dynamicscompanions.com
Dynamics Companions

- 182 -

www.blindsquirrelpublishing.com
© 2017 Blind Squirrel Publishing, LLC, All Rights Reserved

BLIND SQUIRREL
PUBLISHING

DYNAMICS COMPANIONS
BARE BONES CONFIGURATION GUIDES

CONFIGURING ACCOUNTS RECEIVABLE WITHIN DYNAMICS 365 FOR OPERATIONS
MODULE 1: CONFIGURING THE ACCOUNTS RECEIVABLE CONTROLS

Configuring Cash Discount Codes

How to do it...

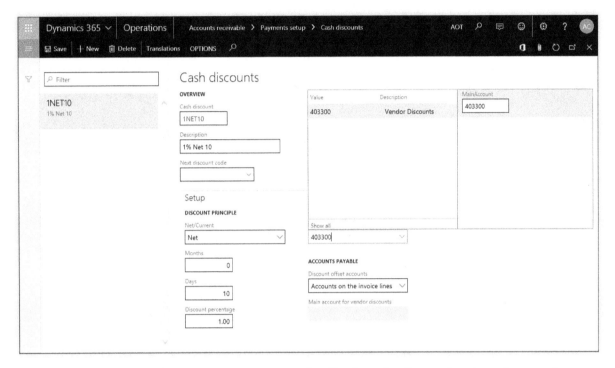

Then assign a **Main Account for Customer Discounts** to identify where the discount is going to be posted to.

In this example, we set the **Main Account for Customer Discounts** to *403300*.

www.dynamicscompanions.com
Dynamics Companions

- 183 -

www.blindsquirrelpublishing.com
© 2017 Blind Squirrel Publishing, LLC, All Rights Reserved

BLIND SQUIRREL
PUBLISHING

DYNAMICS COMPANIONS
BARE BONES CONFIGURATION GUIDES

CONFIGURING ACCOUNTS RECEIVABLE WITHIN DYNAMICS 365 FOR OPERATIONS
MODULE 1: CONFIGURING THE ACCOUNTS RECEIVABLE CONTROLS

Configuring Cash Discount Codes

How to do it...

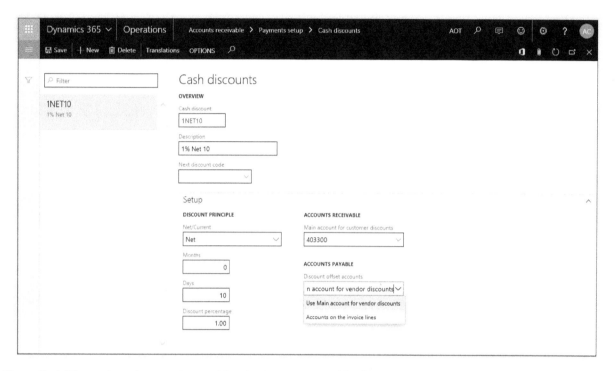

These Cash Discounts codes are also used for the Accounts Payable discounts – no point in reinventing the wheel. So, while we are here we will also configure the AP settings for the discounts so that we don't need to set them up later. To do this, select the **Use Main Account for Vendor Discounts** option from the **Discount Offset Accounts** field.

dyn c

www.dynamicscompanions.com
Dynamics Companions

- 184 -

www.blindsquirrelpublishing.com
© 2017 Blind Squirrel Publishing, LLC, All Rights Reserved

BLIND SQUIRREL
PUBLISHING

DYNAMICS COMPANIONS
BARE BONES CONFIGURATION GUIDES

CONFIGURING ACCOUNTS RECEIVABLE WITHIN DYNAMICS 365 FOR OPERATIONS
MODULE 1: CONFIGURING THE ACCOUNTS RECEIVABLE CONTROLS

Configuring Cash Discount Codes

How to do it...

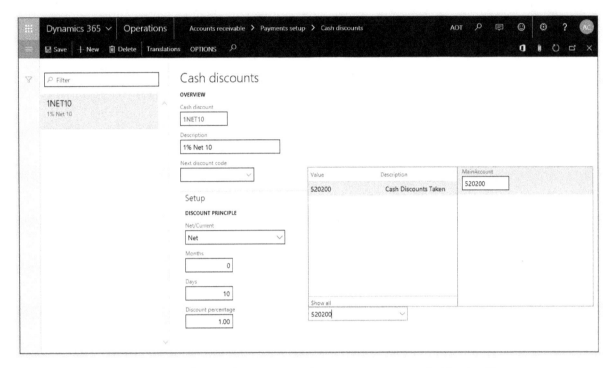

And then select the **Main Account for Vendor Discounts** that you want to post the Vendor Discounts to.

For this example, we set the **Main Account for Vendor Discounts** to *520200* to point to the *Cash Discounts Taken* account.

www.dynamicscompanions.com
Dynamics Companions

- 185 -

www.blindsquirrelpublishing.com
© 2017 Blind Squirrel Publishing, LLC , All Rights Reserved

BLIND SQUIRREL
PUBLISHING

DYNAMICS COMPANIONS
BARE BONES CONFIGURATION GUIDES

CONFIGURING ACCOUNTS RECEIVABLE WITHIN DYNAMICS 365 FOR OPERATIONS
MODULE 1: CONFIGURING THE ACCOUNTS RECEIVABLE CONTROLS

Configuring Cash Discount Codes

How to do it...

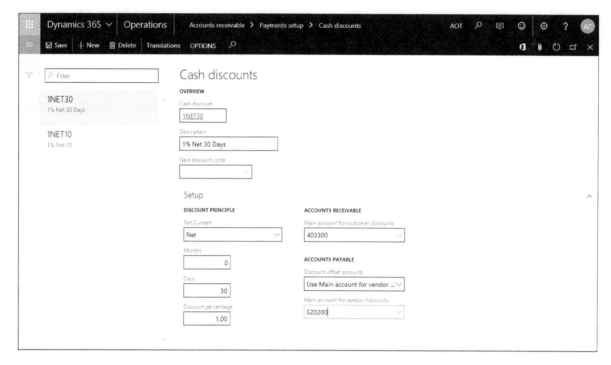

Let's create a few more **Cash discount** codes, starting with another discount that gives the customer 1% off for paying within 30 days.

So click on the **+ New** button in the menu bar and set the **Cash discount** code to *1NET30*, set the **Description** to *1% Net 30 Days*, set the **Days** to *30*, set the **Discount percentage** to *1*, set the **Main Account for Customer discounts** to *403300*, set the **Discount offset account** to *Use Main Account for Vendor Discounts*, and then set the **Main Account for Vendor discounts** to *520200*.

DYNAMICS COMPANIONS
BARE BONES CONFIGURATION GUIDES

CONFIGURING ACCOUNTS RECEIVABLE WITHIN DYNAMICS 365 FOR OPERATIONS
MODULE 1: CONFIGURING THE ACCOUNTS RECEIVABLE CONTROLS

Configuring Cash Discount Codes

How to do it...

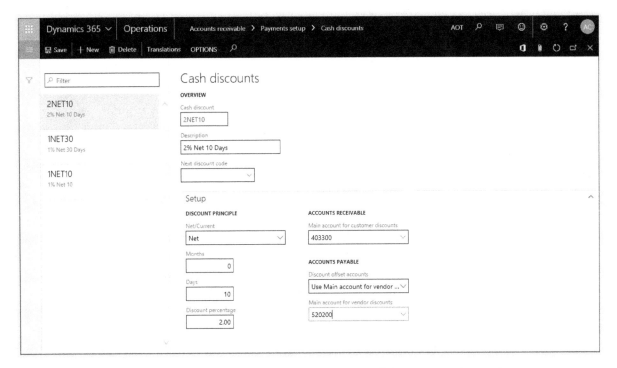

Now create another **Cash discount** code, that gives the customer 2% off for paying within 10 days.

So click on the **+ New** button in the menu bar and set the **Cash discount** code to *2NET10*, set the **Description** to *2% Net 10 Days*, set the **Days** to *10*, set the **Discount percentage** to *2*, set the **Main Account for Customer discounts** to *403300*, set the **Discount offset account** to *Use Main Account for Vendor Discounts*, and then set the **Main Account for Vendor discounts** to *520200*.

www.dynamicscompanions.com
Dynamics Companions

- 187 -

www.blindsquirrelpublishing.com
© 2017 Blind Squirrel Publishing, LLC, All Rights Reserved

BLIND SQUIRREL
PUBLISHING

DYNAMICS COMPANIONS
BARE BONES CONFIGURATION GUIDES

CONFIGURING ACCOUNTS RECEIVABLE WITHIN DYNAMICS 365 FOR OPERATIONS
MODULE 1: CONFIGURING THE ACCOUNTS RECEIVABLE CONTROLS

Configuring Cash Discount Codes

How to do it...

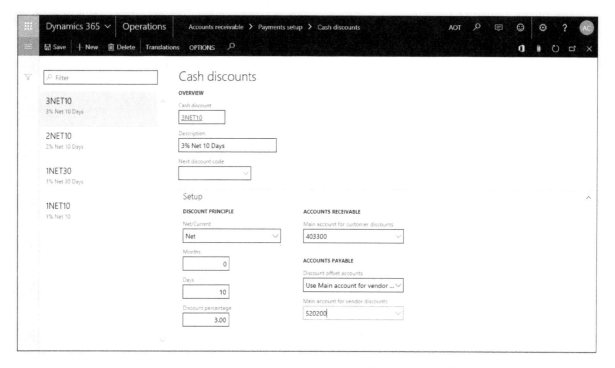

And create one last **Cash discount** code, that gives the customer 3% off for paying within 10 days.

So click on the **+ New** button in the menu bar and set the **Cash discount** code to *3NET10*, set the **Description** to *3% Net 10 Days*, set the **Days** to *10*, set the **Discount percentage** to *3*, set the **Main Account for Customer discounts** to *403300*, set the **Discount offset account** to *Use Main Account for Vendor Discounts*, and then set the **Main Account for Vendor discounts** to *520200*.

You can repeat this process for any other combinations and variations of the discount terms that you want to offer to your customers, and when you a done, just to exit from the form.

dyn©
www.dynamicscompanions.com
Dynamics Companions

- 188 -

www.blindsquirrelpublishing.com
© 2017 Blind Squirrel Publishing, LLC, All Rights Reserved

BLIND SQUIRREL
PUBLISHING

DYNAMICS COMPANIONS
BARE BONES CONFIGURATION GUIDES

CONFIGURING ACCOUNTS RECEIVABLE WITHIN DYNAMICS 365 FOR OPERATIONS
MODULE 1: CONFIGURING THE ACCOUNTS RECEIVABLE CONTROLS

Configuring Cash Discount Codes

Example Data

Field Name	Value
Cash Discount	1NET10
Description	1% Net 10 Days
Days	10
Discount percentage	1
Main Account for Customer Discounts	403300
Discount offset accounts	Use Main Account for Vendor discounts
Main Account for Vendor discounts	520200

Cash Discount: 1NET10 – 1% Net 10 Days

Field Name	Value
Cash Discount	1NET20
Description	1% Net 20 Days
Days	20
Discount percentage	1
Main Account for Customer Discounts	403300
Discount offset accounts	Use Main Account for Vendor discounts
Main Account for Vendor discounts	520200

Cash Discount: 1NET20 – 1% Net 20 Days

Field Name	Value
Cash Discount	2NET10
Description	2% Net 10 Days
Days	10
Discount percentage	2
Main Account for Customer Discounts	403300
Discount offset accounts	Use Main Account for Vendor discounts
Main Account for Vendor discounts	520200

Cash Discount: 2NET10 – 2% Net 10 Days

Field Name	Value
Cash Discount	3NET10
Description	3% Net 10 Days
Days	10
Discount percentage	3
Main Account for Customer Discounts	403300
Discount offset accounts	Use Main Account for Vendor discounts
Main Account for Vendor discounts	520200

Cash Discount: 1NET10 – 1% Net 10 Days

www.dynamicscompanions.com
Dynamics Companions

- 189 -

www.blindsquirrelpublishing.com
© 2017 Blind Squirrel Publishing, LLC , All Rights Reserved

BLIND SQUIRREL
PUBLISHING

DYNAMICS COMPANIONS
BARE BONES CONFIGURATION GUIDES

CONFIGURING ACCOUNTS RECEIVABLE WITHIN DYNAMICS 365 FOR OPERATIONS
MODULE 1: CONFIGURING THE ACCOUNTS RECEIVABLE CONTROLS

Configuring Cash Discount Codes

Summary

Giving customers an incentive to pay early is a great way to get your money just a little bit sooner, and now we have some options available to us to use.

www.dynamicscompanions.com
Dynamics Companions

- 190 -

www.blindsquirrelpublishing.com
© 2017 Blind Squirrel Publishing, LLC, All Rights Reserved

BLIND SQUIRREL
PUBLISHING

DYNAMICS COMPANIONS
BARE BONES CONFIGURATION GUIDES

CONFIGURING ACCOUNTS RECEIVABLE WITHIN DYNAMICS 365 FOR OPERATIONS
MODULE 1: CONFIGURING THE ACCOUNTS RECEIVABLE CONTROLS

Configuring Cash Payment Methods

Now we need to configure a few different methods for receiving cash. The first one that we will configure is a Cash payment method.

How to do it...

To do this, open up the navigation panel, expand out the **Modules** group, and click on **Accounts Receivable** module to see all of the menu items that are available. Then click on the **Methods of Payment** menu item within the **Payment setup** menu group.

Alternatively, you can search for the **Methods of payment** form by clicking on the search icon in the header of the form (or press **ALT+G**) and then type in **methods** into the search box. Then you will be able to select the **Methods of payment** maintenance form from the dropdown list.

This will open up the **Methods of payment** maintenance form.

To create a new **Methods of payment** for our customers, just click on the **+ New** button within the menu bar.

Then give your new record a **Method of payment** code.

For this example, we will set the **Method of payment** code to **CASH**.

Then we will want to give our code a **Description.**

In this example we will set the **Description** to be **Cash Payment**.

Now we will want to click on the **Account type** dropdown list and select the account type that will be used for this method of payment.

For this example, we will want to post the payment to a bank account, so we will set the **Account Type** to **Bank**.

Since we selected the **Bank** as our **Account type** we will now want to select the bank that we want to post the cash to from the **Payment Account** dropdown list.

In this example, we will select the *OPER USD* bank account for the **Payment Account.**

To make your life a little easier later when you start looking at performing Bank Reconciliations, also click on the **Bank transaction type** dropdown list and select the default transaction type that we want to code these transactions to.

Here we will set the **Bank transaction type** to **01**.

dyn c   www.dynamicscompanions.com
Dynamics Companions
- 191 -
www.blindsquirrelpublishing.com
© 2017 Blind Squirrel Publishing, LLC , All Rights Reserved
BLIND SQUIRREL
PUBLISHING

DYNAMICS COMPANIONS
BARE BONES CONFIGURATION GUIDES

CONFIGURING ACCOUNTS RECEIVABLE WITHIN DYNAMICS 365 FOR OPERATIONS
MODULE 1: CONFIGURING THE ACCOUNTS RECEIVABLE CONTROLS

Configuring Cash Payment Methods

How to do it...

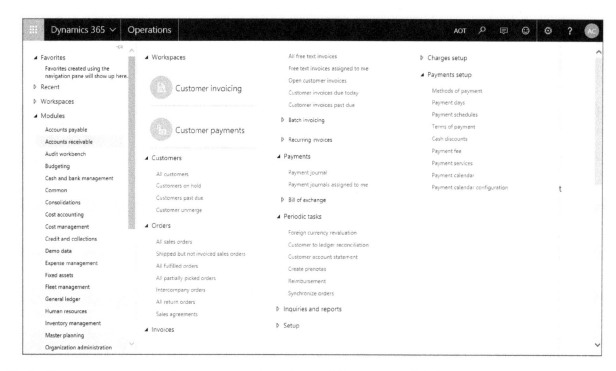

To do this, open up the navigation panel, expand out the **Modules** group, and click on **Accounts Receivable** module to see all of the menu items that are available. Then click on the **Methods of Payment** menu item within the **Payment setup** menu group.

dyn

www.dynamicscompanions.com
Dynamics Companions

- 192 -

www.blindsquirrelpublishing.com
© 2017 Blind Squirrel Publishing, LLC, All Rights Reserved

BLIND SQUIRREL
PUBLISHING

DYNAMICS COMPANIONS
BARE BONES CONFIGURATION GUIDES

CONFIGURING ACCOUNTS RECEIVABLE WITHIN DYNAMICS 365 FOR OPERATIONS
MODULE 1: CONFIGURING THE ACCOUNTS RECEIVABLE CONTROLS

Configuring Cash Payment Methods

How to do it...

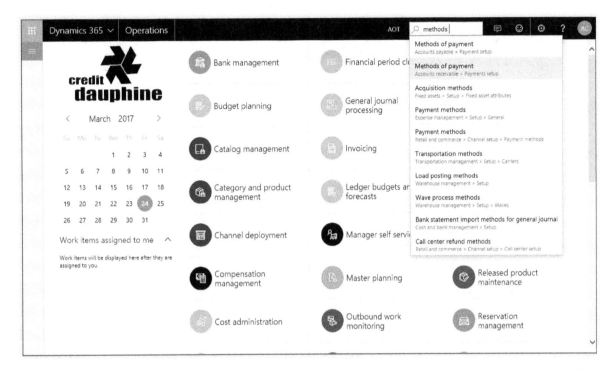

Alternatively, you can search for the **Methods of payment** form by clicking on the search icon in the header of the form (or press **ALT+G**) and then type in **methods** into the search box. Then you will be able to select the **Methods of payment** maintenance form from the dropdown list.

dync
dynamics companions

www.dynamicscompanions.com
Dynamics Companions

- 193 -

www.blindsquirrelpublishing.com
© 2017 Blind Squirrel Publishing, LLC , All Rights Reserved

BLIND SQUIRREL
PUBLISHING

DYNAMICS COMPANIONS
BARE BONES CONFIGURATION GUIDES

CONFIGURING ACCOUNTS RECEIVABLE WITHIN DYNAMICS 365 FOR OPERATIONS
MODULE 1: CONFIGURING THE ACCOUNTS RECEIVABLE CONTROLS

Configuring Cash Payment Methods

How to do it...

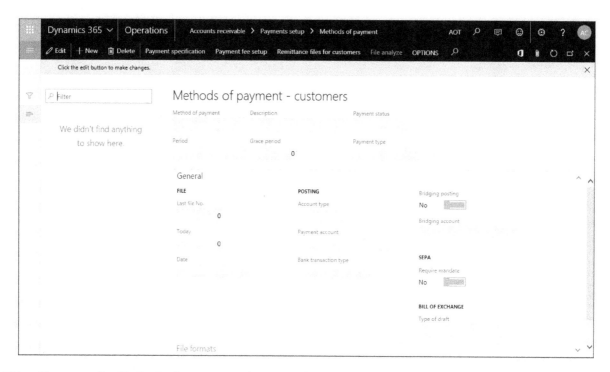

This will open up the **Methods of payment** maintenance form.

dyn⊂

www.dynamicscompanions.com
Dynamics Companions

- 194 -

www.blindsquirrelpublishing.com
© 2017 Blind Squirrel Publishing, LLC , All Rights Reserved

BLIND SQUIRREL
PUBLISHING

DYNAMICS COMPANIONS
BARE BONES CONFIGURATION GUIDES

CONFIGURING ACCOUNTS RECEIVABLE WITHIN DYNAMICS 365 FOR OPERATIONS
MODULE 1: CONFIGURING THE ACCOUNTS RECEIVABLE CONTROLS

Configuring Cash Payment Methods

How to do it...

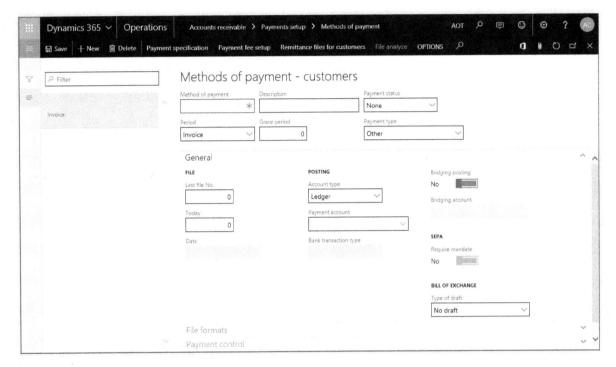

To create a new **Methods of payment** for our customers, just click on the **+ New** button within the menu bar.

dyn c
www.dynamicscompanions.com
Dynamics Companions

- 195 -

www.blindsquirrelpublishing.com
© 2017 Blind Squirrel Publishing, LLC, All Rights Reserved

BLIND SQUIRREL
PUBLISHING

DYNAMICS COMPANIONS
BARE BONES CONFIGURATION GUIDES

CONFIGURING ACCOUNTS RECEIVABLE WITHIN DYNAMICS 365 FOR OPERATIONS
MODULE 1: CONFIGURING THE ACCOUNTS RECEIVABLE CONTROLS

Configuring Cash Payment Methods

How to do it...

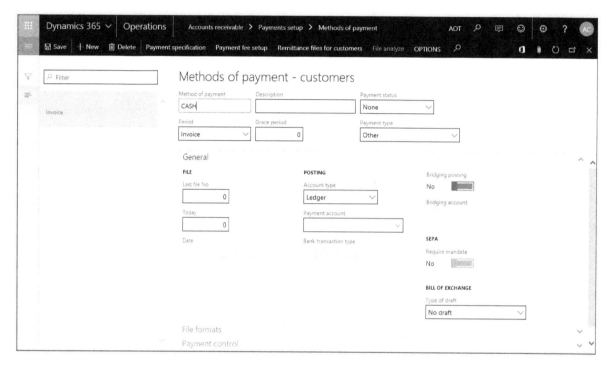

Then give your new record a **Method of payment** code.

For this example, we will set the **Method of payment** code to **CASH**.

dyn￩

www.dynamicscompanions.com
Dynamics Companions

- 196 -

www.blindsquirrelpublishing.com
© 2017 Blind Squirrel Publishing, LLC, All Rights Reserved

BLIND SQUIRREL
PUBLISHING

DYNAMICS COMPANIONS
BARE BONES CONFIGURATION GUIDES

CONFIGURING ACCOUNTS RECEIVABLE WITHIN DYNAMICS 365 FOR OPERATIONS
MODULE 1: CONFIGURING THE ACCOUNTS RECEIVABLE CONTROLS

Configuring Cash Payment Methods

How to do it...

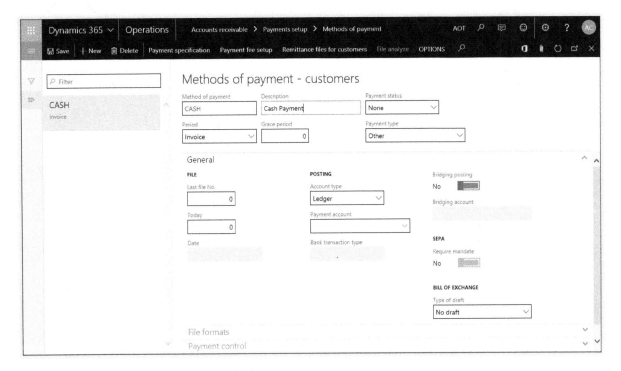

Then we will want to give our code a **Description.**

In this example we will set the **Description** to be **Cash Payment**.

www.dynamicscompanions.com
Dynamics Companions

- 197 -

www.blindsquirrelpublishing.com
© 2017 Blind Squirrel Publishing, LLC , All Rights Reserved

BLIND SQUIRREL
PUBLISHING

DYNAMICS COMPANIONS
BARE BONES CONFIGURATION GUIDES

CONFIGURING ACCOUNTS RECEIVABLE WITHIN DYNAMICS 365 FOR OPERATIONS
MODULE 1: CONFIGURING THE ACCOUNTS RECEIVABLE CONTROLS

Configuring Cash Payment Methods

How to do it...

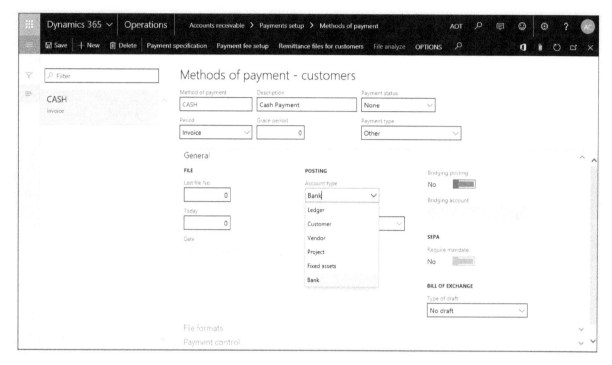

Now we will want to click on the **Account type** dropdown list and select the account type that will be used for this method of payment.

For this example, we will want to post the payment to a bank account, so we will set the **Account Type** to **Bank**.

dyn

www.dynamicscompanions.com
Dynamics Companions

- 198 -

www.blindsquirrelpublishing.com
© 2017 Blind Squirrel Publishing, LLC , All Rights Reserved

BLIND SQUIRREL
PUBLISHING

DYNAMICS COMPANIONS
BARE BONES CONFIGURATION GUIDES

CONFIGURING ACCOUNTS RECEIVABLE WITHIN DYNAMICS 365 FOR OPERATIONS
MODULE 1: CONFIGURING THE ACCOUNTS RECEIVABLE CONTROLS

Configuring Cash Payment Methods

How to do it...

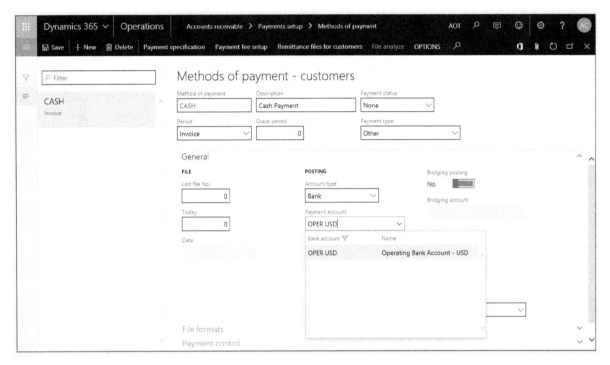

Since we selected the **Bank** as our **Account type** we will now want to select the bank that we want to post the cash to from the **Payment Account** dropdown list.

In this example, we will select the *OPER USD* bank account for the **Payment Account.**

www.dynamicscompanions.com
Dynamics Companions

- 199 -

www.blindsquirrelpublishing.com
© 2017 Blind Squirrel Publishing, LLC, All Rights Reserved

BLIND SQUIRREL
PUBLISHING

DYNAMICS COMPANIONS
BARE BONES CONFIGURATION GUIDES

CONFIGURING ACCOUNTS RECEIVABLE WITHIN DYNAMICS 365 FOR OPERATIONS
MODULE 1: CONFIGURING THE ACCOUNTS RECEIVABLE CONTROLS

Configuring Cash Payment Methods

How to do it...

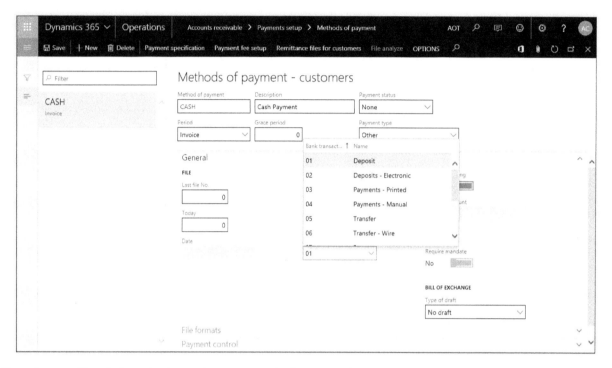

To make your life a little easier later when you start looking at performing Bank Reconciliations, also click on the **Bank transaction type** dropdown list and select the default transaction type that we want to code these transactions to.

Here we will set the **Bank transaction type** to **01**.

dyn⊂
www.dynamicscompanions.com
Dynamics Companions

- 200 -

www.blindsquirrelpublishing.com
© 2017 Blind Squirrel Publishing, LLC, All Rights Reserved

BLIND SQUIRREL
PUBLISHING

DYNAMICS COMPANIONS
BARE BONES CONFIGURATION GUIDES

CONFIGURING ACCOUNTS RECEIVABLE WITHIN DYNAMICS 365 FOR OPERATIONS
MODULE 1: CONFIGURING THE ACCOUNTS RECEIVABLE CONTROLS

Configuring Cash Payment Methods

Example Data

Field Name	Value
Method of Payment	CASK
Description	Cash Payment
Account Type	Bank
Payment Account	OPER
Bank Transaction Code	01

Method of Payment: CASH – Cash Payment

dyn c
www.dynamicscompanions.com
Dynamics Companions

- 201 -

www.blindsquirrelpublishing.com
© 2017 Blind Squirrel Publishing, LLC , All Rights Reserved

BLIND SQUIRREL
PUBLISHING

DYNAMICS COMPANIONS
BARE BONES CONFIGURATION GUIDES

CONFIGURING ACCOUNTS RECEIVABLE WITHIN DYNAMICS 365 FOR OPERATIONS
MODULE 1: CONFIGURING THE ACCOUNTS RECEIVABLE CONTROLS

Configuring Cash Payment Methods

Summary

Cash is king, and now we have a way to track receiving it into the company.

DYNAMICS COMPANIONS
BARE BONES CONFIGURATION GUIDES

CONFIGURING ACCOUNTS RECEIVABLE WITHIN DYNAMICS 365 FOR OPERATIONS
MODULE 1: CONFIGURING THE ACCOUNTS RECEIVABLE CONTROLS

Configuring Check Payment Methods

Another common payment method that you may want to accept are checks. So in this next section we will show how to configure a Method of payment for checks.

How to do it...

Return back to the **Methods of payment** maintenance form and click on the **+ New** button to create a new record.

Then set the **Method of payment** code.

For this example, we will set the **Method of payment** code to **CHECK**.

Then we will want to give our code a **Description.**

In this example we will set the **Description** to be **Check Payment Method**.

For this type of payment we will want to click on the **Payment Type** dropdown field, and select the **Check** option.

Now we will want to click on the **Account type** dropdown list and select the account type that will be used for this method of payment.

For this example, we will want to post the payment to a bank account, so we will set the **Account Type** to **Bank**.

Since we selected the **Bank** as our **Account type** we will now want to select the bank that we want to post the cash to from the **Payment Account** dropdown list.

In this example, we will select the *OPER USD* bank account for the **Payment Account.**

And then set the **Account Type** to be **Bank**, select the bank that you want to deposit the checks into from the **Payment Account** dropdown list and then set the **Bank Transaction Type** to **01.**

After we have done that our **Check Method of payments** has been configured.

www.dynamicscompanions.com
Dynamics Companions

- 203 -

www.blindsquirrelpublishing.com
© 2017 Blind Squirrel Publishing, LLC, All Rights Reserved

BLIND SQUIRREL
PUBLISHING

DYNAMICS COMPANIONS
BARE BONES CONFIGURATION GUIDES

CONFIGURING ACCOUNTS RECEIVABLE WITHIN DYNAMICS 365 FOR OPERATIONS
MODULE 1: CONFIGURING THE ACCOUNTS RECEIVABLE CONTROLS

Configuring Check Payment Methods

How to do it...

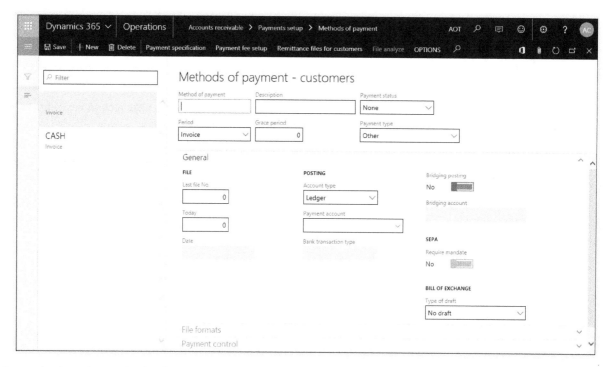

Return back to the **Methods of payment** maintenance form and click on the **+ New** button to create a new record.

www.dynamicscompanions.com
Dynamics Companions

- 204 -

www.blindsquirrelpublishing.com
© 2017 Blind Squirrel Publishing, LLC, All Rights Reserved

BLIND SQUIRREL
PUBLISHING

DYNAMICS COMPANIONS
BARE BONES CONFIGURATION GUIDES

CONFIGURING ACCOUNTS RECEIVABLE WITHIN DYNAMICS 365 FOR OPERATIONS
MODULE 1: CONFIGURING THE ACCOUNTS RECEIVABLE CONTROLS

Configuring Check Payment Methods

How to do it...

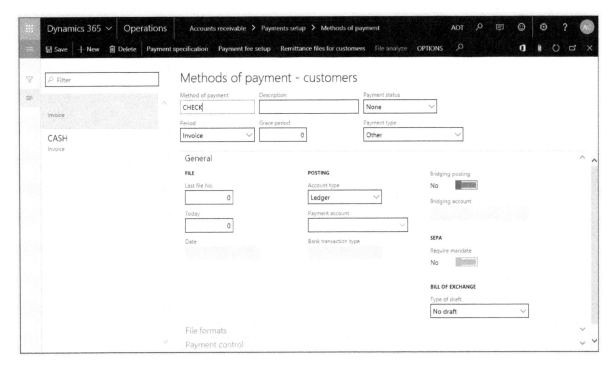

Then set the **Method of payment** code.

For this example, we will set the **Method of payment** code to **CHECK**.

www.dynamicscompanions.com
Dynamics Companions

- 205 -

www.blindsquirrelpublishing.com
© 2017 Blind Squirrel Publishing, LLC, All Rights Reserved

BLIND SQUIRREL
PUBLISHING

DYNAMICS COMPANIONS
BARE BONES CONFIGURATION GUIDES

CONFIGURING ACCOUNTS RECEIVABLE WITHIN DYNAMICS 365 FOR OPERATIONS
MODULE 1: CONFIGURING THE ACCOUNTS RECEIVABLE CONTROLS

Configuring Check Payment Methods

How to do it...

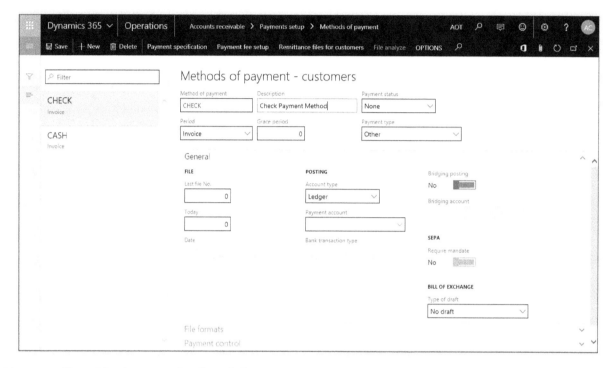

Then we will want to give our code a **Description.**

In this example we will set the **Description** to be **Check Payment Method.**

dyn

www.dynamicscompanions.com
Dynamics Companions

- 206 -

www.blindsquirrelpublishing.com
© 2017 Blind Squirrel Publishing, LLC, All Rights Reserved

BLIND SQUIRREL
PUBLISHING

DYNAMICS COMPANIONS
BARE BONES CONFIGURATION GUIDES

CONFIGURING ACCOUNTS RECEIVABLE WITHIN DYNAMICS 365 FOR OPERATIONS
MODULE 1: CONFIGURING THE ACCOUNTS RECEIVABLE CONTROLS

Configuring Check Payment Methods

How to do it...

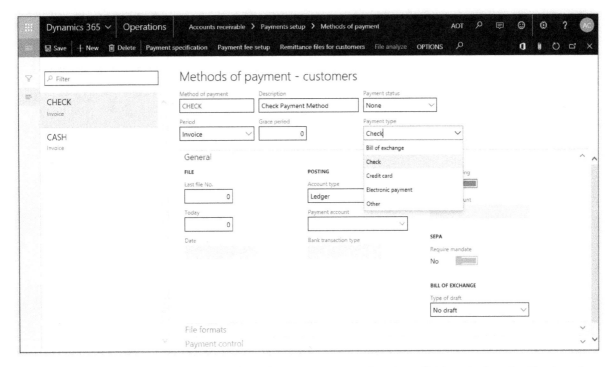

For this type of payment we will want to click on the **Payment Type** dropdown field, and select the **Check** option.

www.dynamicscompanions.com
Dynamics Companions

- 207 -

www.blindsquirrelpublishing.com
© 2017 Blind Squirrel Publishing, LLC, All Rights Reserved

BLIND SQUIRREL
PUBLISHING

DYNAMICS COMPANIONS
BARE BONES CONFIGURATION GUIDES

CONFIGURING ACCOUNTS RECEIVABLE WITHIN DYNAMICS 365 FOR OPERATIONS
MODULE 1: CONFIGURING THE ACCOUNTS RECEIVABLE CONTROLS

Configuring Check Payment Methods

How to do it...

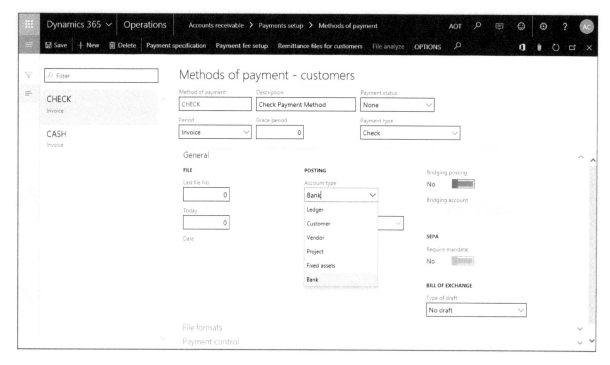

Now we will want to click on the **Account type** dropdown list and select the account type that will be used for this method of payment.

For this example, we will want to post the payment to a bank account, so we will set the **Account Type** to **Bank**.

dync
www.dynamicscompanions.com
Dynamics Companions

- 208 -

www.blindsquirrelpublishing.com
© 2017 Blind Squirrel Publishing, LLC, All Rights Reserved

BLIND SQUIRREL
PUBLISHING

DYNAMICS COMPANIONS
BARE BONES CONFIGURATION GUIDES

CONFIGURING ACCOUNTS RECEIVABLE WITHIN DYNAMICS 365 FOR OPERATIONS
MODULE 1: CONFIGURING THE ACCOUNTS RECEIVABLE CONTROLS

Configuring Check Payment Methods

How to do it...

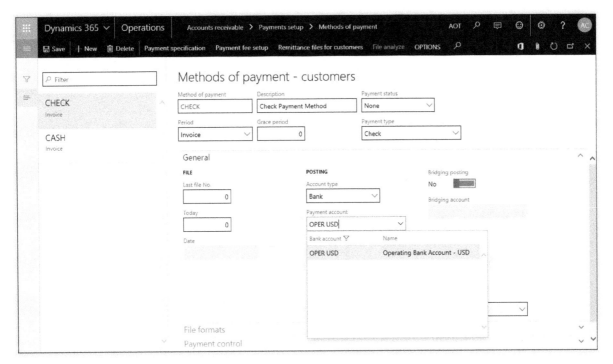

Since we selected the **Bank** as our **Account type** we will now want to select the bank that we want to post the cash to from the **Payment Account** dropdown list.

In this example, we will select the *OPER USD* bank account for the **Payment Account.**

dync
www.dynamicscompanions.com
Dynamics Companions

- 209 -

www.blindsquirrelpublishing.com
© 2017 Blind Squirrel Publishing, LLC , All Rights Reserved

BLIND SQUIRREL
PUBLISHING

DYNAMICS COMPANIONS
BARE BONES CONFIGURATION GUIDES

CONFIGURING ACCOUNTS RECEIVABLE WITHIN DYNAMICS 365 FOR OPERATIONS
MODULE 1: CONFIGURING THE ACCOUNTS RECEIVABLE CONTROLS

Configuring Check Payment Methods

How to do it...

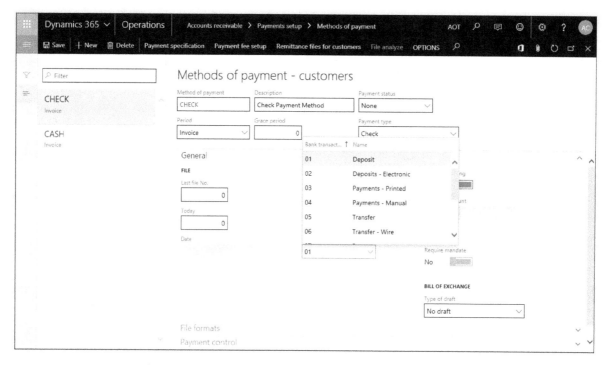

And then set the **Account Type** to be **Bank**, select the bank that you want to deposit the checks into from the **Payment Account** dropdown list and then set the **Bank Transaction Type** to **01.**

www.dynamicscompanions.com
Dynamics Companions

- 210 -

www.blindsquirrelpublishing.com
© 2017 Blind Squirrel Publishing, LLC, All Rights Reserved

BLIND SQUIRREL
PUBLISHING

DYNAMICS COMPANIONS
BARE BONES CONFIGURATION GUIDES

CONFIGURING ACCOUNTS RECEIVABLE WITHIN DYNAMICS 365 FOR OPERATIONS
MODULE 1: CONFIGURING THE ACCOUNTS RECEIVABLE CONTROLS

Configuring Check Payment Methods

How to do it...

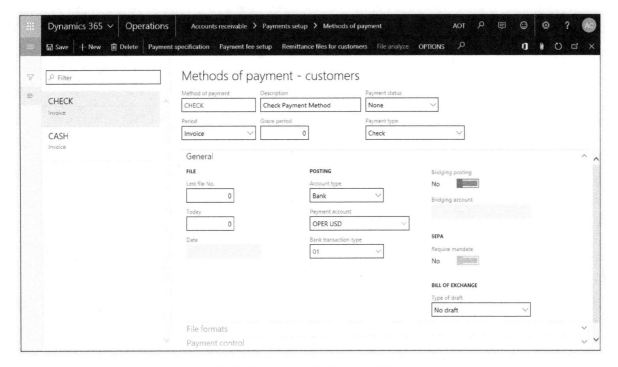

After we have done that our **Check Method of payments** has been configured.

dyn c
www.dynamicscompanions.com
Dynamics Companions

- 211 -

www.blindsquirrelpublishing.com
© 2017 Blind Squirrel Publishing, LLC, All Rights Reserved

BLIND SQUIRREL
PUBLISHING

DYNAMICS COMPANIONS
BARE BONES CONFIGURATION GUIDES

CONFIGURING ACCOUNTS RECEIVABLE WITHIN DYNAMICS 365 FOR OPERATIONS
MODULE 1: CONFIGURING THE ACCOUNTS RECEIVABLE CONTROLS

Configuring Check Payment Methods

Example Data

Field Name	Value
Method of Payment	CHECK
Description	Check Payment Method
Payment Type	Check
Account Type	Bank
Payment Account	OPER
Bank Transaction Code	01

Method of Payment: CHECK – Check Payment Method

dyn

www.dynamicscompanions.com
Dynamics Companions

- 212 -

www.blindsquirrelpublishing.com
© 2017 Blind Squirrel Publishing, LLC , All Rights Reserved

BLIND SQUIRREL
PUBLISHING

DYNAMICS COMPANIONS
BARE BONES CONFIGURATION GUIDES

CONFIGURING ACCOUNTS RECEIVABLE WITHIN DYNAMICS 365 FOR OPERATIONS
MODULE 1: CONFIGURING THE ACCOUNTS RECEIVABLE CONTROLS

Configuring Check Payment Methods

Summary

Congratulations, now you have a way to track when your customers pay you by check.

DYNAMICS COMPANIONS
BARE BONES CONFIGURATION GUIDES

CONFIGURING ACCOUNTS RECEIVABLE WITHIN DYNAMICS 365 FOR OPERATIONS
MODULE 1: CONFIGURING THE ACCOUNTS RECEIVABLE CONTROLS

Configuring Electronic Payment Methods

If you accept payments electronically then you will probably want to configure an Electronic Payment Method.

How to do it...

Return back to the **Methods of payment** maintenance form and click on the **+ New** button to create a new record.

Then set the **Method of payment** code.

For this example, we will set the **Method of payment** code to **ELECTRONIC**.

Then we will want to give our code a **Description**.

In this example we will set the **Description** to be **Direct Debit**.

From the **Payment Type** dropdown field, select the **Electronic Payment** option.

Now we will want to click on the **Account type** dropdown list and select the account type that will be used for this method of payment.

For this example, we will want to post the payment to a bank account, so we will set the **Account Type** to **Bank**.

Since we selected the **Bank** as our **Account type** we will now want to select the bank that we want to post the cash to from the **Payment Account** dropdown list.

In this example, we will select the *OPER USD* bank account for the **Payment Account**.

Then set the **Bank Transaction Type** to **02** for the electronic deposit transaction type.

After we have done that our **Electronic Method of payments** has been configured.

DYNAMICS COMPANIONS
BARE BONES CONFIGURATION GUIDES

CONFIGURING ACCOUNTS RECEIVABLE WITHIN DYNAMICS 365 FOR OPERATIONS
MODULE 1: CONFIGURING THE ACCOUNTS RECEIVABLE CONTROLS

Configuring Electronic Payment Methods

How to do it...

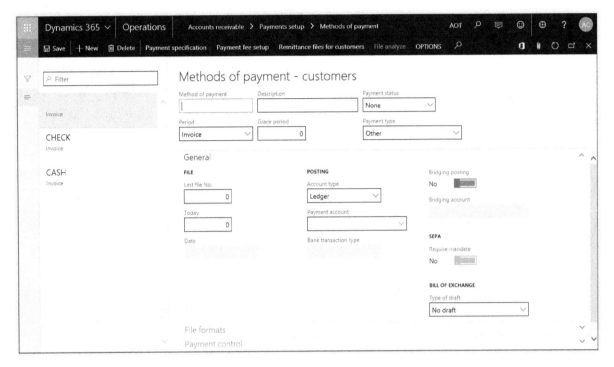

Return back to the **Methods of payment** maintenance form and click on the **+ New** button to create a new record.

dyn c
www.dynamicscompanions.com
Dynamics Companions

- 215 -

www.blindsquirrelpublishing.com
© 2017 Blind Squirrel Publishing, LLC, All Rights Reserved

BLIND SQUIRREL
PUBLISHING

DYNAMICS COMPANIONS
BARE BONES CONFIGURATION GUIDES

CONFIGURING ACCOUNTS RECEIVABLE WITHIN DYNAMICS 365 FOR OPERATIONS
MODULE 1: CONFIGURING THE ACCOUNTS RECEIVABLE CONTROLS

Configuring Electronic Payment Methods

How to do it...

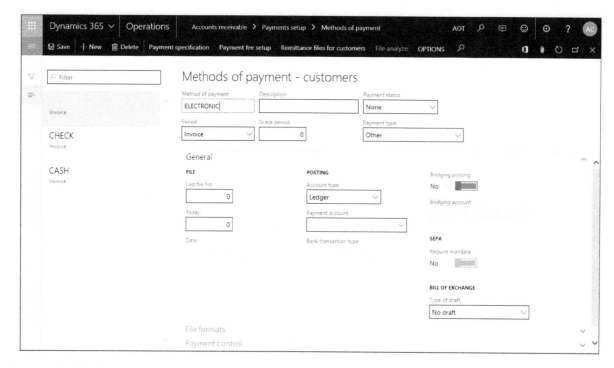

Then set the **Method of payment** code.

For this example, we will set the **Method of payment** code to **ELECTRONIC**.

dyn
www.dynamicscompanions.com
Dynamics Companions

- 216 -

www.blindsquirrelpublishing.com
© 2017 Blind Squirrel Publishing, LLC, All Rights Reserved

BLIND SQUIRREL
PUBLISHING

DYNAMICS COMPANIONS
BARE BONES CONFIGURATION GUIDES

CONFIGURING ACCOUNTS RECEIVABLE WITHIN DYNAMICS 365 FOR OPERATIONS
MODULE 1: CONFIGURING THE ACCOUNTS RECEIVABLE CONTROLS

Configuring Electronic Payment Methods

How to do it...

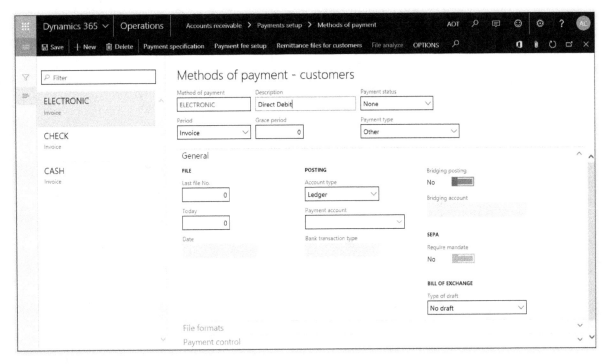

Then we will want to give our code a **Description.**

In this example we will set the **Description** to be **Direct Debit.**

dyn c

www.dynamicscompanions.com
Dynamics Companions

- 217 -

www.blindsquirrelpublishing.com
© 2017 Blind Squirrel Publishing, LLC , All Rights Reserved

BLIND SQUIRREL
PUBLISHING

DYNAMICS COMPANIONS
BARE BONES CONFIGURATION GUIDES

CONFIGURING ACCOUNTS RECEIVABLE WITHIN DYNAMICS 365 FOR OPERATIONS
MODULE 1: CONFIGURING THE ACCOUNTS RECEIVABLE CONTROLS

Configuring Electronic Payment Methods

How to do it...

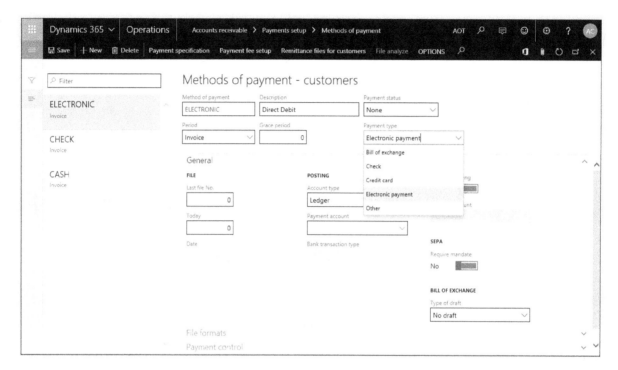

From the **Payment Type** dropdown field, select the **Electronic Payment** option.

dyn

www.dynamicscompanions.com
Dynamics Companions

- 218 -

www.blindsquirrelpublishing.com
© 2017 Blind Squirrel Publishing, LLC , All Rights Reserved

BLIND SQUIRREL
PUBLISHING

DYNAMICS COMPANIONS
BARE BONES CONFIGURATION GUIDES

CONFIGURING ACCOUNTS RECEIVABLE WITHIN DYNAMICS 365 FOR OPERATIONS
MODULE 1: CONFIGURING THE ACCOUNTS RECEIVABLE CONTROLS

Configuring Electronic Payment Methods

How to do it...

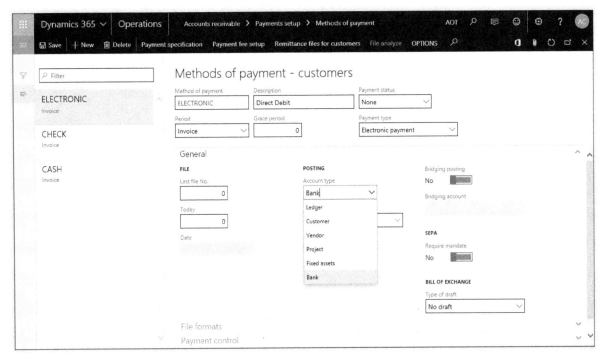

Now we will want to click on the **Account type** dropdown list and select the account type that will be used for this method of payment.

For this example, we will want to post the payment to a bank account, so we will set the **Account Type** to **Bank**.

dync
www.dynamicscompanions.com
Dynamics Companions

- 219 -

www.blindsquirrelpublishing.com
© 2017 Blind Squirrel Publishing, LLC, All Rights Reserved

BLIND SQUIRREL
PUBLISHING

DYNAMICS COMPANIONS
BARE BONES CONFIGURATION GUIDES

CONFIGURING ACCOUNTS RECEIVABLE WITHIN DYNAMICS 365 FOR OPERATIONS
MODULE 1: CONFIGURING THE ACCOUNTS RECEIVABLE CONTROLS

Configuring Electronic Payment Methods

How to do it...

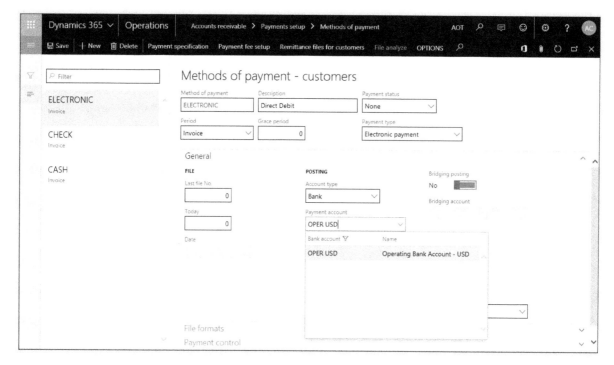

Since we selected the **Bank** as our **Account type** we will now want to select the bank that we want to post the cash to from the **Payment Account** dropdown list.

In this example, we will select the *OPER USD* bank account for the **Payment Account.**

www.dynamicscompanions.com
Dynamics Companions

- 220 -

www.blindsquirrelpublishing.com
© 2017 Blind Squirrel Publishing, LLC, All Rights Reserved

BLIND SQUIRREL
PUBLISHING

DYNAMICS COMPANIONS
BARE BONES CONFIGURATION GUIDES

CONFIGURING ACCOUNTS RECEIVABLE WITHIN DYNAMICS 365 FOR OPERATIONS
MODULE 1: CONFIGURING THE ACCOUNTS RECEIVABLE CONTROLS

Configuring Electronic Payment Methods

How to do it...

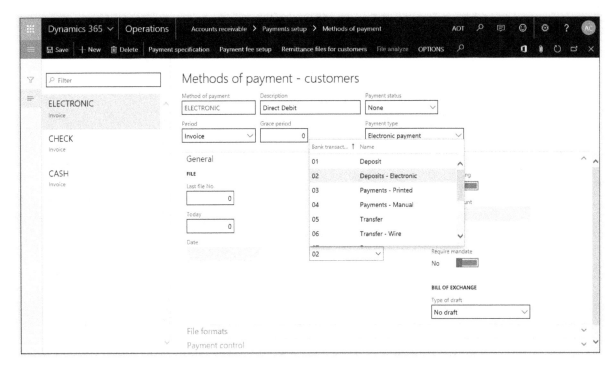

Then set the **Bank Transaction Type** to **02** for the electronic deposit transaction type.

dyn c
dynamics companions

www.dynamicscompanions.com
Dynamics Companions

- 221 -

www.blindsquirrelpublishing.com
© 2017 Blind Squirrel Publishing, LLC, All Rights Reserved

BLIND SQUIRREL
PUBLISHING

DYNAMICS COMPANIONS
BARE BONES CONFIGURATION GUIDES

CONFIGURING ACCOUNTS RECEIVABLE WITHIN DYNAMICS 365 FOR OPERATIONS
MODULE 1: CONFIGURING THE ACCOUNTS RECEIVABLE CONTROLS

Configuring Electronic Payment Methods

How to do it...

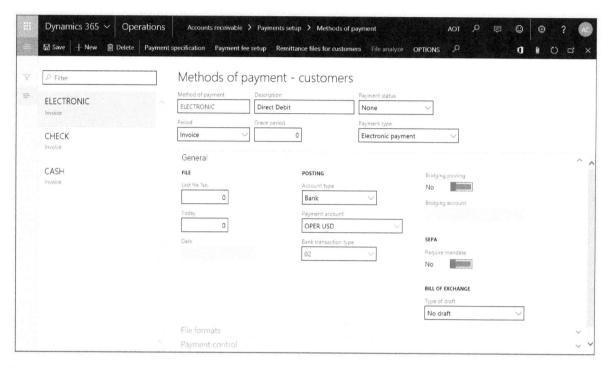

After we have done that our **Electronic Method of payments** has been configured.

dyn
www.dynamicscompanions.com
Dynamics Companions

- 222 -

www.blindsquirrelpublishing.com
© 2017 Blind Squirrel Publishing, LLC, All Rights Reserved

BLIND SQUIRREL
PUBLISHING

DYNAMICS COMPANIONS
BARE BONES CONFIGURATION GUIDES

CONFIGURING ACCOUNTS RECEIVABLE WITHIN DYNAMICS 365 FOR OPERATIONS
MODULE 1: CONFIGURING THE ACCOUNTS RECEIVABLE CONTROLS

Configuring Electronic Payment Methods

Example Data

Field Name	Value
Method of Payment	ELECTRONIC
Description	Direct Debit
Payment Type	Electronic Payment
Account Type	Bank
Payment Account	OPER
Bank Transaction Code	02

Method of Payment: ELECTRONIC – Direct Debit

www.dynamicscompanions.com
Dynamics Companions

- 223 -

www.blindsquirreipublishing.com
© 2017 Blind Squirrel Publishing, LLC, All Rights Reserved

BLIND SQUIRREL
PUBLISHING

DYNAMICS COMPANIONS
BARE BONES CONFIGURATION GUIDES

CONFIGURING ACCOUNTS RECEIVABLE WITHIN DYNAMICS 365 FOR OPERATIONS
MODULE 1: CONFIGURING THE ACCOUNTS RECEIVABLE CONTROLS

Configuring Electronic Payment Methods

Summary

Now we have got another way to receive in our payments, and that's electronically.

DYNAMICS COMPANIONS
BARE BONES CONFIGURATION GUIDES

CONFIGURING ACCOUNTS RECEIVABLE WITHIN DYNAMICS 365 FOR OPERATIONS
MODULE 1: CONFIGURING THE ACCOUNTS RECEIVABLE CONTROLS

Configuring Postdated Check Payment Methods

If you accept postdated checks then there is a slightly different configuration that you want to use, rather than the standard check Payment Method.

How to do it...

Return back to the **Methods of payment** maintenance form and click on the **+ New** button to create a new record.

Then set the **Method of payment** code.

For this example, we will set the **Method of payment** code to **PDC**.

Then we will want to give our code a **Description**.

In this example we will set the **Description** to be **Postdated check**.

And then click on the **Payment Type** dropdown field and select the **Check** option.

Now we will want to click on the **Account type** dropdown list and select the account type that will be used for this method of payment.

For this example, we will want to post the payment to a bank account, so we will set the **Account Type** to **Bank**.

Since we selected the **Bank** as our **Account type** we will now want to select the bank that we want to

post the cash to from the **Payment Account** dropdown list.

In this example, we will select the *OPER USD* bank account for the **Payment Account.**

Then set the **Bank Transaction Type** to **02** for the electronic deposit transaction type**.**

Since this is a Postdated check we will want to check the **Bridging Posting** flag.

This will allow you to select a main account from the **Bridging Account** dropdown to post the postdated check amounts to.

In this example, we set the **Bridging Account** to *130700* to point to the *Other Receivables* account.

And then open the **Payment Control** tab group and check the **Check Number Is Mandatory** option to ensure that the check number is tracked within the system.

After we have done that our **Postdated Check Method of payment** has been configured.

dynᴄ
www.dynamicscompanions.com
Dynamics Companions

- 225 -

www.blindsquirrelpublishing.com
© 2017 Blind Squirrel Publishing, LLC , All Rights Reserved

BLIND SQUIRREL
PUBLISHING

DYNAMICS COMPANIONS
BARE BONES CONFIGURATION GUIDES

CONFIGURING ACCOUNTS RECEIVABLE WITHIN DYNAMICS 365 FOR OPERATIONS
MODULE 1: CONFIGURING THE ACCOUNTS RECEIVABLE CONTROLS

Configuring Postdated Check Payment Methods

How to do it...

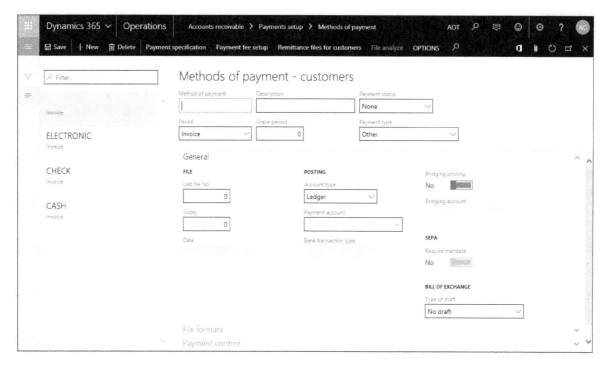

Return back to the **Methods of payment** maintenance form and click on the **+ New** button to create a new record.

www.dynamicscompanions.com
Dynamics Companions

- 226 -

www.blindsquirrelpublishing.com
© 2017 Blind Squirrel Publishing, LLC , All Rights Reserved

BLIND SQUIRREL
PUBLISHING

DYNAMICS COMPANIONS
BARE BONES CONFIGURATION GUIDES

CONFIGURING ACCOUNTS RECEIVABLE WITHIN DYNAMICS 365 FOR OPERATIONS
MODULE 1: CONFIGURING THE ACCOUNTS RECEIVABLE CONTROLS

Configuring Postdated Check Payment Methods

How to do it...

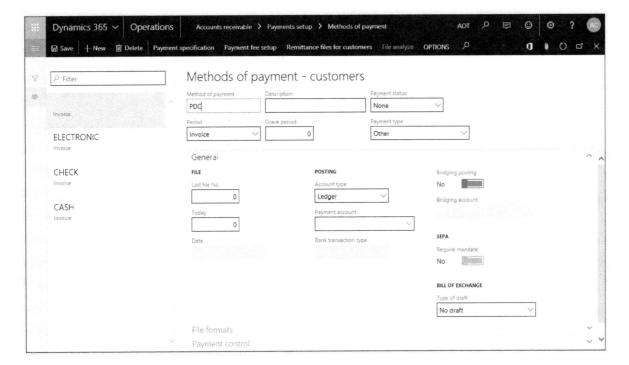

Then set the **Method of payment** code.

For this example, we will set the **Method of payment** code to **PDC**.

dyn c
www.dynamicscompanions.com
Dynamics Companions

- 227 -

www.blindsquirrelpublishing.com
© 2017 Blind Squirrel Publishing, LLC, All Rights Reserved

BLIND SQUIRREL
PUBLISHING

DYNAMICS COMPANIONS
BARE BONES CONFIGURATION GUIDES

CONFIGURING ACCOUNTS RECEIVABLE WITHIN DYNAMICS 365 FOR OPERATIONS
MODULE 1: CONFIGURING THE ACCOUNTS RECEIVABLE CONTROLS

Configuring Postdated Check Payment Methods

How to do it...

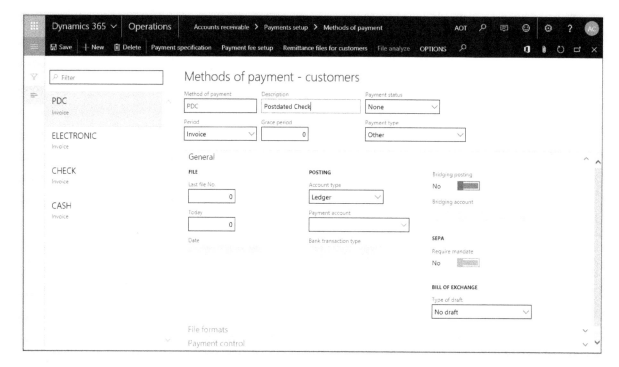

Then we will want to give our code a **Description.**

In this example we will set the **Description** to be **Postdated check**.

dyn☐

www.dynamicscompanions.com
Dynamics Companions

- 228 -

www.blindsquirrelpublishing.com
© 2017 Blind Squirrel Publishing, LLC, All Rights Reserved

BLIND SQUIRREL
PUBLISHING

DYNAMICS COMPANIONS
BARE BONES CONFIGURATION GUIDES

CONFIGURING ACCOUNTS RECEIVABLE WITHIN DYNAMICS 365 FOR OPERATIONS
MODULE 1: CONFIGURING THE ACCOUNTS RECEIVABLE CONTROLS

Configuring Postdated Check Payment Methods

How to do it...

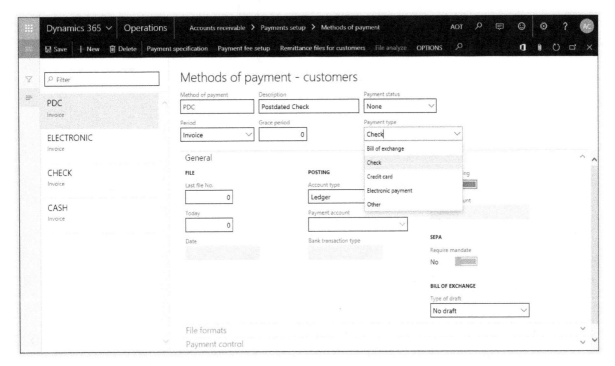

And then click on the **Payment Type** dropdown field and select the **Check** option.

www.dynamicscompanions.com
Dynamics Companions

- 229 -

www.blindsquirrelpublishing.com
© 2017 Blind Squirrel Publishing, LLC , All Rights Reserved

BLIND SQUIRREL
PUBLISHING

DYNAMICS COMPANIONS
BARE BONES CONFIGURATION GUIDES

CONFIGURING ACCOUNTS RECEIVABLE WITHIN DYNAMICS 365 FOR OPERATIONS
MODULE 1: CONFIGURING THE ACCOUNTS RECEIVABLE CONTROLS

Configuring Postdated Check Payment Methods

How to do it...

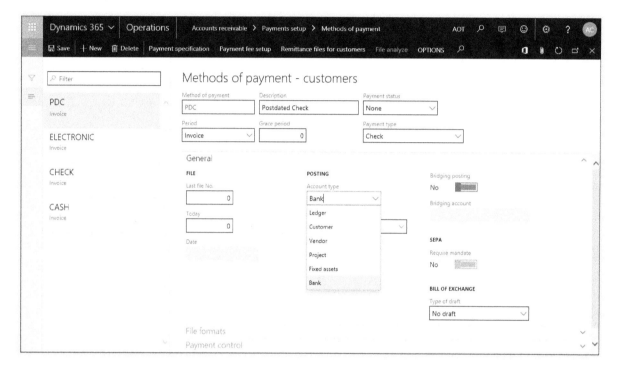

Now we will want to click on the **Account type** dropdown list and select the account type that will be used for this method of payment.

For this example, we will want to post the payment to a bank account, so we will set the **Account Type** to **Bank**.

dyn
www.dynamicscompanions.com
Dynamics Companions

- 230 -

www.blindsquirrelpublishing.com
© 2017 Blind Squirrel Publishing, LLC , All Rights Reserved

BLIND SQUIRREL
PUBLISHING

DYNAMICS COMPANIONS
BARE BONES CONFIGURATION GUIDES

CONFIGURING ACCOUNTS RECEIVABLE WITHIN DYNAMICS 365 FOR OPERATIONS
MODULE 1: CONFIGURING THE ACCOUNTS RECEIVABLE CONTROLS

Configuring Postdated Check Payment Methods

How to do it...

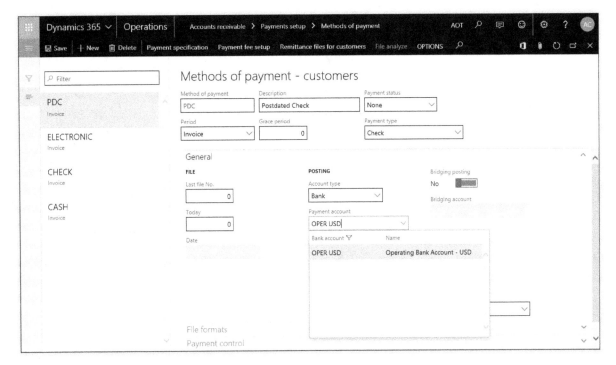

Since we selected the **Bank** as our **Account type** we will now want to select the bank that we want to post the cash to from the **Payment Account** dropdown list.

In this example, we will select the *OPER USD* bank account for the **Payment Account.**

dync
www.dynamicscompanions.com
Dynamics Companions

- 231 -

www.blindsquirrelpublishing.com
© 2017 Blind Squirrel Publishing, LLC, All Rights Reserved

BLIND SQUIRREL
PUBLISHING

DYNAMICS COMPANIONS
BARE BONES CONFIGURATION GUIDES

CONFIGURING ACCOUNTS RECEIVABLE WITHIN DYNAMICS 365 FOR OPERATIONS
MODULE 1: CONFIGURING THE ACCOUNTS RECEIVABLE CONTROLS

Configuring Postdated Check Payment Methods

How to do it...

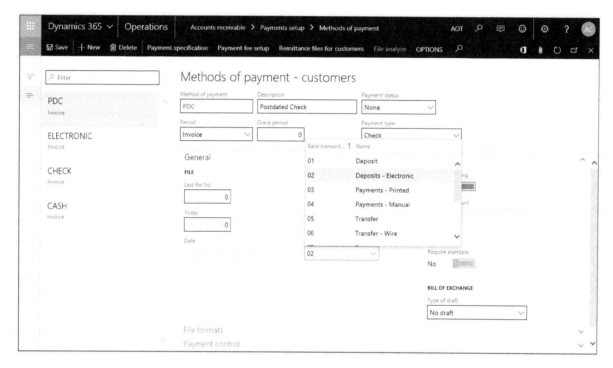

Then set the **Bank Transaction Type** to **02** for the electronic deposit transaction type.

www.dynamicscompanions.com
Dynamics Companions

- 232 -

www.blindsquirrelpublishing.com
© 2017 Blind Squirrel Publishing, LLC , All Rights Reserved

BLIND SQUIRREL
PUBLISHING

DYNAMICS COMPANIONS
BARE BONES CONFIGURATION GUIDES

CONFIGURING ACCOUNTS RECEIVABLE WITHIN DYNAMICS 365 FOR OPERATIONS
MODULE 1: CONFIGURING THE ACCOUNTS RECEIVABLE CONTROLS

Configuring Postdated Check Payment Methods

How to do it...

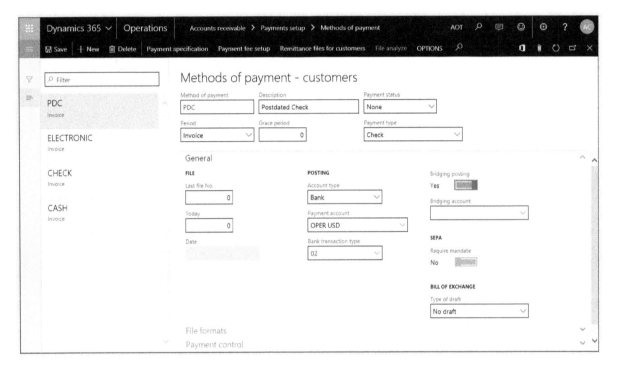

Since this is a Postdated check we will want to check the **Bridging Posting** flag.

dync
www.dynamicscompanions.com
Dynamics Companions

- 233 -

www.blindsquirrelpublishing.com
© 2017 Blind Squirrel Publishing, LLC , All Rights Reserved

BLIND SQUIRREL
PUBLISHING

DYNAMICS COMPANIONS
BARE BONES CONFIGURATION GUIDES

CONFIGURING ACCOUNTS RECEIVABLE WITHIN DYNAMICS 365 FOR OPERATIONS
MODULE 1: CONFIGURING THE ACCOUNTS RECEIVABLE CONTROLS

Configuring Postdated Check Payment Methods

How to do it...

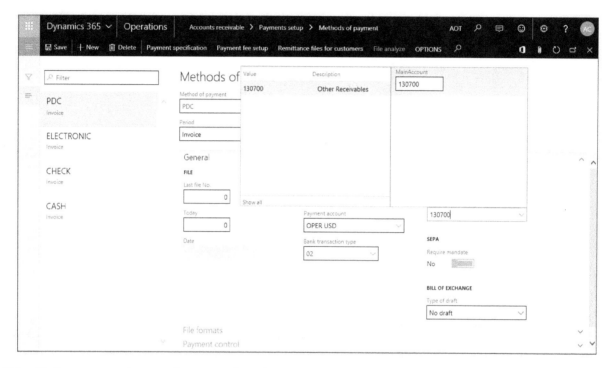

This will allow you to select a main account from the **Bridging Account** dropdown to post the postdated check amounts to.

In this example, we set the **Bridging Account** to *130700* to point to the *Other Receivables* account.

dyn c

www.dynamicscompanions.com
Dynamics Companions

- 234 -

www.blindsquirrelpublishing.com
© 2017 Blind Squirrel Publishing, LLC, All Rights Reserved

BLIND SQUIRREL
PUBLISHING

DYNAMICS COMPANIONS
BARE BONES CONFIGURATION GUIDES

CONFIGURING ACCOUNTS RECEIVABLE WITHIN DYNAMICS 365 FOR OPERATIONS
MODULE 1: CONFIGURING THE ACCOUNTS RECEIVABLE CONTROLS

Configuring Postdated Check Payment Methods

How to do it...

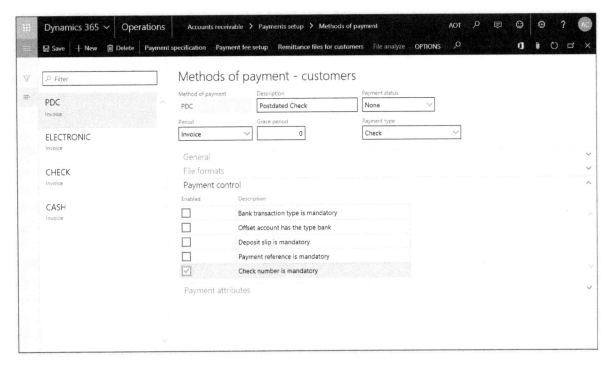

And then open the **Payment Control** tab group and check the **Check Number Is Mandatory** option to ensure that the check number is tracked within the system.

After we have done that our **Postdated Check Method of payment** has been configured.

dyn

www.dynamicscompanions.com
Dynamics Companions

- 235 -

www.blindsquirrelpublishing.com
© 2017 Blind Squirrel Publishing, LLC, All Rights Reserved

BLIND SQUIRREL
PUBLISHING

DYNAMICS COMPANIONS
BARE BONES CONFIGURATION GUIDES

CONFIGURING ACCOUNTS RECEIVABLE WITHIN DYNAMICS 365 FOR OPERATIONS
MODULE 1: CONFIGURING THE ACCOUNTS RECEIVABLE CONTROLS

Configuring Postdated Check Payment Methods

Example Data

Field Name	Value
Method of Payment	PDC
Description	Postdated Check
Payment Type	Check
Account Type	Bank
Payment Account	OPER
Bank Transaction Code	02
Bridging posting	True
Bridging Account	130700
Payment Method.Check Number is Mandatory	True

Method of Payment: PDC – Postdated Check

dyn
www.dynamicscompanions.com
Dynamics Companions

- 236 -

www.blindsquirrelpublishing.com
© 2017 Blind Squirrel Publishing, LLC, All Rights Reserved

BLIND SQUIRREL
PUBLISHING

DYNAMICS COMPANIONS
BARE BONES CONFIGURATION GUIDES

CONFIGURING ACCOUNTS RECEIVABLE WITHIN DYNAMICS 365 FOR OPERATIONS
MODULE 1: CONFIGURING THE ACCOUNTS RECEIVABLE CONTROLS

Configuring Postdated Check Payment Methods

Summary

The Postdated Checks Method of Payment is interesting because it uses the Bridging Account information to track the accrual of the payment until it is really paid within the system. With this configuration though you can make sure that you are accounting for this when a customer wants to pay this way.

DYNAMICS COMPANIONS
BARE BONES CONFIGURATION GUIDES

CONFIGURING ACCOUNTS RECEIVABLE WITHIN DYNAMICS 365 FOR OPERATIONS
MODULE 1: CONFIGURING THE ACCOUNTS RECEIVABLE CONTROLS

Configuring Refund Payment Methods

Although you probably don't want to give refunds, there may be a need for them within the system, so we need to configure one last Payment Method to manage this.

How to do it...

Return back to the **Methods of payment** maintenance form and click on the **+ New** button to create a new record.

Then set the **Method of payment** code.

For this example, we will set the **Method of payment** code to **REFUND**.

Then we will want to give our code a **Description**.

In this example we will set the **Description** to be **Refund**.

And then click on the **Payment Type** dropdown field and select the **Other** option.

Now we will want to click on the **Account type** dropdown list and select the account type that will be used for this method of payment.

For this example, we will want to post the payment to a bank account, so we will set the **Account Type** to **Bank**.

Since we selected the **Bank** as our **Account type** we will now want to select the bank that we want to post the cash to from the **Payment Account** dropdown list.

In this example, we will select the *OPER USD* bank account for the **Payment Account**.

And then set the **Bank Transaction Type** to **04** for the manual payment transaction type**.**

After we have done that our **Refund Method of payment** has been configured.

www.dynamicscompanions.com
Dynamics Companions

- 238 -

www.blindsquirrelpublishing.com
© 2017 Blind Squirrel Publishing, LLC, All Rights Reserved

BLIND SQUIRREL
PUBLISHING

DYNAMICS COMPANIONS
BARE BONES CONFIGURATION GUIDES

CONFIGURING ACCOUNTS RECEIVABLE WITHIN DYNAMICS 365 FOR OPERATIONS
MODULE 1: CONFIGURING THE ACCOUNTS RECEIVABLE CONTROLS

Configuring Refund Payment Methods

How to do it...

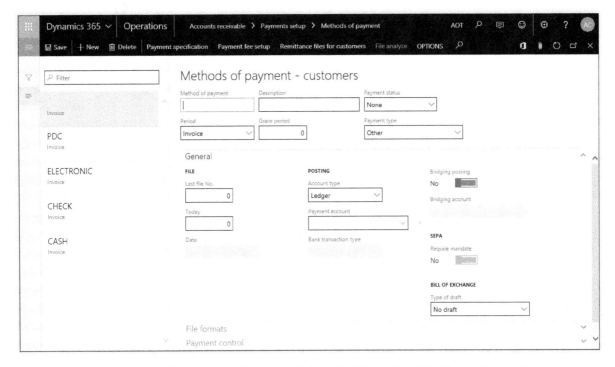

Return back to the **Methods of payment** maintenance form and click on the **+ New** button to create a new record.

www.dynamicscompanions.com
Dynamics Companions

- 239 -

www.blindsquirrelpublishing.com
© 2017 Blind Squirrel Publishing, LLC, All Rights Reserved

BLIND SQUIRREL
PUBLISHING

DYNAMICS COMPANIONS
BARE BONES CONFIGURATION GUIDES

CONFIGURING ACCOUNTS RECEIVABLE WITHIN DYNAMICS 365 FOR OPERATIONS
MODULE 1: CONFIGURING THE ACCOUNTS RECEIVABLE CONTROLS

Configuring Refund Payment Methods

How to do it...

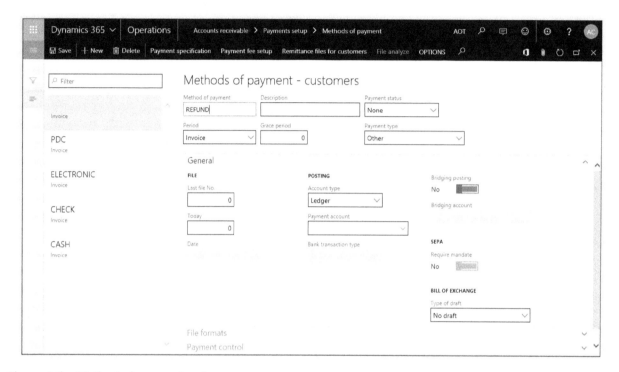

Then set the **Method of payment** code.

For this example, we will set the **Method of payment** code to **REFUND**.

www.dynamicscompanions.com
Dynamics Companions

- 240 -

www.blindsquirrelpublishing.com
© 2017 Blind Squirrel Publishing, LLC, All Rights Reserved

BLIND SQUIRREL
PUBLISHING

DYNAMICS COMPANIONS
BARE BONES CONFIGURATION GUIDES

CONFIGURING ACCOUNTS RECEIVABLE WITHIN DYNAMICS 365 FOR OPERATIONS
MODULE 1: CONFIGURING THE ACCOUNTS RECEIVABLE CONTROLS

Configuring Refund Payment Methods

How to do it...

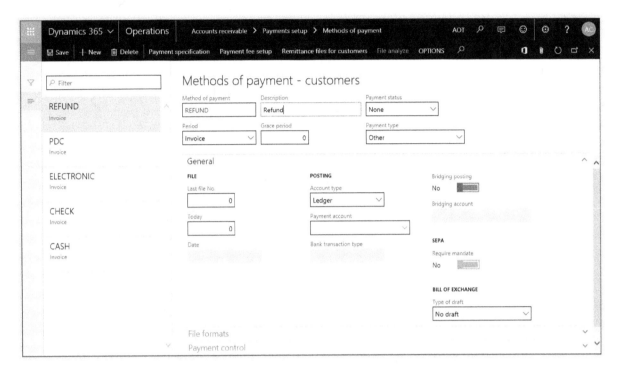

Then we will want to give our code a **Description.**

In this example we will set the **Description** to be **Refund**.

dyn c
dynamics companions

www.dynamicscompanions.com
Dynamics Companions

- 241 -

www.blindsquirrelpublishing.com
© 2017 Blind Squirrel Publishing, LLC , All Rights Reserved

BLIND SQUIRREL
PUBLISHING

DYNAMICS COMPANIONS
BARE BONES CONFIGURATION GUIDES

CONFIGURING ACCOUNTS RECEIVABLE WITHIN DYNAMICS 365 FOR OPERATIONS
MODULE 1: CONFIGURING THE ACCOUNTS RECEIVABLE CONTROLS

Configuring Refund Payment Methods

How to do it...

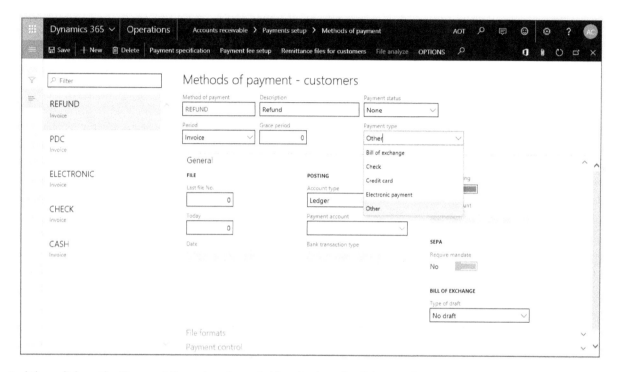

And then click on the **Payment Type** dropdown field and select the **Other** option.

www.dynamicscompanions.com
Dynamics Companions

- 242 -

www.blindsquirrelpublishing.com
© 2017 Blind Squirrel Publishing, LLC, All Rights Reserved

BLIND SQUIRREL
PUBLISHING

DYNAMICS COMPANIONS
BARE BONES CONFIGURATION GUIDES

CONFIGURING ACCOUNTS RECEIVABLE WITHIN DYNAMICS 365 FOR OPERATIONS
MODULE 1: CONFIGURING THE ACCOUNTS RECEIVABLE CONTROLS

Configuring Refund Payment Methods

How to do it...

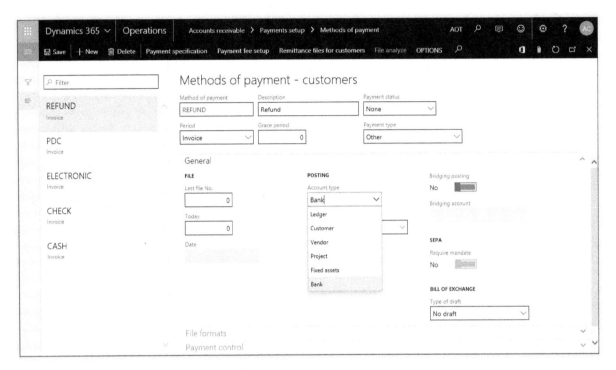

Now we will want to click on the **Account type** dropdown list and select the account type that will be used for this method of payment.

For this example, we will want to post the payment to a bank account, so we will set the **Account Type** to **Bank**.

www.dynamicscompanions.com
Dynamics Companions

- 243 -

www.blindsquirrelpublishing.com
© 2017 Blind Squirrel Publishing, LLC, All Rights Reserved

BLIND SQUIRREL
PUBLISHING

DYNAMICS COMPANIONS
BARE BONES CONFIGURATION GUIDES

CONFIGURING ACCOUNTS RECEIVABLE WITHIN DYNAMICS 365 FOR OPERATIONS
MODULE 1: CONFIGURING THE ACCOUNTS RECEIVABLE CONTROLS

Configuring Refund Payment Methods

How to do it...

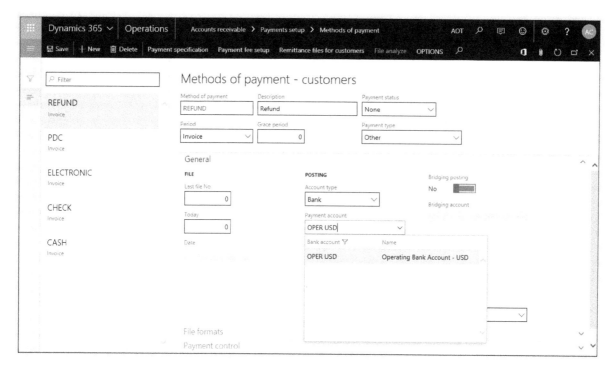

Since we selected the **Bank** as our **Account type** we will now want to select the bank that we want to post the cash to from the **Payment Account** dropdown list.

In this example, we will select the *OPER USD* bank account for the **Payment Account.**

dyn
www.dynamicscompanions.com
Dynamics Companions

- 244 -

www.blindsquirrelpublishing.com
© 2017 Blind Squirrel Publishing, LLC, All Rights Reserved

BLIND SQUIRREL
PUBLISHING

DYNAMICS COMPANIONS
BARE BONES CONFIGURATION GUIDES

CONFIGURING ACCOUNTS RECEIVABLE WITHIN DYNAMICS 365 FOR OPERATIONS
MODULE 1: CONFIGURING THE ACCOUNTS RECEIVABLE CONTROLS

Configuring Refund Payment Methods

How to do it...

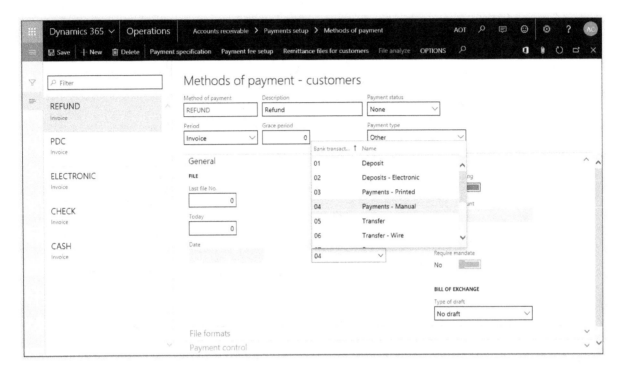

And then set the **Bank Transaction Type** to **04** for the manual payment transaction type.

dyn c
Dynamics Companions

www.dynamicscompanions.com
Dynamics Companions

- 245 -

www.blindsquirrelpublishing.com
© 2017 Blind Squirrel Publishing, LLC , All Rights Reserved

BLIND SQUIRREL
PUBLISHING

DYNAMICS COMPANIONS
BARE BONES CONFIGURATION GUIDES

CONFIGURING ACCOUNTS RECEIVABLE WITHIN DYNAMICS 365 FOR OPERATIONS
MODULE 1: CONFIGURING THE ACCOUNTS RECEIVABLE CONTROLS

Configuring Refund Payment Methods

How to do it...

After we have done that our **Refund Method of payment** has been configured.

dyn

www.dynamicscompanions.com
Dynamics Companions

- 246 -

www.blindsquirrelpublishing.com
© 2017 Blind Squirrel Publishing, LLC, All Rights Reserved

BLIND SQUIRREL
PUBLISHING

DYNAMICS COMPANIONS
BARE BONES CONFIGURATION GUIDES

CONFIGURING ACCOUNTS RECEIVABLE WITHIN DYNAMICS 365 FOR OPERATIONS
MODULE 1: CONFIGURING THE ACCOUNTS RECEIVABLE CONTROLS

Configuring Refund Payment Methods

Example Data

Field Name	Value
Method of Payment	REFUND
Description	Refund
Payment Type	Other
Account Type	Bank
Payment Account	OPER
Bank Transaction Code	04

Method of Payment: REFUND – Refund

www.dynamicscompanions.com
Dynamics Companions

- 247 -

www.blindsquirrelpublishing.com
© 2017 Blind Squirrel Publishing, LLC, All Rights Reserved

BLIND SQUIRREL
PUBLISHING

DYNAMICS COMPANIONS
BARE BONES CONFIGURATION GUIDES

CONFIGURING ACCOUNTS RECEIVABLE WITHIN DYNAMICS 365 FOR OPERATIONS
MODULE 1: CONFIGURING THE ACCOUNTS RECEIVABLE CONTROLS

Configuring Refund Payment Methods

Summary

Now you have a way to track the refund payments within the system.

DYNAMICS COMPANIONS
BARE BONES CONFIGURATION GUIDES

CONFIGURING ACCOUNTS RECEIVABLE WITHIN DYNAMICS 365 FOR OPERATIONS
MODULE 1: CONFIGURING THE ACCOUNTS RECEIVABLE CONTROLS

Configuring the Accounts Receivable Parameters

Now that we have all the main codes and controls configured for the Accounts Receivable area within Dynamics 365, we will tie up the last loose ends by tweaking a couple of the options within the **Accounts Receivable Parameters.**

How to do it...

To do this, open up the navigation panel, expand out the **Modules** group, and click on **Accounts receivable** module to see all of the menu items that are available. Then click on the **Accounts receivable parameters** menu item within the **Setup** menu group.

Alternatively, you can search for the **Accounts receivable parameters** form by clicking on the search icon in the header of the form (or press **ALT+G**) and then type in **accounts re** into the search box. Then you will be able to select the **Accounts receivable parameters** maintenance form from the dropdown list.

This will open up the Accounts receivable parameters form.

Click on the General group on the left had side to view the General parameters.

Then expand out the **Sales order defaults** fast tab. Here we will see a number of defaults related to the Sales order creation.

The first thing that we will do is change the **Default Order Type** from **Journal** to **Sales Order** so that we will be able to ship our orders after entering them.

Next, expand out the **Sales setup** fast tab. These settings control how the sales orders look and are managed within the system.

To make things look nice we will make a small tweak to the "Order Hold" sales order status so that orders that are on hold will show up in a different color.

To do this, click on the color chooser for the "**Order Hold" sales order status** field. When the color chooser is displayed, you can select a less depressing color that will be used to highlight that orders are on hold. Black is too dreary.

After you have done that your general configuration is done.

Next, switch to the **Ledger and sales tax** options page.

From within the **General** tab group, click on the **Posting Profile** dropdown and select the **GEN** posting profile that you set up earlier.

Then expand out the **Payment** fast tab group.

Now select the **PRE** posting profile that you configured earlier from the dropdown list for the **Posting profile with prepayment journal voucher** field.

Now switch to the **Settlement** options page.

Here we will want to check the **Automatic Settlement** flag.

And then set the **Maximum Penny Difference** that we want to accept.

www.dynamicscompanions.com
Dynamics Companions

- 249 -

www.blindsquirrelpublishing.com
© 2017 Blind Squirrel Publishing, LLC , All Rights Reserved

BLIND SQUIRREL
PUBLISHING

DYNAMICS COMPANIONS
BARE BONES CONFIGURATION GUIDES

CONFIGURING ACCOUNTS RECEIVABLE WITHIN DYNAMICS 365 FOR OPERATIONS
MODULE 1: CONFIGURING THE ACCOUNTS RECEIVABLE CONTROLS

Here we set the **Maximum Penny Difference** to **$0.05**.

Then set the Maximum overpayment and underpayment tolerances.

Here we set the Maximum overpayment and underpayment to $0.05 because we will accept 5 cents either way, although you could be stricter or a little more flexible.

After we have done we are done with the configuration of the parameters and we can exit from the form.

DYNAMICS COMPANIONS
BARE BONES CONFIGURATION GUIDES

CONFIGURING ACCOUNTS RECEIVABLE WITHIN DYNAMICS 365 FOR OPERATIONS
MODULE 1: CONFIGURING THE ACCOUNTS RECEIVABLE CONTROLS

Configuring the Accounts Receivable Parameters

How to do it...

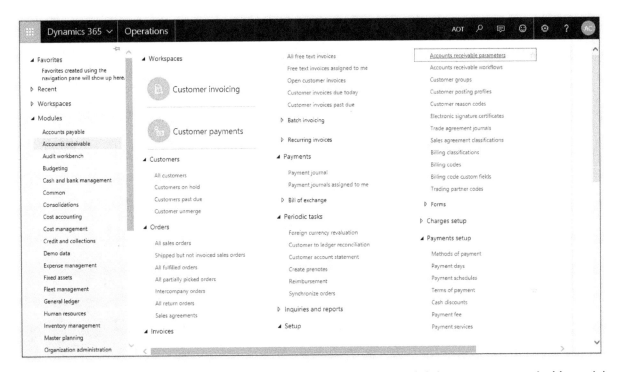

To do this, open up the navigation panel, expand out the **Modules** group, and click on **Accounts receivable** module to see all of the menu items that are available. Then click on the **Accounts receivable parameters** menu item within the **Setup** menu group.

www.dynamicscompanions.com
Dynamics Companions

- 251 -

www.blindsquirrelpublishing.com
© 2017 Blind Squirrel Publishing, LLC, All Rights Reserved

BLIND SQUIRREL
PUBLISHING

DYNAMICS COMPANIONS
BARE BONES CONFIGURATION GUIDES

CONFIGURING ACCOUNTS RECEIVABLE WITHIN DYNAMICS 365 FOR OPERATIONS
MODULE 1: CONFIGURING THE ACCOUNTS RECEIVABLE CONTROLS

Configuring the Accounts Receivable Parameters

How to do it...

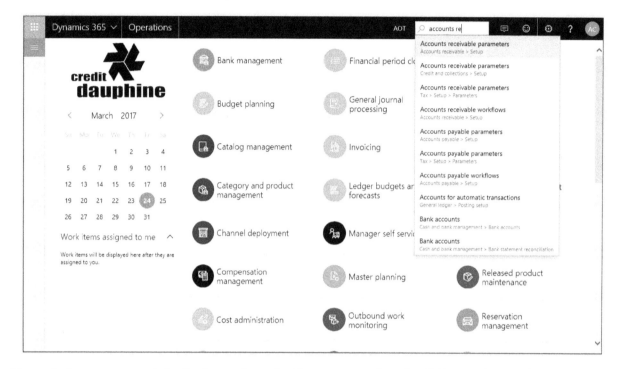

Alternatively, you can search for the **Accounts receivable parameters** form by clicking on the search icon in the header of the form (or press **ALT+G**) and then type in **accounts re** into the search box. Then you will be able to select the **Accounts receivable parameters** maintenance form from the dropdown list.

www.dynamicscompanions.com
Dynamics Companions

- 252 -

www.blindsquirrelpublishing.com
© 2017 Blind Squirrel Publishing, LLC, All Rights Reserved

BLIND SQUIRREL
PUBLISHING

DYNAMICS COMPANIONS
BARE BONES CONFIGURATION GUIDES

CONFIGURING ACCOUNTS RECEIVABLE WITHIN DYNAMICS 365 FOR OPERATIONS
MODULE 1: CONFIGURING THE ACCOUNTS RECEIVABLE CONTROLS

Configuring the Accounts Receivable Parameters

How to do it...

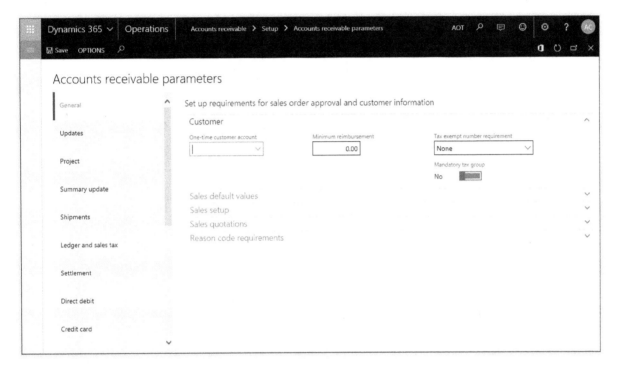

This will open up the Accounts receivable parameters form.

Click on the General group on the left had side to view the General parameters.

dync
www.dynamicscompanions.com
Dynamics Companions

- 253 -

www.blindsquirrelpublishing.com
© 2017 Blind Squirrel Publishing, LLC , All Rights Reserved

BLIND SQUIRREL
PUBLISHING

DYNAMICS COMPANIONS
BARE BONES CONFIGURATION GUIDES

CONFIGURING ACCOUNTS RECEIVABLE WITHIN DYNAMICS 365 FOR OPERATIONS
MODULE 1: CONFIGURING THE ACCOUNTS RECEIVABLE CONTROLS

Configuring the Accounts Receivable Parameters

How to do it...

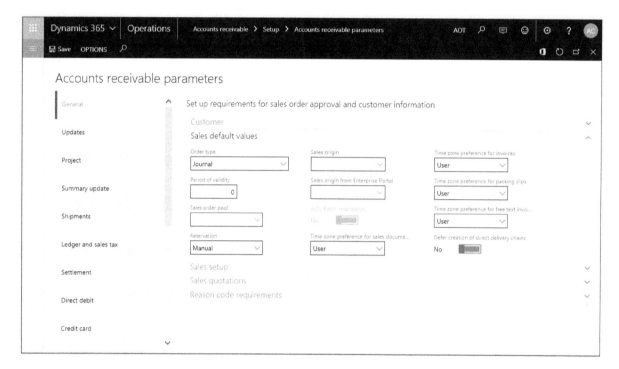

Then expand out the **Sales order defaults** fast tab. Here we will see a number of defaults related to the Sales order creation.

dyn
www.dynamicscompanions.com
Dynamics Companions

- 254 -

www.blindsquirrelpublishing.com
© 2017 Blind Squirrel Publishing, LLC , All Rights Reserved

BLIND SQUIRREL
PUBLISHING

DYNAMICS COMPANIONS
BARE BONES CONFIGURATION GUIDES

CONFIGURING ACCOUNTS RECEIVABLE WITHIN DYNAMICS 365 FOR OPERATIONS
MODULE 1: CONFIGURING THE ACCOUNTS RECEIVABLE CONTROLS

Configuring the Accounts Receivable Parameters

How to do it...

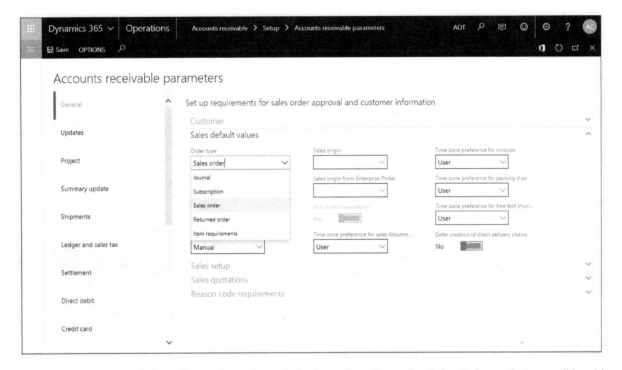

The first thing that we will do is change the **Default Order Type** from **Journal** to **Sales Order** so that we will be able to ship our orders after entering them.

www.dynamicscompanions.com
Dynamics Companions

- 255 -

www.blindsquirrelpublishing.com
© 2017 Blind Squirrel Publishing, LLC, All Rights Reserved

BLIND SQUIRREL
PUBLISHING

DYNAMICS COMPANIONS
BARE BONES CONFIGURATION GUIDES

CONFIGURING ACCOUNTS RECEIVABLE WITHIN DYNAMICS 365 FOR OPERATIONS
MODULE 1: CONFIGURING THE ACCOUNTS RECEIVABLE CONTROLS

Configuring the Accounts Receivable Parameters

How to do it...

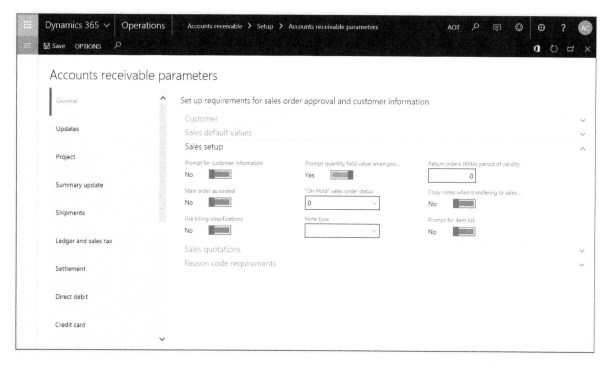

Next, expand out the **Sales setup** fast tab. These settings control how the sales orders look and are managed within the system.

www.dynamicscompanions.com
Dynamics Companions

- 256 -

www.blindsquirrelpublishing.com
© 2017 Blind Squirrel Publishing, LLC, All Rights Reserved

BLIND SQUIRREL
PUBLISHING

DYNAMICS COMPANIONS
BARE BONES CONFIGURATION GUIDES

CONFIGURING ACCOUNTS RECEIVABLE WITHIN DYNAMICS 365 FOR OPERATIONS
MODULE 1: CONFIGURING THE ACCOUNTS RECEIVABLE CONTROLS

Configuring the Accounts Receivable Parameters

How to do it...

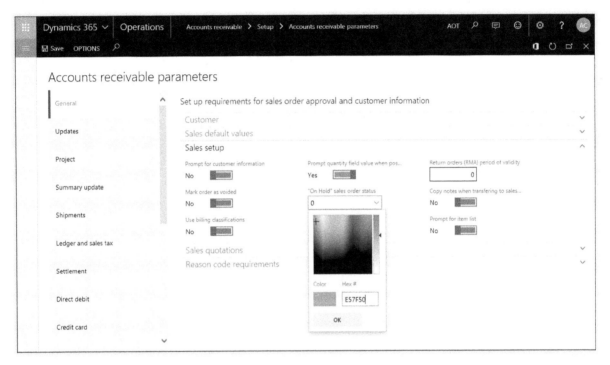

To make things look nice we will make a small tweak to the "**Order Hold" sales order status** so that orders that are on hold will show up in a different color.

To do this, click on the color chooser for the "**Order Hold" sales order status** field. When the color chooser is displayed, you can select a less depressing color that will be used to highlight that orders are on hold. Black is too dreary.

dyn c
dynamics companions

www.dynamicscompanions.com
Dynamics Companions

- 257 -

www.blindsquirrelpublishing.com
© 2017 Blind Squirrel Publishing, LLC , All Rights Reserved

BLIND SQUIRREL
PUBLISHING

DYNAMICS COMPANIONS
BARE BONES CONFIGURATION GUIDES

CONFIGURING ACCOUNTS RECEIVABLE WITHIN DYNAMICS 365 FOR OPERATIONS
MODULE 1: CONFIGURING THE ACCOUNTS RECEIVABLE CONTROLS

Configuring the Accounts Receivable Parameters

How to do it...

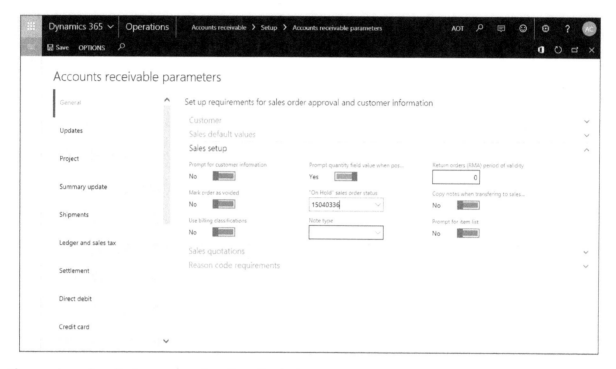

After you have done that your general configuration is done.

DYNAMICS COMPANIONS
BARE BONES CONFIGURATION GUIDES

CONFIGURING ACCOUNTS RECEIVABLE WITHIN DYNAMICS 365 FOR OPERATIONS
MODULE 1: CONFIGURING THE ACCOUNTS RECEIVABLE CONTROLS

Configuring the Accounts Receivable Parameters

How to do it...

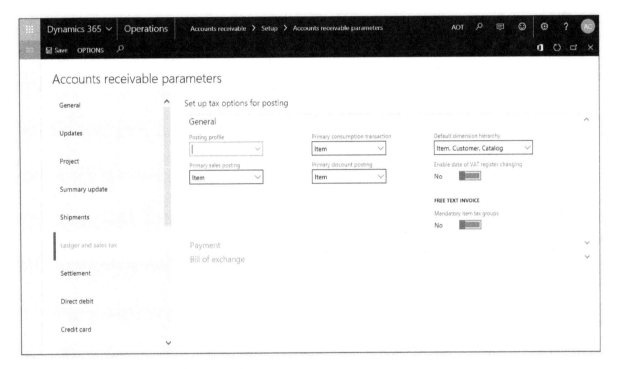

Next, switch to the **Ledger and sales tax** options page.

www.dynamicscompanions.com
Dynamics Companions

- 259 -

www.blindsquirrelpublishing.com
© 2017 Blind Squirrel Publishing, LLC, All Rights Reserved

BLIND SQUIRREL
PUBLISHING

DYNAMICS COMPANIONS
BARE BONES CONFIGURATION GUIDES

CONFIGURING ACCOUNTS RECEIVABLE WITHIN DYNAMICS 365 FOR OPERATIONS
MODULE 1: CONFIGURING THE ACCOUNTS RECEIVABLE CONTROLS

Configuring the Accounts Receivable Parameters

How to do it...

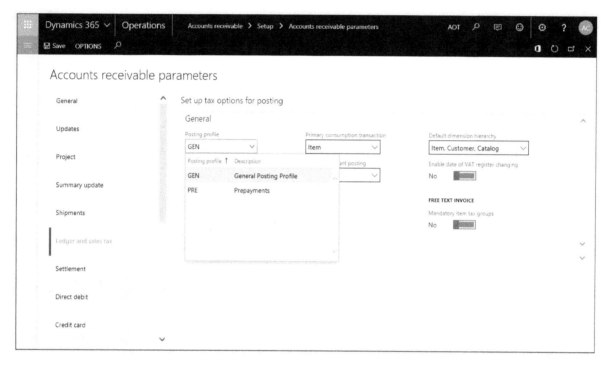

From within the **General** tab group, click on the **Posting Profile** dropdown and select the **GEN** posting profile that you set up earlier.

www.dynamicscompanions.com
Dynamics Companions

- 260 -

www.blindsquirrelpublishing.com
© 2017 Blind Squirrel Publishing, LLC , All Rights Reserved

BLIND SQUIRREL
PUBLISHING

DYNAMICS COMPANIONS
BARE BONES CONFIGURATION GUIDES

CONFIGURING ACCOUNTS RECEIVABLE WITHIN DYNAMICS 365 FOR OPERATIONS
MODULE 1: CONFIGURING THE ACCOUNTS RECEIVABLE CONTROLS

Configuring the Accounts Receivable Parameters

How to do it...

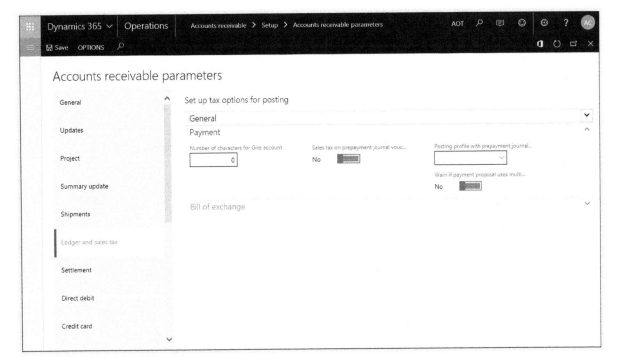

Then expand out the **Payment** fast tab group.

DYNAMICS COMPANIONS
BARE BONES CONFIGURATION GUIDES

CONFIGURING ACCOUNTS RECEIVABLE WITHIN DYNAMICS 365 FOR OPERATIONS
MODULE 1: CONFIGURING THE ACCOUNTS RECEIVABLE CONTROLS

Configuring the Accounts Receivable Parameters

How to do it...

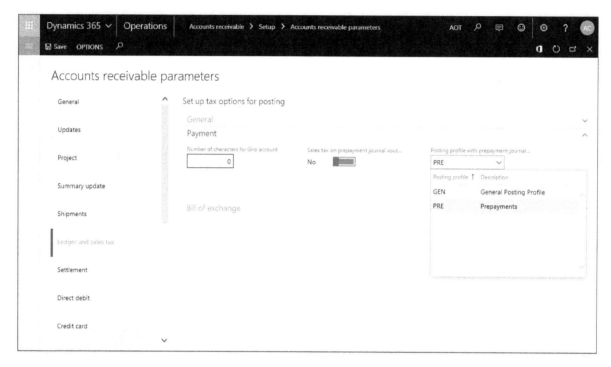

Now select the **PRE** posting profile that you configured earlier from the dropdown list for the **Posting profile with prepayment journal voucher** field.

dyn℮

www.dynamicscompanions.com
Dynamics Companions

- 262 -

www.blindsquirrelpublishing.com
© 2017 Blind Squirrel Publishing, LLC , All Rights Reserved

BLIND SQUIRREL
PUBLISHING

DYNAMICS COMPANIONS
BARE BONES CONFIGURATION GUIDES

CONFIGURING ACCOUNTS RECEIVABLE WITHIN DYNAMICS 365 FOR OPERATIONS
MODULE 1: CONFIGURING THE ACCOUNTS RECEIVABLE CONTROLS

Configuring the Accounts Receivable Parameters

How to do it...

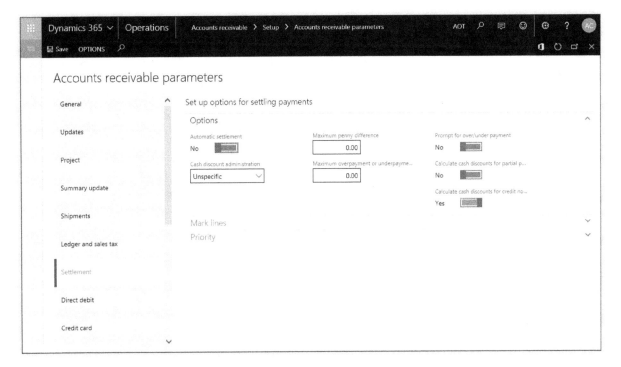

Now switch to the **Settlement** options page.

www.dynamicscompanions.com
Dynamics Companions

- 263 -

www.blindsquirrelpublishing.com
© 2017 Blind Squirrel Publishing, LLC, All Rights Reserved

BLIND SQUIRREL
PUBLISHING

DYNAMICS COMPANIONS
BARE BONES CONFIGURATION GUIDES

CONFIGURING ACCOUNTS RECEIVABLE WITHIN DYNAMICS 365 FOR OPERATIONS
MODULE 1: CONFIGURING THE ACCOUNTS RECEIVABLE CONTROLS

Configuring the Accounts Receivable Parameters

How to do it...

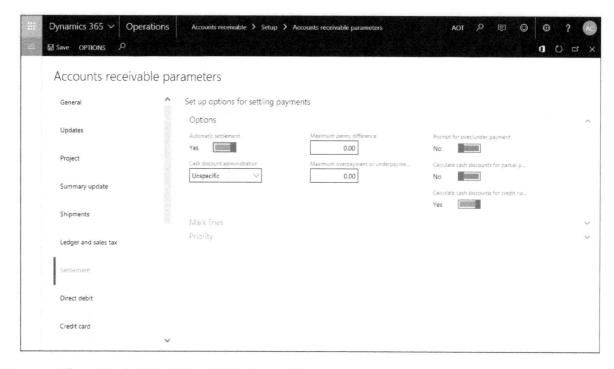

Here we will want to check the **Automatic Settlement** flag.

dyn

www.dynamicscompanions.com
Dynamics Companions

- 264 -

www.blindsquirrelpublishing.com
© 2017 Blind Squirrel Publishing, LLC, All Rights Reserved

BLIND SQUIRREL
PUBLISHING

DYNAMICS COMPANIONS
BARE BONES CONFIGURATION GUIDES

CONFIGURING ACCOUNTS RECEIVABLE WITHIN DYNAMICS 365 FOR OPERATIONS
MODULE 1: CONFIGURING THE ACCOUNTS RECEIVABLE CONTROLS

Configuring the Accounts Receivable Parameters

How to do it...

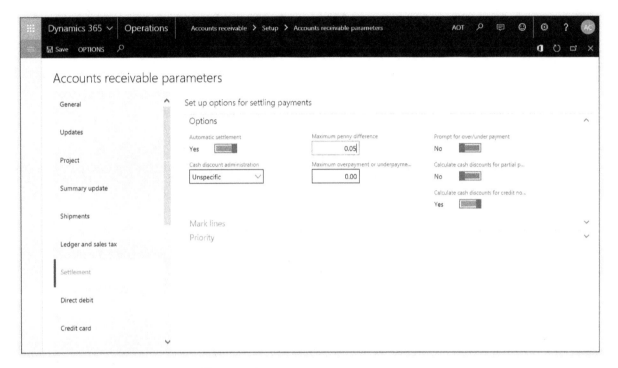

And then set the **Maximum Penny Difference** that we want to accept.

Here we set the **Maximum Penny Difference** to **$0.05**.

dyn c
www.dynamicscompanions.com
Dynamics Companions

- 265 -

www.blindsquirrelpublishing.com
© 2017 Blind Squirrel Publishing, LLC , All Rights Reserved

BLIND SQUIRREL
PUBLISHING

DYNAMICS COMPANIONS
BARE BONES CONFIGURATION GUIDES

CONFIGURING ACCOUNTS RECEIVABLE WITHIN DYNAMICS 365 FOR OPERATIONS
MODULE 1: CONFIGURING THE ACCOUNTS RECEIVABLE CONTROLS

Configuring the Accounts Receivable Parameters

How to do it...

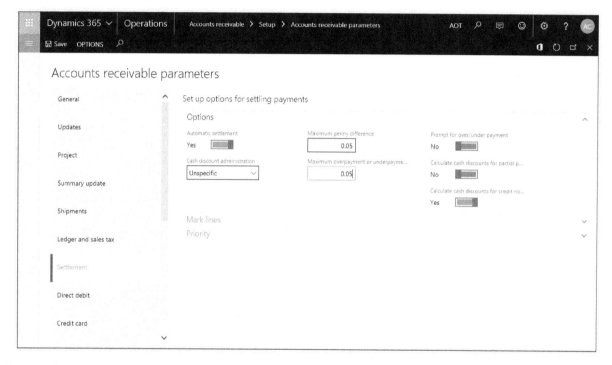

Then set the Maximum overpayment and underpayment tolerances.

Here we set the Maximum overpayment and underpayment to $0.05 because we will accept 5 cents either way, although you could be stricter or a little more flexible.

After we have done we are done with the configuration of the parameters and we can exit from the form.

dyn c

www.dynamicscompanions.com
Dynamics Companions

- 266 -

www.blindsquirrelpublishing.com
© 2017 Blind Squirrel Publishing, LLC, All Rights Reserved

BLIND SQUIRREL
PUBLISHING

DYNAMICS COMPANIONS
BARE BONES CONFIGURATION GUIDES

CONFIGURING ACCOUNTS RECEIVABLE WITHIN DYNAMICS 365 FOR OPERATIONS
MODULE 1: CONFIGURING THE ACCOUNTS RECEIVABLE CONTROLS

Configuring the Accounts Receivable Parameters

Example Data

Field Name	Value
General.Default Order Type	Sales Order
General.Order Hold For Order Status	Orange
Ledger and Sales Tax.Posting Profile	GEN
Ledger and Sales Tax.Posting profile with prepayment journal voucher	PRE
Ledger and Sales Tax.Period between delivery and invoicing	NET1
Ledger and Sales Tax.Invoicing Period	NET1
Ledger and Sales Tax.Settle Period	NET30
Ledger and Sales Tax.Settle Account	110110
Settlement.Automatic Settlement	True
Settlement.Maximum Penny Difference	0.05
Settlement.Maximum Overpayment and Underpayment	0.05

Account Receivable Parameters: TOF

www.dynamicscompanions.com
Dynamics Companions

- 267 -

www.blindsquirrelpublishing.com
© 2017 Blind Squirrel Publishing, LLC, All Rights Reserved

BLIND SQUIRREL
PUBLISHING

DYNAMICS COMPANIONS
BARE BONES CONFIGURATION GUIDES

CONFIGURING ACCOUNTS RECEIVABLE WITHIN DYNAMICS 365 FOR OPERATIONS
MODULE 1: CONFIGURING THE ACCOUNTS RECEIVABLE CONTROLS

Configuring the Accounts Receivable Parameters

Summary

As we set up the parameters for the Accounts Receivable area, we will see that it tied in a lot of the configuration that we did in this section.

DYNAMICS COMPANIONS
BARE BONES CONFIGURATION GUIDES

CONFIGURING ACCOUNTS RECEIVABLE WITHIN DYNAMICS 365 FOR OPERATIONS
MODULE 1: CONFIGURING THE ACCOUNTS RECEIVABLE CONTROLS

Review

Congratulations, you have now set up the Accounts Receivable codes and parameters. Now that we have crossed the t's and dotted the i's we can now move on to setting up the main data within the system and even start recording some transactions as well.

How cool is that?

www.dynamicscompanions.com
Dynamics Companions

- 269 -

www.blindsquirrelpublishing.com
© 2017 Blind Squirrel Publishing, LLC, All Rights Reserved

BLIND SQUIRREL
PUBLISHING

DYNAMICS COMPANIONS
BARE BONES CONFIGURATION GUIDES

CONFIGURING ACCOUNTS RECEIVABLE WITHIN DYNAMICS 365 FOR OPERATIONS
MODULE 1: CONFIGURING THE ACCOUNTS RECEIVABLE CONTROLS

About The Author

Murray Fife is an Author of over 20 books on Microsoft Dynamics including the Bare Bones Configuration Guide series. These guides comprise of over 15 books which step you through the setup and configuration of Microsoft Dynamics including Finance, Operations, Human Resources, Production, Service Management, and Project Accounting.

Throughout his 25+ years of experience in the software industry he has worked in many different roles during his career, including as a developer, an implementation consultant, a trainer and a demo guy within the partner channel which gives him a great understanding of the requirements for both customers and partners perspective.

If you are interested in contacting Murray or want to follow his blogs and posts then here is all of his contact information:

Email:	murray@murrayfife.com
Twitter:	@murrayfife
Facebook:	facebook.com/murraycfife
Google:	google.com/+murrayfife
LinkedIn:	linkedin.com/in/murrayfife
Blog:	atinkerersnotebook.com
Slideshare:	slideshare.net/murrayfife
Amazon:	amazon.com/author/murrayfife

 www.dynamicscompanions.com
Dynamics Companions

- 271 -

www.blindsquirrelpublishing.com
© 2017 Blind Squirrel Publishing, LLC, All Rights Reserved

BLIND SQUIRREL
PUBLISHING

DYNAMICS COMPANIONS
BARE BONES CONFIGURATION GUIDES

CONFIGURING ACCOUNTS RECEIVABLE WITHIN DYNAMICS 365 FOR OPERATIONS
MODULE 1: CONFIGURING THE ACCOUNTS RECEIVABLE CONTROLS

Need More Help with Microsoft Dynamics AX 2012 or Dynamics 365 for Operations

We are firm believers that Microsoft Dynamics AX 2012 or Dynamics 365 is not a hard product to learn, but the problem is where do you start. Which is why we developed the Bare Bones Configuration Guides. The aim of this series is to step you though the configuration of Microsoft Dynamics from a blank system, and then step you through the setup of all of the core modules within Microsoft Dynamics. We start with the setup of a base system, then move on to the financial, distribution, and operations modules.

Each book builds upon the previous ones, and by the time you have worked through all of the guides then you will have completely configured a simple (but functional) Microsoft Dynamics instance. To make it even more worthwhile you will have a far better understanding of Microsoft Dynamics and also how everything fits together.

As of now there are 16 guides in this series broken out as follows:

- Configuring a Training Environment
- Configuring an Organization
- Configuring the General Ledger
- Configuring Cash and Bank Management
- Configuring Accounts Receivable
- Configuring Accounts Payable
- Configuring Product Information Management
- Configuring Inventory Management

- Configuring Procurement and Sourcing
- Configuring Sales Order Management
- Configuring Human Resource Management
- Configuring Project Management and Accounting
- Configuring Production Control
- Configuring Sales and Marketing
- Configuring Service Management
- Configuring Warehouse Management

Although you can get each of these guides individually, and we think that each one is a great Visual resources to step you through each of the particular modules, for those of you that want to take full advantage of the series, you will want to start from the beginning and work through them one by one. After you have done that you would have done people told me was impossible for one persons to do, and that is to configure all of the core modules within Microsoft Dynamics.

If you are interested in finding out more about the series and also view all of the details including topics covered within the module, then browse to the Bare Bones Configuration Guide landing page on the Microsoft Dynamics Companions website. You will find all of the details, and also downloadable resources that help you with the setup of Microsoft Dynamics. Here is the full link: http://www.dynamicscompanions.com/

dync
dynamics companions

www.dynamicscompanions.com
Dynamics Companions

- 273 -

www.blindsquirrelpublishing.com
© 2017 Blind Squirrel Publishing, LLC, All Rights Reserved

BLIND SQUIRREL
PUBLISHING

DYNAMICS COMPANIONS
BARE BONES CONFIGURATION GUIDES

CONFIGURING ACCOUNTS RECEIVABLE WITHIN DYNAMICS 365 FOR OPERATIONS
MODULE 1: CONFIGURING THE ACCOUNTS RECEIVABLE CONTROLS

Usage Agreement

Blind Squirrel Publishing, LLC (the Publisher) agrees to grant, and the user of the eBook agrees to accept, a nonexclusive license to use the eBook under the terms and conditions of this eBook License Agreement ("Agreement"). Your use of the eBook constitutes your agreement to the terms and conditions set forth in this Agreement. This Agreement, or any part thereof, cannot be changed, waived, or discharged other than by a statement in writing signed by you and Blind Squirrel Publishing, LLC. Please read the entire Agreement carefully.

EBook Usage. The eBook may be used by one user on any device. The user of the eBook shall be subject to all of the terms of this Agreement, whether or not the user was the purchaser.

Printing. You may occasionally print a few pages of the text (but not entire sections), which may include sending the printed pages to a third party in the normal course of your business, but you must warn the recipient in writing that copyright law prohibits the recipient from redistributing the eBook content to anyone else. Other than the above, you may not print pages and/or distribute eBook content to others.

Copyright, Use and Resale Prohibitions. The Publisher retains all rights not expressly granted to you in this Agreement. The software, content, and related documentation in the eBook are protected by copyright laws and international copyright treaties, as well as other intellectual property laws and treaties. Nothing in this Agreement constitutes a waiver of the publisher's rights. The Publisher will not be responsible for performance problems due to circumstances beyond its reasonable control. Other than as stated in this Agreement, you may not copy, print, modify, remove, delete, augment, add to, publish, transmit, sell, resell, license, create derivative works from, or in any way exploit any of the eBook's content, in whole or in part, in print or electronic form, and you may not aid or permit others to do so. The unauthorized use or distribution of copyrighted or other proprietary content is illegal and could subject the purchaser to substantial damages. Purchaser will be liable for any damage resulting from any violation of this Agreement.

No Transfer. This license is not transferable by the eBook purchaser unless such transfer is approved in advance by the Publisher.

Disclaimer. The eBook, or any support given by the Publisher are in no way substitutes for assistance from legal, tax, accounting, or other qualified professionals. If legal advice or other expert assistance is required, the services of a competent professional person should be sought.

Limitation of Liability. The eBook is provided "as is" and the Publisher does not make any warranty or representation, either express or implied, to the eBook, including its quality, accuracy, performance, merchantability, or fitness for a particular purpose. You assume the entire risk as to the results and performance of the eBook. The Publisher does not warrant, guarantee, or make any representations regarding the use of, or the results obtained with, the eBook in terms of accuracy, correctness or reliability. In no event will the Publisher be liable for indirect, special, incidental, or consequential damages arising out of delays, errors, omissions, inaccuracies, or the use or inability to use the eBook, or for interruption of the eBook, from whatever cause. This will apply even if the Publisher has been advised that the possibility of such damage exists. Specifically, the Publisher is not responsible for any costs, including those incurred as a result of lost profits or revenue, loss of data, the cost of recovering such programs or data, the cost of any substitute program, claims by third parties, or similar costs. Except for the Publisher's indemnification obligations in Section 7.2, in no case will the Publisher's liability exceed the amount of license fees paid.

Hold Harmless / Indemnification.

7.1 You agree to defend, indemnify and hold the Publisher and any third party provider harmless from and against all third party claims and damages (including reasonable attorneys' fees) regarding your use of the eBook, unless the claims or damages are due to the Publisher's or any third party provider's gross negligence or willful misconduct or arise out of an allegation for which the Publisher is obligated to indemnify you.

7.The Publisher shall defend, indemnify and hold you harmless at the Publisher's expense in any suit, claim or proceeding brought against you alleging that your use of the eBook delivered to you hereunder directly infringes a United States patent, copyright, trademark, trade secret, or other third party proprietary right, provided the Publisher is (i) promptly notified, (ii) given the assistance required at the Publisher's expense, and (iii) permitted to retain legal counsel of the Publisher's choice and to direct the defense. The Publisher also agrees to pay any damages and costs awarded against you by final judgment of a court of last resort in any such suit or any agreed settlement amount on account of any such alleged infringement, but the Publisher will have no liability for settlements or costs incurred without its consent. Should your use of any such eBook be enjoined, or in the event that the Publisher desires to minimize its liability hereunder, the Publisher will, at its option and expense, (i) substitute a fully equivalent non-infringing eBook for the infringing item; (ii) modify the infringing item so that it no longer infringes but remains substantially equivalent; or (iii) obtain for you the right to continue use of such item. If none of the foregoing is feasible, the Publisher will terminate your access to the eBook and refund to you the applicable fees paid by you for the infringing item(s). THE FOREGOING STATES THE ENTIRE LIABILITY OF THE PUBLISHER AND YOUR SOLE REMEDY FOR INFRINGEMENT OR FOR ANY BREACH OF WARRANTY OF NON-INFRINGEMENT, EXPRESS OR IMPLIED. THIS INDEMNITY WILL NOT APPLY TO ANY ALLEGED INFRINGEMENT BASED UPON A COMBINATION OF OTHER SOFTWARE OR INFORMATION WITH THE EBOOK WHERE THE EBOOK WOULD NOT HAVE OTHERWISE INFRINGED ON ITS OWN.